Nani A. Palkhivala was born in January 1920. He was a Professor of Law at the Government Law College, Bombay, and was appointed the Tagore Professor of Law at the Calcutta University. In 1975 he was elected an Honorary Member of The Academy of Political Science, New York, and in 1977, he was appointed Ambassador of India to the United States of America.

In June 1978 the Princeton University, New Jersey (USA), conferred on him the Honorary Degree of Doctor of Laws, describing him as "defender of constitutional liberties, champion of human rights, teacher, author and economic developer." In April 1979 the Lawrence University, Wisconsin (USA), conferred on him the Honorary Degree of Doctor of Laws.

Palkhivala has argued a number of historical cases in the courts of India and abroad. He is also associated with several industrial and business houses as Chairman, Vice-Chairman and Director.

By the same author

The Law and Practice of Income-Tax
Taxation in India
The Highest Taxed Nation
Our Constitution Defaced and Defiled
India's Priceless Heritage
We, the People

We, the Nation
THE LOST DECADES

Nani A. Palkhivala

 UBSPD

UBS Publishers' Distributors Ltd.
New Delhi Bombay Bangalore Madras
Calcutta Patna Kanpur London

UBS Publishers' Distributors Ltd.
5 Ansari Road, New Delhi-110 002
Bombay Bangalore Madras
Calcutta Patna Kanpur London

First Published   1994
First Reprint   1994
Second Reprint   1994
Third Reprint   1994
Fourth Reprint   1994
Fifth Reprint   1994
Sixth Reprint   1994
Seventh Reprint   1994

Cover Design : UBS Art Studio

Lasertypeset in 11 pt. Times at Alphabets, New Delhi and printed at Nutech
Photolithographers, Shahdara, Delhi

To

The millions who, humble and nameless,
the straight, hard pathway plod

"[The Constitution] has been reared for immortality,
if the work of man may justly aspire to such a
title. It may, nevertheless, perish in an hour by the folly,
or corruption, or negligence of its only keepers,
THE PEOPLE."

(Joseph Story's words quoted by Sachchidananda
Sinha in his Inaugural Address, as Provisional
Chairman, to the Constituent Assembly
on December 9, 1946)

CONTENTS

Introduction

Are We Masters of Our Fate?

This volume is intended to be a companion to *We, the People*. Extracts, suitably edited, from my speeches and writings of the last ten years have been reproduced here. Basic ideas and topics recur in different pieces, but I believe such overlapping is unavoidable.

To adapt the words of Malcolm Muggeridge, never was any generation of men intent upon the pursuit of well-being more advantageously placed to attain it, who yet, with seeming deliberation, took the opposite course — towards chaos instead of order, towards breakdown instead of stability, towards death, destruction and darkness instead of life, creativity and light. The current decade has ceased to belong to the category of the lost decades in point of economics, but not in point of national leadership and social cohesion. The following pages bear witness to the three facts which have never ceased to amaze me — the persistent incompetence of governments in charge of one of the most intelligent nations on earth, the abysmal depths to which the nation with the finest spiritual heritage has sunk, and the phenomenal capacity for endurance of our simple, honest, down-trodden poor. One is driven to believe the tenet of ancient Indian culture that the law of *karma* operates not only for individuals but also collectively for groups, nations, and races, in which individuals necessarily participate.

Since nothing is further from my mind than to write hereafter an autobiography, I would like to record here some happenings in my life for which science or rationalism can offer no explanation. I propose to talk about incidents at the risk of exposing myself to thoughtless ridicule.

I believe that the basic pattern of an individual's or a nation's life is predetermined, that very few individuals have the gift of clairvoyance to foresee what is predetermined, and that guidance is sometimes vouchsafed to receptive human beings by means for which there is no scientific explanation. There is the existence of free will but that is again within preordained parameters. The case is similar to that of a dog on a long leash — the dog has the freedom to move about as far as the leash permits, but not beyond.

In *The Times* of July 5, 1993, William Rees-Mogg in a very perceptive article bewails that the inner guide that showed mankind the way forward has fallen strangely silent, and quotes a few examples of the way the voices of destiny spoke in the past. Speaking of the "unknown guest", Maurice Maeterlinck said, "From the darkest corners of our ego it directs our veritable life, the one that is not to die, and pays no heed to our thought or to anything emanating from our reason." Plato quotes Socrates as saying, "In the past the prophetic voice to which I have become accustomed has always been my constant companion, opposing me even in quite trivial things if I was going to take the wrong course." Winston Churchill had a lucky escape from a bomb attack in a car; he chose to sit on the far side from his usual place. Lady Churchill asked him why. "I don't know. I don't know", he replied. Then he said, "Of course I know. Something said to me 'Stop' before I reached the car door which was held open for me. It then seemed to me that I was told I should open the door on the other side and get in and sit there."

In 1968 Mr. Govinda Menon was the Law Minister in the Congress government. He pressed me hard to accept the office of the Attorney General of India. After a great deal of hesitation I agreed. When I was in Delhi I conveyed my acceptance to him, and he told me that the announcement would be made the next day. I was happy that the agonizing hours of indecision were over.

Sound sleep is one of the blessings I have always enjoyed. That night I went to bed and looked forward to my usual quota of deep slumber. But suddenly and inexplicably, I became wide awake at three o'clock in the morning with the clear conviction, floating like a hook through my consciousness, that my decision was erroneous and that I should reverse it before it was too late. Early in the morning I profusely apologized to the Law Minister for changing my mind. In the years immediately following, it was my privilege to argue on behalf of the citizen, under the same Congress government, the major cases which have shaped and moulded the constitutional law of India — Bank Nationalization (1969), Privy Purse (1970), Fundamental Rights (1972-73), among others.

The most incredible experience of clairvoyance or precognition in my life was connected with Mrs. Indira Gandhi's case which culminated in the declaration of the Emergency.

The Allahabad High Court had, in the month of June 1975, decided that the election of Mrs. Indira Gandhi to parliament should be set aside. That meant that she would cease to be a member of the Lok Sabha with a potential risk to her Prime Ministership. Mrs. Gandhi filed an appeal in the Supreme Court and her application for interim relief was argued by me on June 23, 1975. Mr. Justice Krishna Iyer heard the application and passed the order of interim relief on the next day. The interim order was that pending the hearing and final disposal of the appeal Mrs. Gandhi could continue to sit in the Lok Sabha and participate in the proceedings of that House like any other member, and could also continue to be the Prime Minister of India. The only restriction on her was that she was not given the right to vote. The judge mentioned that this did not involve any hardship because parliament was not in session at that time and that I could renew the application for the right to vote when parliament reassembled. The evening of that very day (June 24, 1975) I saw Mrs. Indira Gandhi at her residence and told her that I found the interim order very satisfactory and she should not worry about the case since the judgment of the trial court did not seem to be correct on the recorded evidence.

On the plane which I boarded to return to Bombay, next to me was seated an elderly, simple man dressed in khadi, carrying a khadi cloth bag. He asked me what had happened that day in the Prime Minister's case and I told him briefly what the judge had decided. He related how he was an inmate of a Gandhi ashram in Bangalore and that he had been out of the ashram since May 1975 to conduct one of his periodic tours in different parts of India. He mentioned the name of a clairvoyant in Bangalore who had made some predictions which he thought were rather curious. The conversation between us ran somewhat as follows:

"When I left the ashram in May 1975 the clairvoyant told me that the Prime Minister would lose the case which she was fighting in the Allahabad High Court and yet, after losing the case, she would become the most powerful woman in the world," said my neighbour.

In surprise I asked, "How can Mrs. Indira Gandhi become any more powerful than she is today? When she is already the head of the largest democracy on earth, what can possibly add to her power?"

"I do not know. I am only repeating to you what he said."

Unimpressed, I did not bother even to make a mental note of the name of the clairvoyant. But to carry on the conversation, I asked, "Did the soothsayer say anything else?"

"Yes. He said that the extraordinary power which the Prime Minister is to acquire will end in March 1977."

"Did he mention the precise month and year?"

"Yes, he mentioned specifically that the cessation of the extraordinary power would be in March 1977."

"Did he make any other prediction?"

"Yes he said that Jayaprakash Narayan who is today the most popular figure in India's public life would be stricken by a fatal illness which would carry him away in about two years. He also said that Mr. Y. B. Chavan who aspires to be the Prime Minister of India would never attain that position."

I came home, wondering what the future would bring. In less than 36 hours the Emergency was declared, the invaluable fundamental rights of the people were suspended, and the Prime Minister virtually acquired all the powers of the leader of a totalitarian state. That was the black morning of June 26, 1975.

In the days immediately following the declaration of the Emergency, my mind kept on reverting to the four forecasts. I invited for a quiet dinner at my residence the then Editor of *The Times of India* and a very few other well-known journalists and related to them my conversation with the Gandhian ashramite in the plane. The next month I repeated the story to Ramnath Goenka of the *Indian Express,* who was literally hounded by the Congress government during the Emergency. Those were the days of gloom and despair, and the only streak of light was the prediction that the totalitarianism would end in March 1977. I need hardly mention that all the predictions were accurately fulfilled — the assumption of supremacy which made Mrs. Indira Gandhi the most powerful woman in the world, the cessation of that supremacy in March 1977, the death of Jayaprakash Narayan in October 1979, and Mr. Y.B. Chavan dying in November 1984 without fulfilling his ambition of becoming the Prime Minister.

I did not meet Mrs. Gandhi again till the evening of March 22, 1977 when the results of the election showed that the Janata Party had won a landslide victory and Mrs. Gandhi had to resign as the Prime Minister. I was in Delhi on that day and called on Mrs. Gandhi at her residence. I related to her the incident of my conversation with the total stranger on the plane in June 1975 and said, "Indiraji, if it be any consolation, may I tell you that what has happened since the election case was filed against you in the Allahabad High Court seems to have been preordained." She had tears in her eyes — the only time I saw her in such a sad mood.

It would be preposterous to try to give any explanation for the above episode, except on the hypothesis of preordination and precognition.

The hubris of contemporary science has passed into a byword. In his latest book *Black Holes and Baby Universes*, the brilliant physicist Professor Stephen Hawking writes, "I do not agree with the view that the universe is a mystery." To me it is not only a mystery of the most profound nature, but an infinite cluster of millions and millions of incredible, insoluble mysteries which the human mind (as distinct from the human spirit) will never be able to unravel. Albert Einstein the greatest scientific intellect of our age, had the right attitude: "The most beautiful experience we can have is the mysterious ... the fundamental emotion which stands at the cradle of true art and true science."

Professor Hawking goes on to say, "There are well-defined laws that govern how the universe and everything in it develops in time. Although we have not yet found the exact form of all these laws... I think there is a 50/50 chance that we will find them in the next twenty years." I do not believe that the human brain, which according to Professor Hawking contains "about a hundred million billion billion particles", will ever be able to discover the "set of laws that completely determines the evolution of the universe from its initial state" — until the human spirit reaches a higher stage of evolution which Sri Aurobindo called the supramental stage.

It has become the fashion to aver that you do not believe anything which science cannot prove. I admit that scepticism is healthy and that there are a thousand imposters for every one man with unusual powers. In the latest biography of Harry Houdini which was published in October 1993, it is mentioned that the world-famous magician was so preoccupied with the attempt to reach his beloved mother through spiritualism after her death that he visited several mediums but heard only fake spirit voices which could not trick the master trickster.

However, there are incontrovertible examples of authentic happenings and phenomena which science is wholly unable to explain. Dr. Alexis Carrel, the Nobel Prize winner in Medicine, in his absorbing book *Man, the Unknown*, gives examples of miraculous cures at Lourdes happening even in cases of persons who did not have faith.

Some years ago there was a dinner party in Bombay where among the guests were India's leading scientist, Dr. Homi Bhabha, and a humble simple man from Lucknow who was reputed to have some unusual powers. At the persuasion of some of the guests, Dr. Bhabha consented to test the man's powers. Dr. Bhabha took out a one-rupee note from his wallet and, without looking at it, put it in his side pocket and asked him whether he could tell the number on the note. The man mentioned the number with total accuracy. It could not be a case of mind-reading because Dr. Bhabha had deliberately refrained, from looking at the note. Later, when I met Dr. Bhabha in Delhi I asked him whether there was any scientific explanation for the unusual faculty of the Lucknow man. He confessed that up to now no explanation known to science was available.

In his fascinating autobiographical account *My India*, Jim Corbett relates the story of a hermit in Nepal whose second sight enabled him to locate a lost treasure in a vision, resulting in the treasure being retrieved by a distraught public servant. Jim Corbett observes, "In the Himalayas no one doubts the ability of individuals alleged to be gifted with second sight to help in recovering property lost or mislaid."

When you read Dr. Raynor Johnson's *The Imprisoned Splendour* and Fritjof Capra's *The Tao of Physics* you understand why Sri Aurobindo and Rabindranath Tagore were convinced that India is destined to be the teacher of all lands. Saints never contradict one another and mystics have never been known to disagree. Eastern culture and Western culture share the same heritage of spiritual experience. More and more men have begun to realize that we are the Peeping Toms at the keyhole of eternity. I should like to echo the wish with which Arthur Koestler ends *The Roots of Coincidence* that we would take the stuffing out of the keyhole, which blocks even our limited view.

Bombay   **Nani A. Palkhivala**

1

Addresses at Foreign Universities

Forty-three Years of Independence

*A*t the stroke of midnight on August 14, 1947, Jawaharlal Nehru made his famous speech wherein he referred to India keeping her tryst with destiny and awaking to life and freedom. To review the last three and forty years in an hour is like trying to see the Himalayas at night in one flash of lightning. One thing I promise you — I shall "nothing extenuate, nor set down aught in malice". I would be dishonouring the memory of Pandit Nehru and of his mentor, Mahatma Gandhi, if I try to be economical with the truth.

The greatest achievement of Indian democracy is that it has survived unfractured for forty-three years. Eight hundred and forty million people — more than the combined population of Africa and South America — live together as one political entity under conditions of freedom. Never before in history, and nowhere else in the world today, has one-sixth of the human race existed as a single free nation.

The achievement is all the more creditable, since no other democracy has had such diversity in unity, such a mosaic of humanity. There are twelve great living religions in the world (incidentally, the word "living" is tautologous, since no great religion has ever perished), and all the twelve flourish in India. We have sixteen major languages written in different alphabets and derived from different roots; and, for good measure, our people — whom you can never call taciturn — express themselves in 250

(The Jawaharlal Nehru Memorial Lecture at Trinity College, Cambridge, November 7, 1990)

dialects. English, which is not included in the major languages listed in the Constitution, yet continues to be the only link language for the whole country; it is the only language in which the South is prepared to communicate with the North. British jurisprudence is the matrix of our non-personal laws.

*I*n 1950, we started as a republic with three inestimable advantages.

First, we had 5,000 years of civilization behind us—a civilization which had reached "the summit of human thought" in the words of Ralph Waldo Emerson. We inherited great skills and many-splendoured intelligence, since the genes had evolved over five luminous millennia. We had a superb entrepreneurial spirit, honed over a century of obstacles. A few years ago a World Bank report on India mentioned the two very favourable factors — an unlimited reservoir of skilled labour, and abundance of capital available for investment in new projects. The trader's instinct is innate in Indian genes. An Indian can buy from a Jew and sell to a Scot, and yet make a profit!

Secondly, whereas before 1858 India was never a united political entity, in that year the accident of British rule welded us into one country, one nation; and when independence came, we had been in unified nationality for almost a century under one head of state.

Thirdly, our Founding Fathers, after three long years of laborious and painful toil, gave us a Constitution which a former Chief Justice of India rightly described as "sublime". It was the longest constitution in the world till, a few years ago, Yugoslavia had the impertinence to adopt a longer constitution!

The substance of the Universal Declaration of Human Rights adopted by the United Nations on December 10, 1948, is embodied as Fundamental Rights in our Constitution. The right to equality before the law is guaranteed to citizens and non-citizens alike. In one respect our constitutional law is more secular than that of the

United Kingdom — religion is no bar to the holding of any public office whatsoever in the State. In another respect, our Constitution may claim to be more progressive than that of the USA — equality of the sexes is a guaranteed right in India, whereas the recent attempt to incorporate a similar right in the US Constitution has so far been unsuccessful.

The right to carry on any occupation, trade or business is, again, a guaranteed right. The concept of "socialism" did not figure anywhere in the Constitution as originally enacted. On the contrary, the Constitution provided in the Directive Principles of State Policy that the State shall endeavour to secure that "the ownership and control of the material resources of the community are so distributed as best to subserve the common good" and that "the operation of the economic system does not result in the concentration of wealth and means of production to the common detriment". These words rule out State ownership — the Monolithic State — which is the hallmark of communism, euphemistically called socialism.

India is the only country in the world where, in the States which are governed by the Communist Party, human rights are fully respected — and that is only because the Bill of Rights is firmly ingrained in our national Constitution.

We can proudly say that our Constitution gave us a flying start and equipped us adequately to meet the challenges of the future. Unfortunately, over the years we dissipated every advantage we started with, like a compulsive gambler bent upon squandering an invaluable legacy. I am afraid India today is only a caricature of the noble democracy which Nehru strove to bring to life and freedom in 1947.

Successive governments imposed mindless socialism on the nation, which held in thrall the people's endeavour and enterprise. They respected the shells of socialism — State control and State ownership — while the kernel, the spirit of social justice, was left no chance of coming to life. We shut our eyes to the fact that socialism is to social justice what ritual is to religion and dogma is to truth.

The Economist rightly remarked in January 1987 that socialism as practised in India has been a fraud. Our brand of socialism did not result in transfer of wealth from the rich to the poor but only from the honest rich to the dishonest rich.

We built up State-owned enterprises — called the public sector in India. The sleeping sickness of socialism is now universally acknowledged — but not officially in India. No less than 231 public sector enterprises are run by the Union government, and 636 by the State governments. These public sector enterprises are the black holes, the money guzzlers, and they have been extracting an exorbitant price for India's doctrinaire socialism. There is a tidal wave of privatization sweeping across the world from Bangladesh to Brazil, but it has turned aside in its course and passed India by.

Every segment of the people's enterprise is festooned with red tape. From the very first decade of the republic the steel claws of the permit-licence-quota raj were laid upon the national economy, and even today their grip continues with insignificant relaxation.

The administrative techniques pursued by the government are the same as were cast in a concrete mould more than a century ago. Files and minutes still go perpetually from official to official and from ministry to ministry. In the result, nothing moves except the river Ganges. "Round and round," Lord Curzon the Viceroy noted, "like the diurnal revolution of the earth went the file — stately, solemn, sure and slow." Decades later, Malcolm Muggeridge observed the same phenomenon: "It was government pure and undefiled; endlessly minuting and circulating files, which, like time itself, had neither beginning nor end, but just were."

Today the situation remains unchanged — only the number of files has increased a thousandfold. Millions of man-hours are wasted every day in coping with inane bureaucratic regulations and a torrential spate of amendments.

Legal redress is time-consuming enough to make infinity intelligible. A lawsuit once started in India is the nearest thing to eternal life ever seen on this earth. Close to two million cases are pending in the eighteen High Courts alone, and more than 2,10,000 cases in the Supreme Court for admission or final hearing or miscellaneous relief.

History will record that the greatest mistake of the Indian republic in the first forty years of its existence was to make far less investment in human resources — investment in education, family planning, nutrition and public health — than in brick and mortar, plants and factories. We had quantitative growth without qualitative development. Our gross national product increased, but not gross national happiness.

Different parts of India still live in different centuries, so far as basic amenities and cultural awareness are concerned.

The quality of life cannot improve in India so long as the population keeps on increasing at the present alarming rate. In the time I shall take to deliver this lecture, the population of India will have increased by 2,000.

It has been said that development is the best contraceptive. But development itself would not be possible if the present increase in numbers continues. Education, particularly education of girls, is another excellent contraceptive. But we have totally failed to use education as an instrument of national development. Two-thirds of our people, and four-fifths of our females, are literally illiterate after more than forty years of independence. According to the World Bank, by the turn of the century 54 per cent of all illiterates will be in India.

We keep on tackling fifty-year problems with five-year plans, staffed by two-year officials, working with one-year appropriations — fondly hoping that somehow the laws of economics will be suspended because we are Indians!

"*M*en will do the rational thing," said Lord Keynes, "but only after exploring all other alternatives." After the other alternatives had failed dismally, India in the eighties initiated a policy of liberalization and dismantling of controls. For the first time we talked of economic sanity in place of economic ideology, and we realized the imperative necessity of fruitful egalitarianism instead of sterile socialism of the earlier years.

For years we had suffered crushing rates of income-tax and wealth-tax — the highest in the world in their aggregate impact. We had a supreme ironic procession of budgets — historically retrograde, economically unprogressive, and socially stagnant. Overtaxation corrupted the national character overtly. The nation survived only because the tax system continued to breathe through loopholes and the economy used to breathe through the window of tax evasion.

The Budget of 1985 was epoch-making. It was the finest budget free India ever had. It abolished estate duty. It slashed wealth-tax to a maximum rate of two per cent and personal income-tax to a maximum of 50 per cent. Luckily, the low rates of income-tax and wealth-tax by and large continue in force, though unwise increases have been made in the thinly disguised temporary form of surcharge.

The new budgetary philosophy was eminently suited to prepare and equip India for a place in the 'Prosperity League' in the unfolding future. The new philosophy was that the Government should no longer be the power above the people, to be lobbied, petitioned and propitiated for favours.

Unfortunately, the Government's sensible new policy — the one ray of hope for fast economic growth — was never fairly implemented. It encountered formidable opposition from three quarters: *(a)* the top-heavy bureaucracy reluctant to shed its enormous powers; *(b)* influential politicians who preferred to let socialism remain the opiate of the people and of whom it can be truly said that if ignorance is bliss they should be the happiest men alive; *(c)* quite a few Indian businessmen who were much more interested in their own personal prosperity than in the future of the country and who preferred to flourish in the non-competitive environment.

The result of the working of these three obscurantist forces is that India continues to remain the only significant country in the free world to hold aloft the torn and tattered flag of socialism.

 S mall wonder that after forty-three years of independence, we are still plagued by three basic problems — poverty, unemployment and foreign exchange trade deficit. In the Second Nehru Memorial Lecture delivered here, Lord Mountbatten referred to his first interview with Nehru on March 24, 1947, when he asked Nehru what he thought was the greatest problem confronting India. Nehru replied, "the economic problem". That problem stubbornly refuses to go away.

India has 15 per cent of the world's population, but only 1.5 per cent of the world's income. In the four decades since we became a republic, our per capita income in real terms did not even double but increased by only 91 per cent. Today we are still the twenty-first poorest nation on earth.

Perceptive observers in foreign countries where Indians work and prosper are baffled by one question — how does India, with its great human potential and natural resources, manage to remain poor? The answer is that we are not poor by nature but poor by policy. You would not be far wrong if you called India the world's leading expert in the art of perpetuating poverty.

Sir William Ryrie, the Executive Vice President of the International Finance Corporation, said when he was in India in January 1989 that India has some of "the most creative entrepreneurs . . . the most dynamic business leaders . . . and the sharpest financial brains in the world." These words give you an idea of the magnitude of the effort needed to keep India impoverished.

Most of our politicians and bureaucrats, untainted by knowledge of development in the outside world, have no desire to search for genes of ideas which deserve to be called "a high-yielding variety of economics". We are smugly reconciled, to quote Dr. Sudhir Sen, to low yield from high ideals.

India is rattling — and rattling violently — with spare human capacity. More than 30 million are registered with our 840

Employment Exchanges. According to objective estimates, there must be at least 20 million other unemployed who are not registered.

In 1950, India ranked sixteenth in the list of exporting countries of the world; today it ranks forty-third ! Using another yardstick, in 1950 India had 2.2 per cent of the world export market; today its share stands reduced to 0.45 per cent.

As the Chancellor of the Exchequer pointed out in the House of Commons some time ago, the population of Hong Kong is less than one per cent of India's (0.7 per cent to be precise) and its land area is 0.03 per cent of India's, and yet it has almost three times the trade of India.

Apart from exports, another rich source of foreign exchange earnings can be tourism. Unfortunately, India has less than half of one per cent of the world tourist traffic. We get only 1.2 million tourists a year and earn annually about Rs. 18 billion in foreign exchange from tourism. This is a pathetically deplorable performance for a country which has such fantastic riches to offer tourists.

*N*ever before in our republic's history has violence marked our national life on a scale so widespread as at present. We have enough religion to hate one another but not enough to love one another.

One may apply to India the words used by the late Benigno Aquino about the Philippines — "Here is a land in which a few are spectacularly rich while the masses remain abjectly poor . . . where freedom and its blessings are a reality for a minority and an illusion for the many . . . a land consecrated to democracy but . . . a land of privilege and rank . . . a republic dedicated to equality but mired in an archaic system of caste."

The greatest problem of India is that its finest men — men of calibre and vision, knowledge and character — are not in politics and stand little chance of getting elected having regard to the murky atmosphere of our political life. Caste is the football in the political game which our men in public life play.

Unfortunately, divisiveness has become the Indian disease. Truly, divisiveness is the AIDS of India — a disease which is spreading fast and wide, preys on the public mind and is without a cure in sight. Communal hatred, linguistic fanaticism and regional loyalty are gnawing at the vitals of the unity and integrity of the country. To the growing army of terrorists and professional hooligans, caste or clan, creed or tongue, is a sufficient ground to kill their fellow citizens.

The most crying need of India today is to undergo catharsis, a course of emotional cleansing. We must not allow the moral bedrock of our society to turn to lava.

National integration is born in the hearts of the citizens. When it dies there, no army, no government, no constitution, can save it. States of mind precede states. Inter-faith harmony and consciousness of the essential unity of all religions is the very heart of our national integration.

The soul of India aspires to integration and assimilation. Down the ages, Indian culture — a tremendous force of power and beauty — has been made richer and deeper as a result of absorbing what is best in outside influences and integrating those various influences to grace and enrich its own identity.

*B*ut the landscape is not one of unrelieved gloom. Some measure of the innate potential of the country is afforded by its actual achievements against heavy odds. Among the industrialized nations of the world we are the tenth. The country has set its sights high. It has nuclear reactors and satellites in space. It even exploded an atomic device (1974) — the only one — and learnt the bitter lesson that one explosion activates international reaction but a series of explosions anaesthetizes it. One blast brings discredit, while a sequence brings prestige and power.

Though there is no instant solution for our multitudinous problems and the short-term prospect may only be of shadows lengthening across the path, an objective overview would justify confidence in the long-term future of the country. In the affairs of nations, as in the world of elements, winds shift, tides ebb and flow, the ship rocks. Only let the anchor hold. History records the gloomy forebodings of some of the wisest Britishers in the first half of the nineteenth century about their country's future, but the decades which followed the pessimistic predictions saw Britain rise to the height of its glory. In the first few decades of the USA, the depressing situation led so perceptive a man as Joseph Story to talk of the possibility of the Constitution perishing "before the grave has closed upon the last of its illustrious founders", but the 200-year republic lives on as the most vibrant on earth.

The vitality of India is remarkable. The country does not have a powerful economy, but has all the raw materials to build one.

There are various factors which go to make foreign investments in India very attractive. First and foremost, when you invest in India, you invest in democracy.

Further, our domestic market is itself enormous. Almost all manufacturing units in India with foreign collaboration have garnered golden grain.

Generally speaking, we are a sloppy nation. But there is one surprising thing. If you insist upon nothing but the best, you often get it in India, comparable to world standards. India can and does respond to uncompromising insistence on quality.

Finally, the great appreciation of most foreign currencies against the Indian rupee offers an excellent opportunity of using India as a manufacturing base.

A nation's worth is not measured merely by its gross national product, any more than an individual's worth is measured by his bank account. Ambassador John Kenneth Galbraith remarked that while he had seen poverty in many countries of the world, he found one unusual attribute among the poor of India — "There is richness in their poverty." They do not count their wealth in money alone.

The heart of the nation is sound and the human raw material is excellent. To a western mind, the Indian's inner strength and capacity for patient endurance are almost unbelievable.

Hundreds of millions, who have no standard of living, still have a standard of life. The nation is able to take in its stride situations which would cause a revolution in other countries. The ancient civilization has survived and will survive when the raucous and fractious voices of today are lost in the silence of the centuries.

Nature has been kind to India in one respect. It has endowed the country with the gift of producing great leaders in the darkest hour — leaders with the gift of grace who can arouse the trusting millions to great heights. Look at the galaxy of character and calibre India produced at the time of the struggle for independence in the thirties and the forties.

When the hour struck, the man was found — Mahatma Gandhi — the greatest of our leaders. He lit the imagination of the entire nation. He created men out of dust. He taught the unforgettable lesson that cynicism corrupts and absolute cynicism corrupts absolutely. He made us realize the profound truth that single-minded pursuit of money impoverishes the mind, shrivels the imagination, and desiccates the heart.

There is a basic lesson of Indian history. Our people have always taken their moral standards from their rulers: the people have risen to great heights when they have basked in the glow of noble kings or leaders. The present generation is waiting for a leader who will make it relearn the moral values, and who will inculcate in the people, as Gandhi did, a sense of the responsibilities which fall on every citizen of a free society.

One last thought, and I shall have done. Today, the unity and integrity of India seems to be at stake. But "even this shall pass away". Indian society will, in course of time, acquire the requisite political culture — the attitudes and habits of tolerance, mutual respect and goodwill, which alone can make democracy workable.

The day will come when the 26 States of India will realize that in a profound sense they are culturally akin, ethnically identical, linguistically knit and historically related. The greatest task before India today is to acquire a keener sense of national identity, to gain the wisdom to cherish its priceless heritage, and to create a cohesive society with the cement of Indian culture. We shall then celebrate the 15th day of August not as the Day of Independence but as the Day of Interdependence — the dependence of the States upon one another, the dependence of our numerous communities upon one another, the dependence of the many castes and clans upon one another — in the sure knowledge that we are one nation.

The United Kingdom and India
Past Ties and Promising Future

I feel privileged and honoured to have been invited to deliver the Third GEC Lecture at this renowned College. I thought no subject would be more appropriate than a retrospect of the centuries which our two countries have shared, and a look at the prospect of the unfolding future.

There seems to be a mystical bond which holds us together in real understanding and goodwill. There is something special, in fact providential, in the relationship between Britain and India. The crucial test is this: if the last two hundred years in India's history were to be relived, how many thinking Indians would prefer to have them without British rule? I venture to say that no one, who is not ignorant or partial, would wish the past to be redrawn effacing all traces of the raj.

There was much that was ugly and exploitative in those years. But, on balance, the good far outweighed the evil. The British took enormous wealth out of India, but they left behind legacies which no money could buy. There were six invaluable gifts which you bequeathed to us.

It was the accident of British rule which is responsible for the *unity and integrity* of India today. Whereas before 1858 India was never a unified political entity, the Proclamation of Queen Victoria in that year welded us into one country, one nation; and when independence came, we had been in unified nationality for almost

(The Third GEC Lecture at Imperial College of Science, Technology & Medicine, London, November 3, 1992)

a century under one head of state.

Incidentally, you have only to contrast the disadvantages under which a nation would have to begin its life as a republic, when advantages of the type which accrued to India from British rule do not exist. Take the thirteen colonies in America which won their independence in 1783. Those thirteen colonies were bound together merely by loose articles of confederation. They had no unified nationality, no head of state, no central government, no central judiciary, no common taxation, and no national currency. On all those points, the raj supplied India with the benefits which the USA lacked. India could not, and would not, have reached its present level without the fortuity of British raj.

The largesse of the *English language* enriched Indian culture. It was the cement which bound, and continues to bind, our country together; and it enabled us to deal with the rest of the world from a vantage point. There are sixteen major Indian languages listed in the Constitution, and each of them is used by tens of millions. Those who are following the developments in Canada which has only two languages, English and French, can imagine the multiplication of the problems where sixteen state languages are spoken by different groups who are not unfamiliar with linguistic fanaticism. Even today, the south will not accept any communication from the north in Hindi which is the language of the north, but is willing to accept all communications in English. The authentic text of our Constitution is in English; the laws are passed by our Parliament in English; justice is administered invariably by the Supreme Court in English and usually by the eighteen High Courts in English. It is interesting to note that four of the first thirteen awards of the Booker Prize were either to Indians or for books about India. *The Times* editorially noted on February 11, 1992 —

> ... Indian English is in some ways more correct than British English, because it is taught from old-fashioned text-books by teachers for whom it is not their first language. There may well be fewer unconscious sole-cisms and barbarisms in Indian English than in British. Indians are less casual with the shared language.

The *civil and criminal laws,* apart from personal laws applicable to particular communities, are based upon English jurisprudence. The main instrument of criminal justice — the Indian Penal Code — was drafted by Lord Macaulay when he functioned as the Law Minister of India from 1834 to 1838. It is a tribute to his superb draftsmanship that the Indian Penal Code is one of the least amended statutes of India.

Broadly speaking, the *administrative structure* in India is still as the British left it. The Indian Civil Service (ICS) started by the British was, beyond question, one of the finest civil services the world has ever known. Sardar Vallabhbhai Patel had the good sense to recognize this, and when he introduced the Indian Administrative Service (IAS) it was based on the model of the ICS. At the same time it must be confessed that while the top ICS officers were outstanding, the bureaucratic structure which the British created left much to be desired.

Not the least of the gifts that the British left behind was the institution of the *armed forces* imbued with the tradition of being totally apolitical. Today when we see corruption and degradation all round in India, the one institution of which we can be justly proud is that of the armed forces. In point of discipline and dedication, efficiency and competence, it is the equal of its counterpart anywhere in the world.

Finally, paradoxical as it may seem, if India is a *free republic* today, that is also the consequence of British rule. Indians fought, and fought valiantly, to get rid of foreign domination. But it is probable that up to now India would not have shaken off the domination of Indian rulers but for the notions of freedom imbibed from the days of British rule. Macaulay foresaw this development. He said, "By good government we may educate our subjects [so] that they may in some future age demand European institutions. Whenever such a day comes, it will be the proudest day in English history."

*F*airness begets fairness, and understanding begets understanding. Englishmen have been fair-minded enough to recognize India's right to freedom; and likewise Indians have been fair-minded enough to acknowledge the benefits derived from British rule. It was a Britisher, A.O. Hume, who in 1885 organized the nationalist party of India, the Congress, which has been in power for most of the years of our republic. It was a British constituency which elected Dadabhai Naoroji, exactly a hundred years ago, as the first Indian member of the House of Commons. Such was Dadabhai's faith in Britain's innate sense of justice and fairness that when he published a book in which he bluntly criticized British rule in India, the title he chose was *Poverty and Un-British Rule in India*. Dadabhai said—

> ... the world may rejoice in a glorious chapter added to its history, of the regeneration of an old but long unfortunate race, and India may for ever remember gratefully the benefactors who restored her to more than her ancient splendour and civilization.

The one lesson of history is that sometimes the impossible happens and the inevitable does not happen. Lord Curzon the Viceroy habitually paid major attention to minor details. In 1903, he held a great *durbar* to proclaim the accession of Edward VII to the throne. It was suggested that the hymn "Onward Christian Soldiers" be included for church services during the *durbar*. Lord Curzon rejected the suggestion because of the line in the hymn, "Crowns and thrones may perish, kingdoms rise and wane". It was unthinkable to Lord Curzon that the Indian empire could perish or wane. But in less than fifty years, the unthinkable came to pass. In 1947, within two years of the Second World War coming to an end, Britain overruled Winston Churchill, the greatest Englishman of the age, and with characteristic graciousness conceded the absolute right of self-determination to India.

*I*n 1950, the United Kingdom and the republic of India started a new chapter and began to deal with each other as independent sovereign nations, without rancour or bitterness.

In the history of India which goes back five thousand years, the British connection has been only a short episode. It was a brief interlude lasting less than a century from the Proclamation by Queen Victoria in 1858 to the grant of independence in 1947; less than two centuries if we start with the first significant act of British dominion, the Battle of Plassey in 1757; and less than four centuries if we count from the incorporation of the East India Company in 1600.

What is the future of the relationship which enriched Britain in terms of cash and enriched India in terms of culture?

The year 1992 may witness the start of India flowering into a strong economy. We have at last stopped sleep-walking through history. The biggest metamorphosis — qualitative and not merely quantitative — in the economic climate, both investment and otherwise, came with the enunciation of the New Industrial Policy in July 1991. The New Policy is reflected in the 1992 Budget. The four main thrusts of the Budget are — liberalization, integration of India into the global economy, reduction of taxes, and a stable and healthy balance of payments situation. Mr. P.V. Narasimha Rao the Prime Minister, Dr. Manmohan Singh the Finance Minister, and others in the cabinet are sincere persons totally committed to ushering in an age of economic rationalism in place of economic theology. They mean well and are determined to prepare and equip India for a brighter future. This — the sincerity of the cabinet — is the single biggest asset on the credit side of India's balance sheet.

There are several circumstances which go to make India very attractive to foreign investors.

Investing in India is tantamount to investing in democracy. Around 900 million people live together as one political entity under conditions of freedom. It is not surprising that India is badly governed. What is surprising is that it has been possible to govern this mosaic of humanity at all, as a liberal democracy.

Professor Rostow of the Texas University regards the survival of Indian democracy as the most important phenomenon of the post-war era. That survival ought to be a matter of the most vital concern to you; after all, you were our mentor and we turned out to be your greatest pupil — at least in size! To adapt the words of Cecil Rhodes, investing in India would be philanthropy plus twenty-five per cent. To our British friends we say — we have opened doors with hope: you can ensure that we do not close them with despair. This is a critical moment in our history: you can make it a harbinger of good times to come. The dynamic and far-seeing section of our society is determined to make India the Mexico of Asia.

Our domestic market is continental in size. The population with buying power is at least 250 million out of the total 900 million. Among the countries of the Third World, India is a safe bet.

Not less than 6,500 companies are listed on the 21 recognized stock exchanges of India. We are next only to the USA which had 6,742 domestic companies listed at the end of 1991. The number of our shareholders is over 14 million. India has now become a major player in the emerging markets of the world, second only to Taiwan, Korea and Mexico, in respect of both turnover and market capitalization. There is an enormous infrastructure of free enterprise. New opportunities are at hand, waiting to be seized.

Again, the high appreciation of most foreign currencies against the Indian rupee offers an excellent opportunity of using India as a manufacturing base.

Giant multinational companies are engaged in worldwide competition for the most scarce resource of all — talent. India has never been charged with an inadequate supply of this resource.

*I*t would be futile to pretend that there are no drawbacks or shortcomings. The New Industrial Policy does not go far enough. The Government has measured out liberalization with coffee spoons. Several promises have yet to be implemented. To quote Lord Keynes, "Words ought to be a little wild because they represent the assault of thought upon the unthinking." The Indian governmental machinery may be likened to some prehistoric monster, incapable of intelligently controlling itself. This is not because the Government lacks intelligent and capable officials, but because it is so organized that managerial direction on an all-India outlook is extremely difficult. The general impression, not very wrong, is that India has one of the most obdurate and inflexible bureaucracies the free world has ever known. But a strong and skilful rider can control an unruly horse: fortunately the horse has been in good measure tamed and is less unruly than before.

*I*t is highly probable that the sensible New Policy — the one ray of hope for India's fast economic growth — will be implemented in larger doses by the present government and by any government which succeeds it. The change seems irreversible: fruitful egalitarianism has been irrevocably installed in place of sterile socialism. This is our pledge to the civilized world and the foundation of our belief in a promising future.

Human Rights and Legal Responsibilities

I am grateful for the privilege accorded to me to address this International Conference whose theme is the reassertion of the greatest single idea offered by humans to humanity — the idea of individual human rights.

Freedom is fragile and evanescent. Man has known so little of it in his entire history. The American Civil War was born of the conviction that a nation cannot remain half slave and half free. But the world continues to remain more than half slave and less than half free. Nearly four-fifths of the 160 members of the United Nations do not permit freedom of the press. In half of the countries of the world people are incarcerated for speaking their minds, often after trials that are no more than a sham. Torture — mental, physical, and emotional — is regularly practised by a third of the world's governments, notwithstanding the Declaration Against Torture and Degrading Treatment issued by the United Nations in 1975. In several states, dissenters who are inconvenient to the authorities suddenly disappear and are never seen again. This vanishing act continues to remain widely popular. More millions have died at the hands of their own governments than in war. Human rights violations have created more deaths and more human misery than have all the weapons of mass destruction.

With our incredible scientific progress, we have reached a stage when the only threat to man, left to be met, is man himself. In the

(International Bar Association, New York, September 15, 1986. Later, University of Calgary, Canada, November 11, 1990)

zoo at Lusaka, there is a cage where the notice reads, "The world's most dangerous animal". Inside the cage there is no animal but a mirror where you see yourself.

It is difficult to measure whether repression worldwide is increasing or decreasing. But awareness of that repression has undoubtedly increased, since the human rights movement started as a world movement with the launching of Amnesty International in May 1961. The shifting hemlines of international atrocities are faithfully recorded in the annual reports of that body.

The oldest human rights organization — the Anti-Slavery Society — was founded in 1839. It is still in business, because slavery is still in business. Slavery was abolished in the British Empire only in 1833 and in the United States in 1862; but bonded labour still prevails in parts of India. The Anti-Slavery Society's latest publication, "A Pattern of Slavery: India's Carpet Boys", shows how millions of small children are pressed into bonded labour in India under conditions so abject as to make the distinction between their lot and conventional slavery a matter of semantics.

No doubt it is still a world of brutalities. But the historical perspective would make us realize that ours is a perfecting world, though its progress is painfully slow, sometimes by the millimetre.

There are two gleams of hope. The concept of human rights — the new gospel — has worked its way through the subsoil of human consciousness with speed and strength, and has become one of the great driving forces of our time. But we must be reconciled to the inevitability of gradualness. The slow drip of Amnesty International has begun to work. More and more people the world over realize, and realize more clearly, that there should be increased human rights inspections and publicizing of abuses because, as President Mitterrand said, "Silence nourishes oppression". Secondly, there is a growing solidarity among the nations of the world who believe in freedom. The human rights record of a state has become the legitimate concern of the international community. Today the human rights movement is genuinely worldwide. There is, as Jerome Shestack observed, "a moral inevitability to human rights".

To attempt to define human rights definitively, would be merely to illustrate how the human mind tries, and tries in vain, to give a more precise definition than the subject-matter warrants. Human rights may be summed up in one word — Liberty. But Isaiah Berlin noted that there are more than 200 definitions of liberty; and, as Abraham Lincoln observed, the world has never had a good definition of liberty.

*I*n the Third World today, governments which are the most successful economically are authoritarian ones and veneration for human rights promises to be a cult of slow growth. That is because human rights cannot exist in a cultural and economic vacuum. Their chances of being understood — and respected — improve as the economic and educational level of society rises. It is a noble maxim that it is better for a man to go wrong in freedom rather than go right in chains; but it sounds like empty rhetoric to people who live in economic chains below the minimum subsistence level.

The categories of human rights are never closed. But we must guard against the devaluation of human rights by proliferation. It is good to increase the currency, but not at the cost of depreciating it. In the verbal haze in which we live today, secondary concepts have taken the place of primary ones; relative terms have pushed over absolute ones; and the peripheral has been given the same status as the crucial. Let me illustrate.

The primary idea of human rights involves rights against the government. Modern liberalism has expanded the idea to include rights to be satisfied by the government. "Human rights" should be distinguished from "human needs". Clarity of thought and a sense of priorities would suggest that the essence of liberty which comprises rights *against* the state should not be confused with claims or entitlements which fall to be satisfied *by* the state. Various resolutions and declarations of the United Nations list — as human rights — benefits like full employment, vacations with pay, maternity leave, and free medical care. Such broadbanding enables leftist ideologues to make a specious claim that even totalitarian States respect human rights. They contend that while free democracies have a better record in certain areas of human rights, totalitarian States have a superior record in other areas. It was such depreciation of the currency of human rights which emboldened Lenin to proclaim that the Soviets represent a "higher form of democracy" and Hitler to claim to be an "arch democrat"; and which enables States that practise torture and ruthless repression at home to pay pious lip service to human rights at international forums.

However, this is not to say that economic and social rights evolved by present-day liberalism are irrelevant or unimportant. Rights of men are not only against the government but against the people collectively. Humanity is one enormous extended family, with all the obligations of family membership. One of the basic rights is the right to decent living embodied in Article 25 of the Universal Declaration of Human Rights, 1948. Paul Sieghart who died two years ago, pointed out that the test of rights is not whether the prosperous, with access to the law courts, are well protected, or whether living standards for the majority are improving, but whether the weak are helped by the strong. "The ultimate measure of whether a society can properly be called civilized," he concludes, "is how it treats those who are near the bottom of its human heap."

Violations of economic needs occur from negligence, such as the failure to save large numbers of people from famine or floods. But mostly they occur when governments — wedded to the eighth deadly sin, ideology — pursue economic policies which deprive the poor of employment and education, nutrition and health care.

*D*emocracy and freedom are not synonymous. Adult franchise may merely amount to the right to choose your tyrants. In Lord Hailsham's words, you may have "Elective Dictatorship". Hence the conviction shared by several countries about the sovereign virtue of having a Bill of Rights in the Constitution — which would guarantee basic human freedoms including economic, social and cultural rights. Even in England where freedom is bred in the bones of the people, eminent judges like Lord Devlin, Lord Gardiner, Lord Hailsham, Lord Salmon, and Lord Scarman have advocated the incorporation of a Bill of Rights in British law.

The very purpose of a Bill of Rights is to withdraw certain subjects from the vicissitudes of political controversy, to place them beyond the reach of majorities and officials, and to establish them as legal principles to be applied by the courts. One's right to life, liberty and property, to free speech, a free press, freedom of worship and assembly, and other fundamental rights may not be submitted to vote; they depend on the outcome of no elections. (Per Jackson, *West Virginia State Board of Education v Barnette* 319 U.S. 624, 638).

It is interesting to note that in the states of India which have been governed by the Communist Party, human rights have continued to be fully respected — only because the Bill of Rights is firmly entrenched in the Indian Constitution. Incidentally, the right to equality of the sexes, which the United States has been recently attempting — so far unsuccessfully — to incorporate in its Constitution, has been provided for in the Indian Constitution right from its inception in 1950.

Since freedom cannot be passed on in the bloodstream, and is never more than one generation away from extinction, it is essential that the power to amend the Constitution should not extend to abrogating the Bill of Rights. The permanence of the core of human rights has been ensured in India by our Supreme Court which held in *Kesavananda v State of Kerala (A.I.R. 1973 S.C. 1461)* that Parliament, in exercise of the power to amend the Constitution, cannot destroy or alter its basic structure. A constitution is not a jellyfish; it is a highly evolved organism. It has an identity and integrity of its own, the evocative Preamble to the Indian Constitution being its identity card. It cannot be made to lose its identity in the process of amendment. The Fundamental Rights are the very heart of our Constitution — taking them away would deprive the Constitution not only of its identity but of its life itself. Parliament, when it claims the right to amend the constitutional law, cannot set itself up as the official liquidator of the Constitution.

Dr. Konrad Adenauer, the former Chancellor of West Germany, remarked that in creating man, God had hit upon a very poor compromise. If he had made man more intelligent, he would have known how to behave; if he had made man less intelligent, he would have been easier to govern. This remark neatly sums up the dilemma of democracy. Till man rises higher in the process of evolution, the world situation will continue to remain fouled up.

Since man does not know how to behave, the necessity arises of legal responsibilities to prevent liberty from degenerating into licence. No virtue is absolute — not even freedom. One man's freedom fighter is another man's terrorist.

It is true that eternal vigilance is the price of liberty. But it is true, in even a deeper sense, that eternal responsibility is also part of the price of liberty. Excessive authority, without liberty, is intolerable; but excessive liberty, without authority and without responsibility, soon becomes equally intolerable. De Tocqueville made the profound observation that liberty cannot stand alone but must be paired with a companion virtue: liberty and morality; liberty and law; liberty and justice; liberty and the common good; liberty and civic responsibility.

Let us make this gathering a Conference of Introspection. While we are commendably concerned with the issue of human rights, we may ask ourselves — are we equally mindful of the paramount need of legal responsibilities? Have we reduced the inalienable rights of man — to life, liberty and the pursuit of litigation?

Liberty has a hypnotizing sound; while, unfortunately, responsibility has no sex appeal. Freedom is like alcohol — it must be taken in moderation. Perhaps we are making life too easy for criminals and too difficult for law-abiding citizens. In free societies, too many crooks break the law, blight young lives, traffic in drugs, and claim the fundamental right to exploit commercially sex and violence. Our values today are drastically eroded, because too many men — with no more moral backbone than a chocolate éclair — claim the freedom of expression and action which results inevitably in increasing the numbers of violent criminals. American, British, and Indian societies lit up the moral imagination of the world in the past; why are they crime-ridden today? Is not alienation — alienation of the individual from society, of the child from the family — too high a price to pay for the freedom to be a permissive society? Are we right in thinking that hard evidence, if collected illegally, cannot be used against a criminal in a trial even when there is no other way of securing a conviction? We have to strike an acceptable balance between the proper interests of society which wants criminals to be put out of harm's way and the equally proper instincts of libertarians anxious that nothing should imperil the rights of the citizen.

These questions have been debated over decades, but admit of no easy solution. The sun never sets on these debates. In the present state of human consciousness — when man continues to be merely a caricature of man to be — there is a certainty of freedom being abused unless legal responsibilities are given the same prime importance as human rights. Since the continuous intellectual enjoyment of the debate must depend to a large extent upon its inconclusiveness, it would be boorish as well as presumptuous of me to suggest a final conclusion.

The Ideal of Human Unity
and
The North-South Dialogue

*I*n a century which has witnessed two World Wars resulting in the breaking of nations and the deaths of tens of millions, and at a time when so many countries have not even achieved national integration, the ideal of human unity seems light years away. Even now, not a year passes without violent conflicts and skirmishes erupting in some part of the world. In Plato's phrase, we are still like cavemen, with our backs turned to the light, watching the shadows on the wall. Modern man exists in what Ezra Pound called "a botched civilization". Professor Gunnar Myrdal towards the end of his long life observed that the world was "really going to hell in every possible respect".

Occasionally we have the triumph of hope over experience but those are short-lived moments of Pollyanna optimism, and even the cheer-mongers are driven to rejoin the ranks of "despairing optimists".

The world is witnessing today two basic confrontations — one vertical and the other horizontal. The vertical is between the East and the West, the horizontal between the North and the South. The East-West conflict is between tyranny and freedom, just as the North-South confrontation is between affluence and poverty. The solution of the first would release the resources necessary to pave the way for a solution of the second. The temperature of the world

(1984-85 Hagey Lectures, University of Waterloo, Canada, October 31 and November 1, 1984. Later, Twelfth J.N. Tata Lecture at Bangalore, September 30, 1987)

is determined by the thermostat of East-West relations.

The expressions "North" and "South" passed into the current coin of global thought in the early 1970s. They are more or less synonymous with "developed economies" and "developing economies" respectively.

Out of the developed countries which constitute the North, twenty-four are members of the Organization for Economic Co-operation and Development (OECD). Although the North has only a quarter of the world's population, it has 70 per cent of the wealth, over 80 per cent of the trade, 90 per cent of the industry, and close to 100 per cent of the finest and most advanced centres of learning and technology. It holds 94 per cent of the registered patents.

"South" is generally applied to the countries of South and South-Asia, Africa, and Latin America, and it includes the oil-rich countries of the Middle East which have formed the Organization of Petroleum Exporting Countries (OPEC). The South is a cluster of 116 countries which present a picture of enormous diversity and contrast in basic features. The infinite variety is marked in every conceivable way. The poor countries of the South are united more by attitude than by geography. Underlying that unity is a common sense of anger against the North and a deep sense of frustration.

Sometimes the North is referred to as the First World, the Second World being the Soviet Union and East European countries which believe in what is euphemistically called 'socialism'. The South is often called the Third World. It also goes under the anachronistic name "Group of 77" though now it comprises well over a hundred members. It is impossible to arrive at a precise categorization, because the North and the South are not formal organizations.

To Candide's optimistic dictum, "This is the best of all possible worlds", the pessimist's reply was "I am afraid so." The South accepts neither Candide's optimism nor the reply. It would like to break the sorry scheme of things entire, and remould it nearer the South's desire.

The North-South dialogue began in 1974. The aspiration of developing countries to secure an international co-operative system culminated in the formulation of a New International Economic Order (NIEO) which was declared at the Plenary Meeting of the General Assembly on May 1,1974.

Sometimes the North-South dialogue has lapsed into a dialogue of the deaf, frequently into a soliloquy of the South, and occasionally into a confrontation. In a lighter vein I may repeat the remark of C. Rajagopalachari, one of the wisest and greatest Indians of this century, who was asked why there is generally a confrontation between the north and the south in different countries of the world. His reply was, "It is the fault of the geographers. They always put the south at the bottom."

The issues involved in the North-South dialogue have never been brought out more beautifully or more cogently than by the Independent Commission on International Development issues, under the Chairmanship of Willy Brandt (the Brandt Commission). The two Reports of the Brandt Commission — *North-South: A Programme for Survival* (1980) and *Common Crisis of North-South: Co-operation for World Recovery* (1983) are *the* documents of the decade. They were not merely the work of economists but of thinkers and statesmen who strongly felt the need for humanizing world economics. As *The Economist* of London said, "Brandt is not for burning."

The most voracious consumer of money today is nuclear weapons and other armaments. It is expenditure on armaments — the most sterile of all forms of spending — which results in poor countries' development being kept in cold storage. President Eisenhower said, "Every gun that is made, every warship launched, every rocket fired, signifies in the final sense a theft from those who are hungry and are not fed, those who are cold and are not clothed." Today around 1,000 billion US dollars are spent annually on arms and armies — much more than two billion dollars a day.

It is a platitude that the two Super Powers possess over-saturation and over-kill nuclear capacities. Their present stock-pile is of 50,000 nuclear warheads. Military experts speak of "Mutual Assured Destruction" between the two Super Powers. The acronym is MAD, an abbreviation of symbolic significance.

The waste of human ability, energy and money on armaments will continue unabated, and diversion of world resources to development will remain a pipe-dream, so long as man does not learn the great lesson which Mahatma Gandhi preached so convincingly in our own times — viz., non-violence is the law of our species. The exhortation to divert resources from weaponry to development stands no practical chance of being heeded unless and until the balance of terror is replaced by the balance of reason.

The Brandt Commission pointed out that (a) the military expenditure of only half a day would suffice to financè the entire malaria eradication programme of WHO; (b) the cost of one modern tank — roughly a million dollars — could provide a thousand classrooms; (c) the price of one jet fighter (20 million dollars) could set up 40,000 village pharmacies. But these chilling truths present threatened nations with a false choice between what is unavoidable and what is desirable. Though spending on armaments is undoubtedly both wasteful and highly dangerous in the world of today, the vast majority of nations must necessarily defend themselves against external threats or internal uprisings, for reasons which the Brandt Report did not consider.

It is noteworthy that the Brandt Commission's 1980 Report suggested that in the dialogue on the international economic system the participation of the Soviet Union, China and East European economies would be desirable. China would come in as a member of the South, and the Soviet Union as a member of the North. After the Brandt Report, the People's Republic of China has taken its seat in the International Monetary Fund and the World Bank, thereby improving the degree of global representation on those twins of Bretton Woods.

The Brandt Commission made 59 recommendations, falling broadly under three heads: (i) a large transfer of resources to the less developed countries involving an increase in official aid to reach 0.7 per cent of developed countries' GNP by 1985 and one per cent by the year 2000, and a doubling of World Bank loans; (ii) an international energy strategy; and (iii) major reforms in international economic systems.

Unfortunately, the debate on the New International Economic Order has been heavy on rhetoric and light on analysis, long on emotion and short on reason.

The South symbolizes humanity's immemorial pain. Its situation may be summed up in the staccato style of Micawber: Votes doubled, expectations multiplied, income stationary, result misery.

The case of the South is so strong that it almost argues itself. It is an instance of what lawyers call *res ipsa loquitur* — the thing speaks for itself. The absolute gap between rich countries and poor countries widens every year.

In the European Economic Community they do not know what to do with all the milk that they produce: the total weight of their milk powder surplus is a million tonnes, while their embarrassing butter mountain is of 1.5 million tonnes. There are 20 million tonnes of surplus food in European warehouses. At the same time more than one-third of the people in the world suffer from serious malnutrition. Despite the World Food Programme, despite the Food and Agriculture Organization (the largest specialized agency of the United Nations), despite the United Nations Disaster Relief Organization (itself something of a disaster), despite the International Fund for Agricultural Development, and despite bilateral aid programmes, Oxfam and other private charities — starvation persists and famines occur with distressing frequency. Three people out of four in the Third World have no proper sanitation and few have clean drinking water.

A billion people are trapped in what the World Bank, in its first Development Report calls absolute poverty: "a condition of life so characterized by malnutrition, illiteracy, disease, squalid surroundings, high infant mortality and low life expectancy as to be beneath any reasonable definition of human decency." Three-quarters of the "absolutely poor" are to be found in Commonwealth countries.

There was a time when one-half of the world did not know how the other half lived. But today television pictures successfully translate a continent's distant agony into humanly comprehensible horror. The tragedy of Africa would move the sands of the Sahara to tears — a tragedy too full for sound and foam. And in some areas it is getting even worse. The average per capita income of Africans in some recent years was four per cent below the level in 1970.

Unfortunately, some countries of the North seem to be suffering from what may be called "compassion fatigue". In some years the United States spent annually more on potted plants and flowers than they did on aid to the Third World.

In the language of studied moderation, the South has a good case on merits. But it is a good case spoilt by bad advocacy. Self-criticism is not the strong point of the South, and it is about time it stopped thinking that anyone who agrees with NIEO is a friend of the South and anyone who disagrees is an enemy. The South has chosen to fight, as happened in the Vietnam war, a wrong war with the wrong weapons against the wrong enemy on the wrong battlefield. So sympathetic a friend as Professor W. W. Rostow of the University of Texas at Austin said, "In my view — and I say this as one who has crusaded for over thirty years on behalf of development in the South — the whole NIEO process has been rooted in an inappropriate ideology, it has operated with an agenda destined to frustrate both South and North; and it has been conducted by negotiations unlikely to generate a productive result."

*I*t is not as if justice is only on the side of the South. The North has a rational viewpoint which demonstrates that the air is not merely thick with alibis for inaction. The North feels — and with justification — that the South has been its own greatest enemy. The charge-sheet against the developing countries makes sorry reading:

(a) The South has been demanding revolutionary reforms as of right and behaving as if it has an indefeasible title to share the wealth of the North. Considering the New International Economic Order as its "economic Magna Carta", it has made demands which are strident and static, "one-sided and unrealistic".

(b) The South maintains double standards. The rich and the super-rich of the South show far less compassion for their own poor countrymen than the North has displayed towards the South. Even the oil-rich OPEC countries do not significantly help the other countries of the South except for assisting their co-religionists and, in particular, the Arab world against Israel.

(c) The North, wedded to freedom, is expected to finance communist regimes of the South, while the Soviet Union and its satellites do little to help those countries of the South where state-controlled economy prevails. The Council for Mutual Economic Assistance — consisting of East European communist countries — hardly assists the countries of the South. As OECD's 1983 review notes, "For the bulk of the Third World, the Eastern European communist countries have played practically no role at all in the major resource transfer developments of the last ten to fifteen years."

(d) Corruption prevents the benefits of aid from trickling down to the poor. Aid goes into private pockets. This is not to say that there is no corruption in the North; but there are degrees of corruption, and a different set of considerations arise when politicians ask another country to finance the corruption in their own state. The Argentine President, Raul Alfonsin, says of the billions of dollars Argentina borrowed in the late seventies, "The foreign debts' most irritating feature for the Argentines is that the money was not converted into the expansion of the economy and the creation of capital. Quite the contrary."

Researchers at America's Federal Reserve Board reckon that over one-third of the 252 billion dollars' increase in the debt of Argentina, Brazil, Chile, Mexico and Venezuela between 1974 and 1982 went into buying assets overseas or was salted away in private foreign bank accounts.

(e) The governments of the South are inefficient and make hopeless investors and the North is expected to finance their grandiose ego-inflating projects, with the inevitable waste and muddle. Most of them cannot manage men, materials or money. Dr. Drucker uttered a penetrating truth when he said, "There are no under-developed countries. There are only undermanaged ones." Of course, the truth needs to be sugar-coated. Myint observes, "If one were to tell the politicians of the under-developed countries that their people are lazy, stupid, lacking in initiative and adaptability, one would be branded as an enemy; but if one were to re-phrase [this] in another way and say that the people lack entrepreneurial capacity, one would be welcomed for giving scientific support for economic planning."

Many of the countries of the South preach and practise outdated socialism and State control which turns the sale of every commodity into a bureaucratic struggle, subject to political dominance and graft.

(f) The South continues to persist in its cardinal blunder of taking no effective steps to make investment in family planning, education, public health and nutrition, despite repeated pleas that investment in human development is far more important than physical investment; and that without an adequate investment in the former, investments in the latter would prove infructuous. It is of paramount importance that the countries of the South set their own houses in order with all convenient speed. What is needed is not so much a New International Economic Order as New Domestic Economic Orders. The greatest thing for a nation is self-help. Eradication of corruption, mobilization of available internal funds, efficient use of human resources — as have been done by South Korea and Hong Kong, Taiwan and Singapore — would be far more rewarding than a confrontation with the North.

(g) Aid is no substitute for self-help. The poverty of a nation has never been cured by a massive transfer of wealth. No country, however rich, can develop another country merely through finance. In fact, official aid accounts for only 13 per cent of the total investment in developing countries.

*T*he international meetings today seem to produce mainly recriminations and bad tempers. There have been unseemly squabbles between the North and the South. The South rattles the borrowing bowl and denigrates its creditors for not displaying further munificence. The poor countries charge the rich nations with hypocrisy, criminal irresponsibility, arrogance and insensitivity. The North has been driven to say that the verbal violence of the South represented "the babbling of economic illiterates seized by a fit of passion", and would make the UN "fade into the shadow of world rhetoric." The outspoken Ambassador Daniel P. Moynihan criticized the South for practising "the politics of resentment and the economics of envy." Even granted that some of the railing of the less developed countries against the North is meant for domestic consumption, and they want to find northern scapegoats for their own inefficiency or corruption, their harsh tone and temper have been hardly conducive to a rational debate. Condemning the North is hardly a brilliant strategy for eliciting its generous response. The victims of the current deadlock are the 38 lowest-income States.

It is time to end on both sides this exhibition of frayed tempers. A conciliatory tone would be statesmanlike and productive of far better results. As India's representative said at the UN Assembly's special session on NIEO in September 1975: "Let us not confront each other, but let us together confront the problems facing us."

If one brings the historical perspective to bear on the problems inherent in the North-South dialogue, one would see room for hope. The most significant verities are most commonly missed. The profound and satisfying truth is that the ideas of inter-dependence and inter-assistance have made greater and faster progress than almost any other global idea in world history.

How many centuries did it take Western Europe to stop the lunacy of wars and live in peace together as a common economic community? How many centuries did it take India to pass a law abolishing the disgraceful concept of untouchability, and how many more generations will it take for the still surviving vestiges of it to disappear in practice? Have Catholics and Protestants in the North, and Shias and Sunnis in the South, yet learnt that they should love one another since they are the followers of the same Prophet?

By contrast, the concept of inter-dependence of nations has penetrated and permeated the stratum of human consciousness with unusual speed and strength. It is only four decades since the last World War ended. Yet the international institutions symbolizing the inter-dependence of nations, started after the war, have become as firmly rooted in the human psyche as any of the centuries-old organizations. The World Bank and the International Monetary Fund have served the Third World well. Their annual meetings are milestones along the road to global growth.

The picture of inter-assistance, especially aid by the North to the South, is again, not one of unrelieved gloom. "Nothing is here for tears, nothing to wail or knock the breast." Ours is a perfecting world, but its progress is painfully slow, sometimes by the millimetre. The famous anthropologist Margaret Mead concluded that it takes about a generation, say three decades, for a new idea to strike roots in the public mind. The impatient dialogue between the North and the South started only thirteen years ago. We must be reconciled to the inevitability of gradualness. Brandt's passionate plea has begun to work. More and more people of the North realize more clearly, that the economically desperate of today are the international flashpoints of tomorrow. There is a growing consciousness that, as Rabindranath Tagore reminded us, the weak in their weakness can do no less harm to the strong than the strong in their strength to the weak.

The greatest gift the North can confer on the South is the gift of knowledge. Transfer of technology can be the most fruitful type of assistance. An old Asian adage says, "Give a boy some fish to eat and you will assuage his hunger for a day, but teach a boy to catch fish and he will never be hungry." Shared responsibility should beget a shared programme for development and an adequate, collective response.

The South has to abandon its wild rhetoric and engage in conciliatory negotiation. And the North has to realize that the search for solutions is not an act of benevolence, but a condition of mutual survival. In the historical perspective, that search has had a good start and must continue with redoubled vigour. In the words of Arnold Toynbee, "Our age will be well remembered not for its horrifying crimes nor its astonishing inventions, but because it is the first generation since the dawn of history in which mankind dared to believe it practical to make the benefits of civilization available to the whole human race."

*I*f mankind is to live in minimum comfort as a single family and the internecine tensions and strains are to be avoided, population control is not only desirable but necessary.

There can be no doubt that the frightening growth of world population is one of the strongest forces shaping the future of human society. It took mankind one million years to reach the first billion: that was the world population around the year 1800. By 1900 — in just a hundred years — a second billion was added. The twentieth century by itself has already added another three billion. The present world population is five billion. According to the *Global 2000 Report* to the American President, "three-quarters of the people who have ever lived since life on earth began are alive today." The number is expected to increase to 6.3 billion by 2000 A.D., and nine-tenths of the increase will be in developing countries. Every five days the world population increases by one million. Fertility falls as incomes rise, education spreads and health improves.

The rich get richer, and the poor get children which helps to keep them poor. More children does not mean more workers but more people without work. The World Bank's World Development Reports rightly suggest that population control is one of the first imperatives of development, since economic advance is so severely diluted by rapid population growth. It is not suggested that human beings should be treated like cattle and compulsorily sterilized. But there is no alternative to family planning at a human level without introducing an element of physical coercion. The choice is really between control of population and perpetuation of poverty.

No one familiar with the conditions in the South would have any doubt that the hope of the people there would die in their hungry hutments unless population control is given the topmost priority.

*T*he three basic factors militating against translation of the ideal of human unity into action are religion, nationalistic politics and economic ideologies.

Religions are different roads converging to the same destination. Mahatma Gandhi said, "The need of the moment is not one religion, but mutual respect and tolerance of the devotees of different religions. We want to reach not the dead level but unity in diversity. The soul of all religions is one, but it is encased in a multitude of forms. The latter will persist to the end of time."

The free countries rightly believe in freedom as the only sensible way of organizing society. They believe that even "tragic freedom" is preferable to· "compulsory happiness". But this need not come in the way of free nations living in harmony and tolerance with authoritarian regimes. Unfortunately, enmity and hatred persist among nations even after the root cause has been relegated to the limbo of the forgotten past. Speaking of the Schleswig-Holstein question in the 19th century, Lord Palmerston observed, "Only three people had ever understood it. One was dead. The other was in a lunatic asylum. I am the third and I have forgotten it."

As a species, we can no longer afford the luxuries of strident nationalism and the fundamentalism of religions and of economic ideologies. Citizens of the world are far more needed than nationalists. Ideologists can never solve the problem of Man on Earth. In the words of Dr. Jung, "All isms are lethal."

I am never tired of repeating that ancient India was far more civilized than modern India with its satellites in space. The hallmark of our generation is spiritual sterility and moral illiteracy.

In his masterly writings *The Human Cycle* and *The Ideal of Human Unity* Sri Aurobindo expresses his prescient views as regards the human family and its future. Today everyone knows about the European Common Market or the European Economic Community, and the credit for bringing about the union of free European countries is rightly given to the French thinker, Jean Monnet. But few know that it was as early as 1916, when the First World War was raging and the European countries were locked in a conflict bloodier than any previous one, that Sri Aurobindo foresaw the birth of those unifying forces which have now led to the creation of the European Economic Community. He called it the United States of Europe. In his message on the day of our independence — August 15, 1947 — Sri Aurobindo referred to his dream of "a world union forming the outer basis of a fairer, brighter and nobler life for all mankind." He added, "That unification of the human world is under way; there is an imperfect initiation, organized but struggling against tremendous difficulties. But the momentum is there and it must inevitably increase and conquer."

In another place, Sri Aurobindo said, "Mankind has a habit of surviving the worst catastrophes created by its own errors or by the violent turns of Nature; and it must be so if there is any meaning in its existence, if its long history and continuous survival is not the accident of a fortuitously self-organizing Chance, which it must be in a purely materialistic view of the nature of the world. If man is intended to survive and carry forward the evolution of which he is at present the head and, to some extent, a half-conscious leader of its march, he must come out of his present chaotic international life and arrive at a beginning of organized united action; some kind of World-State, unitary or federal, or a confederacy or a coalition, he must arrive at in the end. . . . The ideal of human unity would be no longer an unfulfilled ideal but an accomplished fact and its preservation given into the charge of the united human peoples."

Already, Sri Aurobindo's incredible prediction about the "United States of Europe" has almost come true. His prophecy about a World-State will take a little longer.

Man, whatever may be his scientific and technological advance, is pathetically small and insignificant in the scheme of the Universe. Each one of us is condemned to death, and lives under a stay of execution for an unknown length of time. Man is an unfinished creature — he is only a caricature of Man to be. When he evolves further, he will shed his ego and his penchant for aggrandizement. There is no doubt that a race weary of its own bloodshed and divisiveness will ultimately grope its way to a system which offers the only chance for the survival of the species.

2

Prime Ministers

Prime Minister in Office
but not in Power

*T*his year, when the world is celebrating the 2500th anniversary of the birth of democracy, the greatest crisis facing the free world is that there is no real leadership. Men, smaller than life, are strutting and fretting their hour upon the stage in the democratic States of the East and the West. It is difficult to recall a time when so many heads of government had so little public support and commanded so little public respect. Instead of real leadership, we have just "holes in the air", to use the expressive phrase of George Orwell. India is no exception to the world trend — a plethora of politicians and paucity of statesmen.

An allegation regarding the integrity of our Prime Minister is dangerous at all times but is disastrous at this critical juncture when the need for moral leadership is greater than ever before. In the last forty-five years our standard of living has been rising, but our standard of life has been falling. No country can survive without a functioning Head of State. Today the Prime Minister is shell-shocked: he may continue in office, but he is no longer in power. The Congress is counting its tomorrows.

At present it is impossible to say definitely whether the tainted money changed hands or whether Mr. Harshad Mehta was only trying to divert attention from the enormity of his own misdeeds.

If the allegation of the payment having been made is false, it is clearly not enough for the Prime Minister to deny it. He must

(The Times of India, June 24, 1993)

take active steps to bring home to Mr. Harshad Mehta, in either
civil or criminal proceedings, the charge of defamation. The arrears
in courts are such that obviously it would not be enough merely
to file a case. A judicial proceeding once started in India, as I have
said before, is the nearest thing to eternal life ever seen on earth.
The Prime Minister would have to use the enormous resources at
his command to ensure that the civil or criminal proceeding comes
immediately to a hearing. Such a step would be pre-eminently in
the public interest. It is not only the Prime Minister who would
be the plaintiff or the complainant, but the entire Indian people.
They are entitled to live under a head of government who is seen
to have decency and legitimacy.

On the other hand, if Mr. Harshad Mehta's allegation is true,
the Prime Minister has lost a great opportunity of rendering a
signal service to Indian democracy. Mr. Narasimha Rao has
integrity and moral standards far above those of the average Indian
politician. He should have made the important point that though
he did accept the donation, he had not the slightest motive of
favouring the donor. (It must be remembered that the donation was
made in November 1991 when the scam had not yet exploded.) Mr.
Narasimha Rao should have put the blunt question — is there any
member of the Lok Sabha who has got elected without financial
support from others? We have lived so long in an atmosphere of
misrepresentations and falsehoods that we are reconciled to the
thought that the only commandment a politician should not break
is "Thou shalt not be found out".

It is interesting to draw a parallel between what happened in
India and what happened, by a strange coincidence, in Britain in
the same week. Mr. Asil Nadir has an unanswerable claim to be
regarded as no less crooked than Mr. Harshad Mehta; and his
company Polly Peck was run on no more ethical lines than Mr.
Mehta's Growmore. He gave substantial donations to the Conservative party. Threatening to spill the beans, Mr. Nadir spoke to *The
Times* in words which are very similar to those used by Mr.
Harshad Mehta: "Everything that I will be showing will be
substantiated by relevant documents: We have already gathered the

material, and I am very happy with it. . . I will not be pushed into making these details public. The timing will be of my own choosing." (Incidentally, it is most probable that the key to the suitcase was deliberately "forgotten" by Mr. Harshad Mehta, so that a telephone call which would be received later could be tape-recorded.)

What was the attitude of the Conservative party when Mr. Asil Nadir threatened to unleash a 'Watergate'? The Treasurer of the Conservative Party frankly admitted that he was wrong in accepting the donations and had "misjudged" the situation. The party said that it would repay any money donated by Mr. Asil Nadir if it turned out to be tainted money.

A statement by the Prime Minister that even he could not fight the election without donations would have given a jolt to our self-complacency and made us realize that the present system of conducting elections is bound to breed greater and greater degradation in our public life. Politics tends to corrupt; Indian politics tends to corrupt absolutely.

Under Indian law it is not a crime for any politician or for any political party to accept donations from an individual or a company. Further, a person would not be guilty of any wrong if he accepts a donation and forwards it to his own party to spend on elections including his own personal election.

It is *not* suggested that it is right for the Prime Minister to accept a donation from a private individual, much less if he is a shady character. What is suggested is that it is better to make a clean confession than falsely deny having received the money.

Consider the hypocrisy and humbug involved in our administratively framed rules and forms. All members of the Lok Sabha are asked to declare that they have not spent more than Rs. 1,50,000 on their election campaign — apart from the amount spent by the party. The Prime Minister could have well asked whether there was any member of the Lok Sabha who had made an honest declaration as regards expenditure on his own election.

Again, all members of the Rajya Sabha have to declare that they ordinarily reside in the State from which they get elected. This is merely a requirement of the prescribed form, and not of the substantive law. But we will not have the intellectual honesty to change the form, despite our prolonged experience that it involves the making of a patently false declaration in a sizeable number of cases. The latest example is that of the Finance Minister Dr. Manmohan Singh, a perfectly honest man, who had to make an untrue declaration that he "ordinarily resides in Assam". Similarly, palpably false declarations had to be made in the past by Dr. Pranab Mukherjee, Mr. Shiv Shankar, the late Mr. L. K. Jha, and several others. Cases challenging their election were filed but have not been decided for one reason or another.

When simple problems created by mere forms or regulations, which are administratively prescribed, remain unresolved, is there any hope of our making desirable changes in our substantive election law? Small wonder that a nation so apathetic about honesty in public life and having such scant regard for truth, has an unacceptably large number of corrupt officials, venal politicians, and swindlers in the business community.

Far too long, we have suffered from "the unawakened heart", to use the poignant expression of E. M. Forster. The Harshad episode will serve a great national purpose if it prods us to ensure that a member of Parliament can start his public life with a clear conscience, instead of being compelled to make a declaration which constitutes a mockery of our national motto, "Truth Shall Prevail".

Tribute to Rajiv Gandhi

*T*he most illustrious martyr to the cult of violence which is tearing our country apart is no more. Rajiv Gandhi has been snatched away from India in circumstances which are so tragic as to touch the least tender to tears and the most incredulous to prayer.

I had known Rajiv personally for about two decades; and my memory retains what was good and gracious about this fine human being.

Before he entered politics, he was simplicity and gentleness personified. During the dark days of the Emergency (1975 to 1977), he kept himself totally aloof from the tyranny which stalked the land. Then his brother Sanjay died. Between 1980 and 1984 there was no Indian politician who was more universally loved and respected. At that time he almost achieved the impossible — he earned rich tributes even from his political opponents.

He began his tenure as the Prime Minister of India in a blaze of glory and proved that he had the right vision and decent basic instincts. The first twelve months of his rule, commencing from November 1984, constituted the brightest period in the chequered history of our republic. He was responsible for the Union Budget of 1985 which was the finest budget since we became independent in 1947. It was better conceived and more nutritive than any earlier budget. He dismantled controls and introduced liberalization — the only policy which could ever in practice break the stranglehold of

(Doordarshan, May 23, 1991)

poverty on our hapless and helpless people. He entered into pacts with the Sikhs in the Punjab, and the militants in Assam, which could have been the foundation of lasting peace and goodwill. But the Fates ruled otherwise. A number of factors (most of them within his own control) were responsible for the non-fulfilment, in his later years as the Prime Minister, of the golden promise of his first twelve months. Rajiv had the right ideas but chose the wrong people to surround him. The decay of the state which had begun in his mother's time was accentuated, and the country went down the inclined plane with alarming acceleration.

His untimely death is a grim reminder that the land with the noblest heritage has become the most criminalized and the most violent democracy in the world.

3

Governors

C. Subramanian — The Ideal Governor

*I*f one were to sum up in a single sentence the work done by Mr. C. Subramanian as the Governor of Maharashtra, one would say he proved himself to be an ideal Governor.

Mr. V. P. Singh has much to answer for, but his wisest act as the Prime Minister was to appoint in February 1990 Mr. C. Subramanian as the Governor of Maharashtra.

Those who have come in close contact with Mr. Subramanian will agree that he is the living embodiment of true Indian culture. Decades of perceptive thinking and experience in India's public life have given him *buddhi* which sets apart a statesman from a politician. Knowledge of our ancient culture has endowed him with an instinctive yearning for the higher values.

I may bring to the surface of my mind one incident which happened in New York. There were on the dais the late Mr. Hidayatullah, Vice President of India, and some swamis. Mr. Subramanian prefaced his talk by mentioning the swamis first and the Vice President later. He explained, for the benefit of the Western audience, that according to our ancient culture the man of God came first and the man who had attained worldly distinction came later.

Mr. Subramanian exemplifies in his own personal life the philosophy of plain living and high thinking. Unlike the typical Indian politician, he is allergic to "the noise that men call fame, the dross that men call gold". Even as the Governor he continued to maintain the incredible simplicity of his normal style of living. Not for him the pomp and circumstance of high public office. Within the first month of his coming to Bombay as the Governor, he made it clear that he was sincerely embarrassed by being called "Your Excellency". The people thereafter referred to him only as the Honourable Governor.

One of his last acts as the Governor was again characteristic. In Goa, he divested himself of his black convocation robe, and the distinguished gathering got the message that what counts is the grey matter, enriched by study, and not the raiments.

Mr. Subramanian's tenure as the Governor was stamped by one great quality. He practised gubernatorial activism. He was never content to be merely a namby-pamby figurehead. He regarded himself as the guardian of the welfare of the State and actively took all those measures which were necessary to promote public welfare. No one worked harder to advance the cause of the essential unity of all religions. If despite his unremitting efforts there is widespread violence in Bombay today, it is a measure of the depths of degradation to which our people have sunk in point of cultural illiteracy. If the Governor and the Chief Minister of every State had the vision, knowledge and capability of Mr. Subramanian, India would be transformed into a wholly different country.

In the course of a full political life, Mr. Subramanian had held many portfolios and made many decisions which left their mark on our history. As the Agriculture Minister he was the main architect of the Green Revolution. His decisions as the minister, at different times, in charge of finance, commerce, defence and steel have contributed to the growth and development of India. Those were great memories but he laid them down. It was after years of retirement that he was called back to active public life. We in Maharashtra like to think that in all his crowded life his finest hour was the three-year stint which he had as the head of our State.

His manner of quitting the high office which he occupied was again characteristic of him. He was in Goa to attend the meeting of the Indian Science Congress. The news editor of a local daily happened to be present and in the worst tradition of cheap journalism he published a report of what Mr. Subramanian is supposed to have said. According to the newspaper report Mr. Subramanian observed that the Prime Minister had reserved to himself so many portfolios and that he undertook so many less crucial engagements that efficiency of government could not be maintained. This was not a criticism but a statement of fact which no thinking Indian can possibly disagree with. The observation was made not at a press conference but at an informal tea party.

My own view is that the incident did not amount to such an indiscretion that it necessitated Mr. Subramanian's resignation. The local newspaper editor thought that he was entitled to publish the report without the permission of the man whose public life was at stake. Since the large majority of governors are boneless wonders, I can only hope that the episode will not serve as a precedent, deterring governors from honestly expressing their views on what is needed to promote high standards in public administration.

But if the resignation of Mr. Subramanian was uncalled for, the acceptance of the resignation by the government was a blunder of the first magnitude. When the history of India comes to be written, the acceptance of Mr. Subramanian's resignation will rank with the grievous mistake of the acceptance of Mr. Chidambaram's resignation. These two incidents bear witness to the genius of India for getting rid of persons who are most needed at a critical moment in our history.

The people of Maharashtra will sorely miss Mr. Subramanian's statesmanship and his vision, his healing guidance and his unswerving commitment to the betterment of the people in every way. Dr. P.C. Alexander will have a hard act, indeed, to follow.

Ram Lal — The Shameless Governor

*N*ineteen eighty-four may go down in Indian history as the year of disintegration. After having successfully alienated all the neighbouring countries, we have now turned our gift for alienation to our own states. Federalism is in peril.

During 1984 we have piled up an ominously large heap of dangerous precedents which diminish democracy and devalue the Constitution; and among them the dismissal of Chief Minister N. T. Rama Rao by Ram Lal as the Governor of Andhra Pradesh takes the palm. People's faith in democratic institutions has been violently shaken and they have begun to wonder whether the office of Governor is worse than an expensive superfluity.

A Chief Minister duly elected by a spectacular majority has been summarily removed and the State has been entrusted to the care of a new ministry which has never been proved to enjoy the confidence of the Assembly. The heart of the democratic process has been stilled. These happenings are light years away from the way in which the architects of the Constitution intended the democratic process to function.

Under the Constitution the Governor is to the State what the President is to the Union. As one who symbolizes the State and is its head, he should obviously and necessarily be above the maelstrom of party politics.

There has to be a Governor for each State (Article 153). The

(The Times of India, August 30, 1984)

Governor is appointed by the President (Article 155) and he holds office during the pleasure of the President (Article 156).

According to the judgment of the Supreme Court in *Dr. Raghukul Tilak's* case (A.I.R. 1979 S.C. 1109), the relationship of employer and employee does not exist between the Government of India and the Governor, and the Governor's office "is not subordinate or subservient to the Government of India". While this is the true constitutional position, among the various prestigious institutions which we have devalued is the office of Governor. In practice the Governor has been reduced to virtually the same position as that of the resident agent in a native state in the days of the British raj. Several Governors have debased their high office by lending their services to fulfil the partisan objectives of the political party in power at the Centre.

The Constitution intended that the Governor should be the instrument to maintain the fundamental equilibrium of the people of the State and to ensure that the mandates of the Constitution are respected in the State. Instead, the Governors of Sikkim, Jammu and Kashmir, and of Andhra Pradesh removed the Chief Minister of each of the three States who had not been defeated, and could not have been defeated, on the floor of the house.

The removal of Rama Rao is only the latest incident in this fast-moving and disgrace-abounding scenario. In the language of studied moderation, it was an unmitigated crime against the Constitution. It was an act both indefensible in point of constitutional legality and marked by black turpitude in point of constitutional morality.

Repeated violations of the Constitution are bad enough; but even worse is the acceptance and approval of the violations, in high quarters.

Consider the defence of Ram Lal's misconduct by the Union Home Minister, Mr. Narasimha Rao, who proclaimed last week that it was the "unfettered right" of the Governor to dismiss Rama Rao once he was convinced that the Chief Minister had lost his majority, and that Ram Lal's "subjective satisfaction" was enough. For good measure, Mr. Narasimha Rao went on to add that "the

Governor could not have acted otherwise at the given moment". This pretentious view is diametrically contrary to the patent and elementary legal position.

First, all public acts are required under the rule of law to be performed fairly and impartially. If by the Governor's "unfettered right" is meant that he can act whimsically or arbitrarily or for extraneous reasons, such a right is unknown to the Constitution and to the rule of law. A long series of recent decisions of the House of Lords in England and of our own Supreme Court have established that "subjective satisfaction" is not final but has to be the satisfaction of a reasonable man. In other words, the facts must be such that a reasonable man could possibly come to that conclusion.

Secondly, to dismiss Rama Rao on the ground that he did not enjoy the confidence of the House, without acceding to his request to be given an opportunity of proving his majority on the floor of the House within two days, was the ultimate in contempt for the Constitution. To appoint Bhaskara Rao as the Chief Minister and to give him a month to procure support (while turning down Rama Rao's request to prove immediately his majority) was to mock at the democratic process.

Almost every State is plagued by power-seekers and power-brokers, by unholy alliances and fleeting loyalties. Can the Governor be permitted to trivialize the constitutional process by virtually acting as the *agent provocateur* to assist a new claimant to engineer defections, desertions and disloyalties? The Constitution never intended the Governor to have the "unfettered right" to act as the official liquidator of national character.

Thirdly, under Article 164 (1) of the Constitution, the Chief Minister has to be appointed by the Governor, and under Article 164(2) the Council of Ministers has to be collectively responsible to the State Assembly. Reading the two clauses together, it is clear that the Governor can only appoint a Chief Minister who enjoys the confidence of the House. The most significant point here is that a majority can be proved only on the floor of the House and not in the Raj Bhavan. The idea of seeking to parade MLAs before the

Governor is infantile and wholly unworthy of the world's largest democracy. The essence of the matter is that the Governor has no right to remove a Chief Minister on the ground that he has lost his majority when the Chief Minister has not been defeated in the Assembly. A majority is an objective fact to be proved in the Assembly and not a matter for the "subjective satisfaction" of the Governor.

Fourthly, it is futile to search for an express constitutional provision enjoining the Governor not to pursue his own nose-counting method but to be solely guided by a vote in the Assembly. To look for such an express provision is to admit that we have lost the spirit of discernment, the spirit of perspicacity, the spirit of understanding. In a constitution what is left unsaid is as important as what is said. Do we need an express provision that the Governor shall not usurp the function of the Assembly? Since our legislature is fundamentally based on the Westminster model, it is relevant to ask whether anyone can imagine MPs being paraded before the Queen by a claimant who proposes to supplant Mrs. Thatcher.

To claim that "the Governor could not have acted otherwise at the given time" is too absurd to be seriously refuted. The plain position is that under the Constitution the Governor could not possibly have acted as he did at the given moment.

The nationwide outcry against Rama Rao's removal indicates that the average Indian is not tainted by the total unscrupulousness and plain wickedness which have become the hallmark of Indian politics. Ram Lal's resignation as the Governor "to uphold the dignity of the office" shows that whatever faculties he might have lost, he has not lost his sense of humour. But what was first enacted as a tragedy in Sikkim and in Jammu and Kashmir is too tragic to be enacted again as a farce in Andhra Pradesh.

Let us never forget that it is not the Constitution which has failed the people; it is our chosen representatives who have failed the Constitution. Our Constitution is not a structure of fossils like a coral reef, and is not intended merely to enable politicians to play their unending game of power. What is needed is not a change in the Constitution but a change of heart in our unworthy politicians.

We have woefully failed to build up healthy constitutional traditions and have proved ourselves alarmingly deficient in self-discipline or for that matter in any other type of discipline. The power of self-discipline is the very opposite of the fatal arrogance of power which confidently asserts that whatever is technically possible is licit. We need to build up salutary conventions to preserve our nation from the temper which hardens the heart and perverts the understanding. Decency in public life is the only solution if we are to preserve the true spirit of democracy and not be left merely with the husk of a comatose Constitution. We are faced with the stark alternatives of either *dharma* in public life or the twilight of Indian democracy.

Dismissal of Governor Patwari

*P*ersonalities apart, the dismissal of Governor Patwari raises two crucial issues. It was constitutionally unauthorized, and the manner of the dismissal was not only uncivil but uncivilized.

The Supreme Court has expressly laid down that governorship "is an independent constitutional office which is not subject to the control of the Government of India." In other words, the Governor of a State is not subordinate or subservient to the Central Government. Again, the Supreme Court's judgments leave no doubt that when the Constitution says that the Governor shall hold office "during the pleasure of the President", it does not mean the whim and fancy of the President. The President cannot terminate a Governor's tenure merely because there is a change in the ruling party at the Centre or in the State.

Governor Patwari was dismissed at a late hour on Sunday evening and the next incumbent was sworn in within an hour. In the words of a Bombay Judge, the dark hours of the night are associated in the public mind with dark deeds, and there is no reason why the legitimate activities of the Government cannot be carried out in broad daylight. During the last fifteen years, we have piled up an ominously large heap of dangerous precedents which diminish democracy and devalue the Constitution. The latest incident is not only an affront to the office of Governor but is an insult to the worth and dignity of the human person. Even a subordinate deserves to be treated with more courtesy.

(Press Release, October 28, 1980)

4

The Ayodhya Years

Ayodhya — From Conflict to Co-operation

*T*he subject of today's Seminar is of such vital importance, and the consequences of taking a wrong turn at Ayodhya are so mind-boggling, that I have chosen, departing from my normal practice, to reduce to writing what I have to speak. Departing, again, from the hallowed tradition of the Indian legal profession, I shall come straight to the point.

History will refer to our times as the Ayodhya Years — the years when the nation had to choose between conflict and co-operation. This Seminar has been organized as a clearing-house of ideas as to which is the path indicated by *buddhi* — a word for which there is no exact equivalent in the English language.

Two forces are working simultaneously in India's public life. On the one hand we have Ayodhya as an example of confrontation. On the other hand, national integration is symbolized by the Sarva Dharma Maitri Yatra organized by the Bharatiya Vidya Bhavan and the Gandhi Smarak Nidhi on the same day that we are holding this Seminar. The Sarva Dharma Maitri Yatra could not have been scheduled for a more appropriate day than the 15th December — the day when the greatest integrator of India, Sardar Vallabhbhai Patel, passed away 41 years ago.

Ayodhya is shorthand for a civil dispute with rich potential for a civil war. Catastrophe, and not merely conflict, is the alternative to co-operation. The urgent need for India today is to undergo

(Seminar under the auspices of Forum for National Consensus, New Delhi, December 15, 1991)

catharsis, a course in emotional cleansing, and create a unified nation with the bond of Indian culture.

The soul of India yearns for inter-religious harmony and respect. Over 5,000 years, Indian civilization has been made richer and deeper as a result of absorbing what is best in outside influences and integrating them. This is what has made Indian culture such a living force of ineffable beauty. As Dr. K. M. Munshi said in his monumental book, *Pilgrimage to Freedom,* —

> Indian culture is not merely Aryan culture but very much more, though the latter glistens like a thread of gold through many and varied elements which now go to make up our way of life. We cannot repudiate the Gandhara Art because of Greek influence. We cannot disown the Taj Mahal because of its Islamic inspiration. We cannot reject the art, the manners, the institutions, which Hindu-Muslim adjustments have given birth to. We cannot even throw off the Western influences and institutions which have grown into our life.

Sarva Dharma Maitri — friendship and goodwill among all religious communities — is a condition precedent to *Ekta*, Oneness. National integration lives in the hearts of the citizens.

Those who do not hesitate to spread over the bedrock of Indian society the lava spewed from Ayodhya in the name of *Hindutva*, should reconsider their position. *Hindutva* as propagated today is the very antithesis of true Hinduism.

The Lord says in the *Gita*, "Whatever may be the form in which each devotee seeks to worship Me with faith, I make their faith steadfast in that form alone." The Vedas proclaim, "That which exists is only One; the sages speak of it variously."

Hinduism as preached by its greatest exponents aims at universal harmony and goodwill and regards the world as one family. Adi Sankaracharya said that as different rivers flow into the ocean, different individuals reach the *Paramatma* through different paths.

Muslim leaders have been no less emphatic in their teaching

that Hindus and Muslims must live in peace and harmony. Sayyid Ahmed Khan (1817-1898) uttered the following memorable words:

> Centuries have passed since God desired that Hindus and Musalmans may share the climate and the produce of this land and live and die on it together. So it appears to be the will of God that these two communities may live together in this country as friends, or even like two brothers.... I have frequently said that India is a beautiful bride and Hindus and Muslims are her two eyes.... If one of them is lost, this beautiful bride will become ugly.

Maulana Abul Kalam Azad (1888-1958) told our countrymen in 1921 that Hindu-Muslim partnership was sanctioned by the Prophet's own example. Trusted by the divergent groups within the Congress, Maulana Azad was asked to preside when the Congress met in September 1923 to decide its future course. No one younger had been, or would be, given the honour. Maulana Azad was clear as to what was vital to the struggle for *swaraj*, and what was indeed greater than the struggle itself. His stirring words which came from the heart were:

> If an angel descends from the heavens today and proclaims from the Qutab Minar that India can attain *swaraj* within 24 hours provided I relinquish my demand for Hindu-Muslim unity, I shall retort: 'No my friend, I will give up *swaraj*, but not Hindu-Muslim unity, for if *swaraj* is delayed, it will be a loss for India, but if Hindu-Muslim unity is lost, it will be a loss for the whole of mankind.'

Mahatma Gandhi emphasized the religion which underlies all religions and brings us face to face with our Maker. "This religion transcends Hinduism, Islam, Christianity, etc. It does not supersede them. It harmonizes them and gives them reality." "Religions are different roads converging to the same point.... The soul of all religions is one, but it is encased in a multitude of forms. The latter will persist to the end of time."

Ayodhya could be the first step on the journey from conflict to co-operation if only we bear in mind the words of Mahatma Gandhi:

> Gather together under one banner all men from all religions and races of India and infuse into them the spirit of solidarity and oneness to the utter exclusion of all communal and parochial sentiments.

We are at a turning point in world history. Great thinkers have looked upon Indian culture as affording the only way out of the ills which afflict mankind. It was this belief in the panacea of Indian culture which made Professor E.P. Thompson observe that India is not only an important but perhaps *the* most important country for the future of mankind. Unfortunately, the action proposed by some to be taken at Ayodhya is an insult to Indian culture.

No one knows whether the great mystic-saint Sai Baba of Shirdi was a Hindu or a Muslim. Likewise, no one knows whether the great poet-saint Kabir was a Hindu or a Muslim. The story goes that when Kabir died, both the Hindus and the Muslims claimed his body; the Hindus wanted to cremate it according to Hindu rites, and the Muslims were desirous of burying the *pir* in the Muslim way. But when they came to take charge of the earthly remains of the saint, both groups discovered that there was only a heap of flowers under the shroud! If the story is not true, it deserves to be true. In the words of Dr. S. R. Sharma, "How like Kabir again — dead or alive — a divine weaver of the hearts of men, who alchemised old hatreds into the gold of love. . . ."

Five beacon lights may serve to illuminate our path and enable us to see the Ayodhya problem steadily and see it whole:

(1) Whatever injustices may have been done in the past and whatever wrongs perpetrated, it is not possible for us to redress them after centuries. Two wrongs do not make a right; two injustices do not make justice.

(2) As Swami Vivekananda wrote in a letter dated June 10, 1898 to Mohammed Sarfarez Husain, "For our motherland a junction of the two great systems, Hinduism and Islam — Vedanta brain and Islam body — is the only hope. . . The perfect India of the future will arise out of this chaos and strife, glorious and invincible, with Vedanta brain and Islam body."

(3) The great destiny of India is to lead mankind to the place where the Vedas, the Koran and the Bible are harmonized, and again in Swami Vivekananda's words, "where man has learned that religions are but the varied expressions of THE RELIGION which is Oneness, so that each may choose the path that suits him best."

(4) Litigation is no solution at all to the Ram Janmabhoomi-Babri Masjid dispute. Civil suits already filed have been pending for decades; and old and new legal proceedings will go on for at least a century.

(5) The only solution is for men of vision, goodwill, integrity, and knowledge (in that order) in both communities to come together and resolve not to disperse till they agree upon a compromise. It would be a good test of the fairness of their decision if it keeps both sides equally unsatisfied.

Dragging the Supreme Court into the Political Arena

*T*he Constitution of India provides for a just balance between the legislature, the executive and the judiciary. Each has a specific field to cover. The courts are there to maintain the most fundamental equilibriums of our society. They are the agency of a sovereign people to enforce the laws; to expound the Constitution and to ensure that its mandates are respected.

It is the primary duty of the executive, and of the executive only, to maintain order. All recorded history has one clear lesson to teach — freedom cannot last long unless it is coupled with order. Order can exist without freedom, but freedom can never exist without order. That freedom and order may co-exist, it is essential that freedom should be exercised under authority and order should be enforced by authority. Under the Constitution of India, as under every other constitution, authority is vested solely in the executive, popularly known as the government.

Time and again the government has to make those hard decisions which are essential for the maintenance of order. The making of such decisions cannot be avoided by shifting the responsibility to the judiciary.

The Supreme Court as well as the eighteen High Courts of India are vested with the widest possible powers. (I am not aware of any constitution of the world which confers wider powers on its higher judiciary.) But the courts can decide only questions of fact or of law. They cannot decide, and should never be called upon to

(The Illustrated Weekly of India, January 2-8, 1993)

decide, questions of opinion or belief or political wisdom. It is not the court's role to be an extended arm of the executive. Public opinion or public beliefs may weigh with the executive in shaping governmental policies. But it is not for the court to decide whether there are cogent grounds for opinions or beliefs which the people may choose to entertain. In fact, in every country the majority of the people are unable to think for themselves. Some years ago a survey conducted by the Rockefeller Foundation came to the conclusion that even among the educated classes 97 per cent of the people could not think for themselves. They derived their opinions and beliefs from what they heard on the radio or television or read in the newspapers.

It is true that many questions which arise before a court can, in a sense, be regarded as political questions or questions of policy. But this is where perception and clarity of mind should come into play. Diamonds are nothing but carbon, but on that account those who deal in diamonds are not called carbon merchants.

It is to my mind absurd to suggest that the highest court in the country should be asked to decide questions of history or archaeology. But the government has now asked the Supreme Court to give its opinion under Article 143 of the Constitution, whether a temple existed centuries ago on the site where the Babri Masjid stood before its demolition. The correct position in law is that the Supreme Court should decline to entertain such a matter under Article 143, and emphatically state that it is not within the jurisdiction of the court to hear the matter and not within the ambit of Article 143 to be asked to express an opinion on such an issue. Such strong attitude of the Supreme Court would prevent abuse of Article 143 in the years to come.

Consider the ridiculous length to which our Cabinet Ministers are prepared to go in order to shift the responsibility to the courts for matters which the government is too weak, too timid or too confused to decide for itself. Recent newspaper reports suggest that some Cabinet Ministers are of the view that the Supreme Court should be called upon to decide the following questions:

(i)   Whether the devotees should be allowed to have *darshan* of

Ram Lalla at the makeshift temple on the disputed site at Ayodhya.

(ii) Whether the government should rebuild the mosque which was dismantled.

(iii) Whether a mosque and a temple should both co-exist at Ayodhya.

Is it the function of the court to decide such questions? Historians have expressed widely divergent views on the issue whether there was a pre-existing temple on the site on which the mosque was built by Babar. Much less are they agreed that Ram was born at that place. There is even a greater difference of opinion on the question whether Ram actually lived as a human being or whether he was the supramental ideal created by mythology to represent the perfect man. To ask the Supreme Court or the Allahabad High Court to decide such questions of mythology or history, or mixed questions of mythology and history, is to bear witness to the bankruptcy of our political institutions.

It is a measure of the degradation to which we have reduced our third-rate democracy that we have lost all sense of propriety, and are not only willing but eager to call upon the courts to decide questions of opinion or belief, history, mythology, or political expediency. Never in the history of any country have courts been approached to deal with the type of questions which are now suggested as fit to be referred to the courts in connection with the incidents at Ayodhya.

The consequences of asking the Supreme Court or the Allahabad High Court to deal with the type of questions which are suggested for reference would be disastrous in the long run.

First, it would thrust upon the court a task for which it is not qualified by training or experience. Courts can deal with questions of law or of fact. They are not qualified to deal with questions in other fields like archaeology or history. A judge can decide only upon documentary evidence or evidence given by a witness as to what he himself saw or heard. It is well established that hearsay evidence is inadmissible in a court of law under the Indian Evidence Act.

Secondly, no government is entitled to shift the responsibility which the Constitution has squarely placed upon its shoulders, to any other agency of the State which was created for a wholly different purpose. Judicial pronouncements can never be a cover for inadequacy of government.

Thirdly, if the court is pushed into the political arena, it would impair the image and undermine the status of the court. During the working of our Constitution for forty-two years, we have devalued every single institution except that of the armed forces. Do we want even the small remnant of public respect, which providentially still attaches to the higher courts, to be dissolved in the murky waters of the cesspool which we are pleased to call the Indian democracy?

Fourthly, large organizations with millions of followers have officially and openly stated that they would not be bound by any verdict of the court of law. The question is not whether they are right or wrong in adopting this attitude. The real point is that if a certain issue essentially involves a question of opinion or belief, the people are entitled to say that a court of law cannot deal with the issue, and if it does its opinion would be without jurisdiction and not binding on the group which is adversely affected.

Fifthly, the decision of the court would not be reached for decades. Cases pertaining to Ayodhya were filed in the Allahabad High Court more than forty years ago and they are still pending. Numerous new cases about Ayodhya have been recently filed and no one knows when they would be decided. More than two and a half lakh cases are pending in the Supreme Court, and an equally unacceptable number in the Allahabad High Court. This country has a genius for so arranging its affairs that the administration of justice is bound to break down before the end of the century. Reference to court would aggravate the problem and ensure communal bitterness and hatred during this generation and the next. If at all a decision is reached in our lifetime, it may be like the Supreme Court's majority decision in the Mandal case which has only revived the very scourge of casteism which the Constitution emphatically intended to end.

The blunt truth is that the failure of the political process can never be either concealed or supplemented by any reference to any court.

The Supreme Court has to decide the issue whether there was a pre-existing temple on the disputed site before the mosque came into existence. Even a finding on this single point issue would leave at large various other questions which are bound to crop up, irrespective of the Court's finding on the question referred for its consideration:

(i)   If evidence is conflicting or non-existent that a temple stood on the site, should it be presumed that no such temple existed? Five hundred years of bloody history may efface marks and traces.

(ii) Should any religious place of worship be razed to the ground because a structure pertaining to another religion stood in its place before?

(iii) Archaeology is the study of the art, customs and beliefs of ancient times. It can afford a ground for a belief or an opinion but never for universal certainty. Cannot two minds come to different conclusions on the same archaeological evidence? How can a conclusion reached by a judge be binding on people whose opinions or beliefs go counter to those of the judge? Does it help in any way to confuse separate and distinct questions? Whether Ram was born at a particular place is wholly distinct and different from the issue whether a temple existed at that place. Therefore, are we in any way dislodging the beliefs of those who hold a certain spot to be the birthplace of Ram by saying that no temple existed there?

When a man loses his memory he necessarily becomes disoriented. The Indian people have lost their memory of their profound culture and have consequently become alarmingly disoriented.

We love to have instant solutions for every can of worms which we open up. Under a democratic set-up, I see no short-term solution whatever to the problems we are facing. The only solution is a long-term one. We have to educate our people on the essential unity of all religions, instead of letting them remain cultural ignoramuses.

There are times in a country's history when inaction and silence can be a culpable wrong, and we are living in such times. The nation is standing on the escalator of anarchy and chaos. At this perilous moment it is the duty of every right-minded citizen to raise his voice against the devious endeavour of politicians to relieve themselves of their own duty to make wise and strong decisions.

Today we are faced with two big questions — will democracy survive in India, and second, if it does, whether the States will remain united? "Probably" is the answer to the first question. "Likely" is the answer to the second.

Saving India's Soul — Maulana's Formula

*I*n the five and forty years of its independence, India has never had to face a crisis of the magnitude and far-reaching effect comparable to what it is facing today. We must awake from our apathy and realize that there is a grave threat to the unity and integrity of the country — even to the very survival of our democratic system. The devil must be an optimist if he thinks he can incite India to continued violence without tearing it apart.

Democracy is of three types. Democracy, as India knew it in the first fourteen years of its independence. Guided democracy, as Singapore has known it under Lee Kuan Yew. And misguided democracy, of which India is the prime example today. The Hindu community and also the Muslim community have forgotten the lofty teachings of their own faith and are misguided by fanatics and dogmatists who have not imbibed the true essence of their own religion. India is passing through a phase of disorder which makes you recall the pregnant words of Lord Wavell: "India can be governed firmly, or not at all."

Before his life's dream of independence was fulfilled, Sri Aurobindo said that things looked "ominous" and that India might lapse into *goonda* raj involving atrocities by one community upon another. The still, small voice of humanity is not heard in the din of arms and warring fanaticisms. It is difficult to recognize today's India as the same country whose culture had reached such vertiginous heights.

(The Times of India, February 12, 1993)

The basic question which faces India today is whether it will ever be a nation, or continue to be merely a collection of communities. The supreme reality of our time and land is our indivisibility as joint heirs to the finest composite culture the world has ever known, and the mind-boggling vulnerability of our State if it continues with the bloodbath unchecked.

Power politics has been called the diplomatic name for the law of the jungle. How long do we want to run the circus from the tiger-cage? A reasonable solution can emerge from men of vision, wisdom and learning. It will not come from politicians who put their party and themselves before the State; and are more concerned with votes than with welfare of the people, more interested in the short-term prospects of their own party than in the long-term future of the country.

The main purpose of this piece is to commend to all right-thinking Hindus and to all right-thinking Muslims the formula suggested by Maulana Wahiduddin Khan — a man of compassion and not of passion, a scholar who can give moral leadership in sanity instead of fanning the flames of communal hatred. Incidentally, the formula suggested by the Maulana is not very different from what was suggested by Mr. L. K. Advani himself sometime ago. The Maulana's three-point formula may be summarized in a few words.

First, the movement launched by Hindus in the name of *masjid-mandir* should stop at Ayodhya and should not be allowed to go beyond Ayodhya in any circumstances. It should not be repeated at Varanasi or at Mathura or at any other place. An assurance to this effect should take the form of a written declaration signed by the four Sankaracharyas and by other Hindu leaders.

Every country must learn to live with its past history and to cherish it instead of trying to rewrite it. Chaos would be the only result of trying to undertake "correction of history", or to undo the past, or to seek to remedy past wrongs. Britain was invaded by the Romans, and centuries later by the Normans. But the British still look upon their history with reverence and with a desire to preserve every trace of the invasions. Can we Indians not have the nobility and greatness to preserve our past history instead of taking upon ourselves the impossible task of righting past wrongs?

Secondly, Muslims should, in the larger national interest, forget altogether the wrong done at Ayodhya. They should not ask for the masjid to be reconstructed at the original site or at any other site in Ayodhya. If the protection of the Babri Masjid was their responsibility, they have discharged it by the sufferings they have undergone and the sacrifices they have made.

Thirdly, the Maulana suggests that the aforesaid first point — which is already the law of the land embodied in The Places of Worship (Special Provisions) Act, 1991 — should be enacted as a part of our Constitution.

While I am in favour of the first two points, I would appeal to the Maulana not to press the third point. I understand the reason why Muslims would like to have the principle enacted as part of our constitutional law. Let us face the unpleasant truth that we Indians as a nation have no sense of honour towards our own countrymen. Was it honourable for us to have amended the Constitution to abolish the privy purses (which in those days cost the country less than Rs. 5 crore a year and would today cost a fraction of that amount), after having persuaded the rulers to give up their kingdoms (which constituted two-thirds of India) on the basis of a cast iron guarantee embodied in the Constitution regarding privy purses? But while I appreciate the misgiving which underlies the demand for constitutional amendment, there are good reasons for not pressing this issue. A constitutional amendment would need a two-thirds majority (in each House of Parliament) which, in the present state of affairs, would be difficult to muster. Moreover, if a nation has no sense of shame, it can delete the amendment any time in the future, just as it deleted the provision for payment of privy purses. A constitutional amendment is no substitute for national conscience.

Time is running out. If any compromise is to be effected which would put an end to the present state of unrest and instability which is so patently deterring the world from investing in India, the solution should be found urgently before emotions are further inflamed to unacceptable levels.

Let us remember the wise words of Mahatma Gandhi:

> Religion is outraged when an outrage is perpetrated in
> its name. Almost all the riots in this unhappy land take
> place in the name of religion, though they may have a
> political motive behind them. There is no room for
> *goondaism* in any religion worth the name, be it Islam,
> Hinduism or any other. If religion dies, then India dies.
> Today the Hindus and Muslims are clinging to the husk
> of religion. They have gone mad.

On another occasion, the Mahatma said: "Let me warn you that
if you let the fact of the Hindu majority turn your head and attempt
to eliminate other people, Hinduism is not going to benefit
anyway. On the contrary, it would perish . . . . If you are
worshippers of Ram, you must accept that Ram belongs to all. He
is the saviour of all, whether Hindus, Muslims, Christians or
Parsis." Only a man who has a greater claim to patriotism and
wisdom than Mahatma Gandhi should dare to express his dissent.

When Bombay Burned

*I*n its history going back over three serried centuries, Bombay had never witnessed scenes of such violence and beastliness, such wanton destruction and ruthless savagery, as during the black days following December 6, 1992 and January 6, 1993, followed by the bomb blasts on March 12.

Newspapers recorded those macabre events in grisly detail. But when it is difficult to cope even with today's newspapers, predictably yesterday's papers are consigned to oblivion. And public memory retains nothing beyond a fortnight. It is, therefore, imperative that the blots on Bombay's fair name should be recorded within the covers of a book.

The Times of India has rendered a distinct public service by bringing out *When Bombay Burned*. It is edited by Mr. Dileep Padgaonkar and represents a vivid contemporaneous record by the top journalists of that paper. It is a bird's eye view — in words, cartoons and photographs — of the gruesome happenings, but the eye is that of an eagle.

Those were the days when the still, small voice of sanity was not heard in the din of arms and warring factions. Never before were prejudices more widely mistaken for truth, passion for reason, fundamentalism for religion, and myth for history. Both Hindus and Muslims lost sight of the essentials of their respective religions, and allowed themselves to be misled by bigots and fundamentalists whose activities represented the very antithesis of

---

(Book Review, The Times of India, June 4, 1993)

the true teachings of their religion.

The end is not yet. What happened before can happen again — and again.

The book has two lessons which ought to be written as with a sunbeam on the minds of all Indians. First, if we continue to go the same way — stupid and stubborn and mulish — we shall never become an integrated nation but continue to be a group of communities.

On the other hand, if we have any capacity to learn, we can make the burning of Bombay the harbinger of a new India which "will arise out of this chaos and strife — glorious and invincible — with Vedanta brain and Islam body." That would be a consummation devoutly to be wished for. Can we not look with pride upon our great destiny as joint heirs to the finest cultural melange the world has ever known? If this book can make our people realize the enormity of the frightening nexus between politicians and the underworld, and the depths of degradation to which the city was allowed to sink, it will serve a great public purpose.

Secondly, it is beyond hope that the correct guidance can ever come from our politicians. They are self-centred and have their minds glued on their own personal prospects and those of their party; and shamelessly look upon people as vote banks and not as human beings entitled to disinterested guidance from their so-called political leaders. Citizens will have to take the lead if Bombay is to be saved from a recrudescence of the disorder.

The solution is not far to seek. There is a formula which must appeal to every Indian who is not wedded to bigotry or fanaticism. As Maulana Wahiduddin rightly suggested, the movement launched by Hindus should stop at Ayodhya and should not be repeated at any other place. We can never rewrite or "correct" history. Again, Muslims should, in the larger national interest, forget altogether the wrong done at Ayodhya. The site at Ayodhya should be marked by a garden and a school which would be a great monument to true Indian culture and where regular and insightful instruction should be imparted regarding "The Essential Unity Of All Religions". That is the title of a perceptive book written by Dr. Bhagwan Das on whom the Bharat Ratna was posthumously and most deservingly conferred.

5

From Sterile Socialism to
Fruitful Egalitarianism

The Economic Environment in India

I feel privileged to be invited to deliver a lecture in memory of India's outstanding Professor of Management — Prof. A. Dasgupta. He was a teacher par excellence. To him teaching was not a vocation but a mission. He attracted — like a powerful magnet — friends, students and professors.

The only major factor impelling Prof. Dasgupta was love of the country and good of the people. He was not wedded to any particular ideology. He has been acclaimed as the Father of Management Education in India. To his students, he was a "great thinker, great teacher, and humanist" and to his colleagues "mentor and friend".

In the last forty years, the world economy has grown at a pace faster than in the earlier 4,000 years. The capacity of India to make its economy surge to new heights is undeniable. But in order to achieve the potential, the three top priorities have to be population control, education, and changes in our policy even more drastic than those proposed by the present government, who have been understandably moderate in the reforms they have announced.

Without population control, the problems of India would never be resolved but would only be aggravated. Perpetuation of poverty is the twin sister of a burgeoning citizenry.

Without education it is impossible to fulfil the four noble ideals on which our Constitution was built — liberty, equality, fraternity,

(The First Prof. A. Dasgupta Memorial Lecture, New Delhi, September 30, 1991)

and justice. Yet no significant nation of the world attaches such low priority to education as India. Our Government spends 2.7 per cent of its total expenditure on education, as compared to 18.5 per cent spent by South Korea and 19 per cent by Singapore.

Fast economic growth would be impossible with woolly, outworn socialism which betrays a severe hardening of intellectual arteries and a pathetic lack of knowledge of the revolutionary changes which have recently swept across the world.

During the last 25 years, China's economic growth, despite its communism, has been more than twice as fast as India's. The annual investment in China by foreign companies exceeds the total investment in India in the last 44 years. There are already more than 2,500 foreign enterprises operating in the 27 hi-tech industrial parks recently started in China.

I have the highest opinion of Indian capacity and potential. But I find it impossible to refute the universal criticism that our two besetting sins are self-complacency and obstinate refusal to face the truth.

The survey on India, published by *The Economist* on May 4, 1991, showed the tiger "caged". It should be made compulsory reading in every school and college, as well as for those adults who choose to enter Parliament or the civil service. The jugular vein of the article is that if India has more than its fair share of the world's misery, it is not the fault of former colonial masters or wicked western capitalists or the cruel hand of fate: it is largely India's own doing.

One of the main reasons for our failure to fulfil our export potential is the maddening instability of our fiscal and economic laws. A new Stable Export-Import Policy was announced in April 1985 and a second Stable Policy in April 1988, followed by a new Policy in 1990. But since 1985 the enormous number of Notifications which have amended the Stable Policy works out to one change every alternate working day. The present government has recently announced a reformed trade policy. It remains to be seen whether the reformation will inject stability into the policy.

We are slipping behind the rest of the world — except in

population growth. This truth can hardly be better illustrated than by the fact that the present per capita income in South Korea is 13 times, and in Hong Kong 30 times, that in India, though the three countries started at about the same level.

What we miss is not merely growth but development. Growth is quantitative; development is qualitative.

The United Nations Development Report, published last June, ranks the nations of the world by reference to the Human Development Index (HDI). In determining a nation's position in the list, the HDI takes into account the expenditure incurred by the state on human priority sectors — health, water, sanitation, daily calorific intake, literacy, and education at primary and secondary levels. Having regard to the HDI, India is placed, for the second year running, pretty much at the bottom of the list — 123rd out of 160 countries.

Legislative work expands so as to fill the time available for its completion. This is a branch of Parkinson's Law and its operation has caused Parkinson's Disease in the body of our economic laws. The avalanche of ill-conceived changes and complications, which may be compendiously called "legal litter", is the highlight of our economic environment.

G. K. Chesterton, in his brilliant essay "The Mad Official", analyses how a society goes mad. The rot begins, he says, when wild actions are received calmly by society. "These are people that have lost the power of astonishment at their own actions. When they give birth to a fantastic passion or foolish law, they do not start or stare at the monster they have brought forth . . . . These nations are really in danger of going off their heads *en masse*, of becoming one vast vision of imbecility." India is one such country in respect of economic and fiscal laws. Today the monster of our direct and indirect tax structure has become more monstrous than ever before.

Truly, we Indians are a "low arousal" people. We endure injustice and unfairness with feudalistic servility and fatalistic resignation. The poor of India endure inhuman conditions which would lead to a bloody revolution in any other country. The rich endure foolish laws and maddening amendments which benefit none except the legal and accountancy professions, and instinctively prefer to circumvent the law than to fight for its repeal.

*H*owever, the New Industrial Policy of the present government is a step in the right direction. India is no longer in a state of "suspenseful indecision". We have left behind the terminal stage of our forty-year affair with shabby state socialism. I am making a prediction, and not expressing a hope, when I say that doctrinaire socialism will soon be dust on the shelf of Indian history. As in the rest of the world, liberalization has come to stay and there can be no retracing of steps.

The potential of India is fantastic. As Lee Kuan Yew observed, the Indian economy is like a sleeping giant who, if awakened, could make a powerful impact on the global economy. It would not be mere chauvinism to say that India is a giant with a bad cold, not a pygmy with cancer.

Affluence has never been the yardstick for measuring the contribution of a nation to the growth and development of human civilization. Besides, in recorded history, nations and civilizations have perished through affluence; but no nation, no civilization, has died of adversity.

*T*oday the nation is in a state of moral decay and suffers from a flabby degeneration of conscience. In India, as in the rest of the world, consumer culture has consumed humanity. We need to relearn the values which are the lifeblood of our imperishable heritage.

The economic environment will change beyond recognition when businessmen can engage in commerce, without having a commercialized outlook. A new generation has to grow up, the youth of which will cultivate its mind — not merely with a view to offering it as a commodity for sale in the marketplace. We need entrepreneurs who will contribute not only to the gross national product but also to gross national happiness. The most attractive face of capitalism was depicted by Mahatma Gandhi — and that was the face loved by Prof. A. Dasgupta — the man who goes into business to do well but stays in it to do good.

India and Israel

*I*srael is 44 years old. India's full diplomatic ties with Israel came only four months ago. The delay in recognizing one of the most dynamic peoples of the world may be regarded by history as one of the great mistakes in India's foreign policy.

Like India, Israel is an old country but a young nation. We have a lot to learn from that country as to how democratic institutions should function, just as we have a lot to teach it, by our own sad example, how they ought not to function.

Israel is to India what quality is to quantity. Its population is less than five million, i.e., half that of the single city of Bombay. By another yardstick, Israel's population is only 200th of India's, but they make up for it by the people's sense of total dedication, devotion to duty and eagerness to work.

The ultimate resource of a nation is the character of the people, and it is in this resource that Israel is so rich. We Indians are endowed by Nature with, I believe, no less intelligence than the Israelis, but we lack character and the sense of duty and dedication which makes all the difference.

A few million Israelis live outside Israel. Quite voluntarily and out of a sense of moral duty the majority of them send a percentage of their income as their annual contributions to Israel. Contrast that with non-resident Indians. Fifteen million of them live outside India. Have you heard of any of them sending a voluntary

(Indo-Israel Seminar on "The Role of Trade Unions and Co-operatives in Development", Bombay, September 21, 1992)

contribution to the Indian exchequer?

Egalitarianism is widely practised by Israel — perhaps on a wider scale and in a more meaningful way than in any other country.

The kibbutz is an admirable institution peculiar to Israel. The people in a kibbutz own and enjoy their property jointly and each member of the kibbutz gets what he needs from the common property and income of the kibbutz. There are only 1,25,000 members of the 270 kibbutzim which are in operation today. They represent 2.7 per cent of Israel's population, but they are responsible for 35 per cent of the agricultural produce and 8 per cent of the manufactured articles. Communism, which is based on the same ideology has failed hopelessly because it wants to compel people, in fact tyrannize them, into accepting common ownership. By contrast, kibbutzim succeeded because their members are voluntary workers but, out of their sense of duty and social justice, are willing to live their lives as members of a joint family. That brings to my mind the thought that the Hindu undivided family is no different, in its concept, from the kibbutz. In a Hindu undivided family the members of the family own the family property jointly and the *karta* is expected to satisfy the varying needs of the different members. Today, unfortunately, the Hindu undivided family has become merely a device for reducing or avoiding tax; and thus what was noble in concept has been put to a nefarious use.

6

Sharing Thoughts
with Shareholders

Fluctuating Fortunes of Cement

(December 19, 1984)

I am addressing you under the shadow of a national tragedy — a tragedy too full for sound and foam. The fatal shots that were fired on October 31 still echo round the country and will continue to do so for many a long day. The soul of Indira is not slain. Still her spirit walks abroad. She is still a haunting presence; her memory still a rallying ground.

We had the traumatic experience; and if we do not miss the meaning, she would not have laid down her life in vain. Hark to Mahatma Gandhi's lesson — non-violence is the law of our species as violence is the law of the brute. None of our problems can be solved by physical force. The brutal assassination and the backlash of burnings and killings have brought home the lesson that the first priority of the government has to be order. And the future of India depends wholly on the secular ethic. Secularism is the very heart of our republic. The foundation of our democracy, the source of its vitality, and the imperative of our national integrity — all lie in the concept of multiplicity, of plurality and tolerance, of union rather than unity. Let us remember that the Constitution was meant to *constitute* the nation. Auden's words remain true — we must love one another or die.

(Extracts from Chairman's Statements at the Annual General Meetings of the Shareholders of The Associated Cement Companies Limited)

*T*he cement industry affords the finest case-study of the incalculable damage which irrational controls can cause to an industry and the nation at large. You have only to see the transformation effected by partial decontrol in March 1982. In the very first year of what I had earlier called the New Deal for cement, the industry achieved a record increase of 15 per cent in installed capacity. If the embers of confidence and optimism can be set aglow so luminously by partial decontrol, what can be not achieved by total removal of controls?

The case for total decontrol. rests on three unanswerable grounds:

(a) Cement production has increased to such an extent that it is wholly adequate to meet the demand. Higher production has already resulted in keen competition, while new million-tonne plants are the order of the day. There is no likelihood of a shortage in the foreseeable future.

(b) Levy cement purchased by the government is at a price below the cost of production and the loss is expected to be made up by the manufacturer out of sales of non-levy cement at higher prices to the public. How long can the people be expected to subsidize the government in such a patently unfair fashion?

(c) Some part of levy cement finds its way into the free market. Such seepage brings corruption in tow. A government which aims at a clean administration must plug every hole through which filth blows.

The time has come to show our capacity for change and for learning from experience. If we are to get the nation's adrenalin going again, we must end the era of stiff talks, frozen postures and unbending minds. Looking into our own hearts we must realize the profound truth of M. Visveswaraya's dictum, "The genius of our people is for standing still." We must rid ourselves of the habit of merely collecting a harvest of lofty resolutions to do great things for the national economy, followed by public amnesia.

In economics nothing sprouts overnight without its back-roots in time. The mould of economic fundamentalism — miscalled socialism — which is cast in concrete, has to be broken. The anti-enterprise culture must be given its quietus. The remaining controls on cement must go.

Gone are the days when cement sold itself. It is all to the good that it has become a buyer's market where the purchaser can insist upon quality and a fair price. Consumer pressures are welcome, particularly the consumer's appetite for value. In a free market a product moves forward at the command of the consumer.

As Dr. Peter Drucker observed, "Business has only two functions — marketing and innovation." We expect all our Works to perform both these functions and find better ways to fulfil the needs of the public.

(December 18, 1985)

A year has rolled by since Mr. Rajiv Gandhi became the Prime Minister. No fanfare at the outset; no drum roll at the conclusion. The most striking feature of this memorable year has been the quiet dignity of his success. He has proved himself to be dedicated to purpose and principle, rather than to doctrine and definition.

The threat of a nuclear winter cannot be allowed to overshadow the truth that we are living through the most exciting period in human history. Nine times as much scientific knowledge has been generated since the end of the Second World War as mankind was able to produce in all the previous eras. "The amount of information in the world now doubles every eight years. Prosperity goes to countries that have a mechanism to put it to use."

Nineteen eighty-five saw the redesigning of India to meet the challenges of the 21st century which is just a little over 5,000 days away. The year witnessed an epoch-making budget. Earlier budgets had imposed such draining direct taxes that thrift, once a virtue, had become a vice, and there was a danger of Envy, one of the seven deadly sins, being canonized. The twin begetters of black money had been inane controls and insensate fiscal levies. This year India indicated that it would be kissing goodbye to both. It was some change from the last 30 years in which posture politics had compelled entrepreneurs to breathe in an atmosphere of oxygen, nitrogen and odium!

John Kenneth Galbraith observed in *A Life in our Times,* "Economics is not a durable truth; it requires constant revision and accommodation. Nearly all its error is from those who cannot change . . . . The experience of being wrong is salutary; no economist should be denied it, and not many are."

The cement industry should be one of the major beneficiaries of the rethinking in our own land. The industry has been nursed back to health. Primarily as a result of partial decontrol, the installed capacity of the industry zoomed from 29.3 million tonnes at the end of 1981-82 to 42 million tonnes by the end of 1984-85, and production jumped from 21.1 million tonnes to 30.1 million tonnes. This was more than what was achieved during the preceding ten years!

If partial decontrol can launch India on such a big market-driven wave of development, what a full harvest of benefits would not be garnered by total decontrol! There is no reason for the continuation of partial control on cement except the reluctance of the bureaucracy to let go its powers and the national penchant for sticking to arsenic and old lace.

(December 17, 1986)

*O*ur recent history has hardly been the march of enlightenment. It has been as much a story of precipitate regression in human values as of tardy progression on the economic front.

The year 1986 has seen India slip into stridency. We specialize in elevating disagreements about minor matters into clashes of principles and tests of religiosity. The world's largest democracy has yet to learn the simple truth that communal chauvinism, linguistic fanaticism and parochial loyalty are the surest prescription for national disintegration.

We are squandering the treasure of our national identity. The whole nation plays the piper, while the extremists are calling the tune. "From the beginning of time," said Barbara Ward, "people have heard the 'still, small voice' of obligation and brotherhood. When they have listened, society has worked. When they have refused to listen, society has broken up."

This happens to be the Golden Jubilee year of your Company. Nothing would have given me greater pleasure than to have been able to present a resplendent picture of the Company's present working. But it would be a closer approximation to truth if I told you that for 'bright sunshine' read 'grey and chilly'.

*R*eason dictates that three painful decisions would have to be made and implemented in the long-term economic interests of the country.

First, tens of thousands of sick units in the country bear witness to the fact that we have been paying dearly for our shortsighted policy of trying to preserve jobs at the cost of modernization and rationalization. Jobs do not have to be merely protected, but they have to be productive. The mischief of an excessive labour force is compounded by the fact that the basic wages are sought to be increased periodically — over and above the rise in dearness allowance on account of an increase in the cost of living index. Such a policy is dead against the long-term interests of the workers themselves.

The labour productivity in Indian cement plants is abysmally poor. In our old cement plants, with a number of small kilns, we employ between 3,000 and 5,000 workers for an annual production of one million tonnes. In the new dry process plants recently installed in this country, the figure would be around 500 to 700 workers for a million-tonne plant, as compared to 100 to 200 persons in a similar plant in the developed countries of Europe, the USA and Japan.

Secondly, the greatest roadblock to the development of the cement industry is the erratic supply of coal and electricity, not to speak of the deplorably low quality of coal. The ash content of Indian coal can be as high as 40 per cent. Luckily for India, the public sector has ceased to be the sacred cow — it is no longer beyond criticism. In the words of T. S. Eliot, "Humankind cannot bear very much reality." But, under the present Prime Minister, we are able to bear far more reality than before. In talking about the public sector we can now speak the blunt economic truth — without calling a spade an agricultural implement.

Thirdly, controls — financially crippling, economically indefensible, and morally corrosive — have plagued the cement industry for almost 40 years. The remaining controls must go. The industry must be enabled to generate the financial resources for modernization. The system of "levy cement" which is virtually a military solution to an economic problem must be scrapped. Like other easy solutions to economic problems, it is neat, plausible, and wrong.

(December 17, 1987)

The time has come to cast India's balance sheet of forty years of freedom, presenting a true and fair view of the national potential and the dim reality.

In 1984, Prime Minister Rajiv Gandhi wisely initiated the policy of liberalization and dismantling of the controls which had been dictated by socialism. The Prime Minister should say to the Congress Socialist Forum what Attlee said in 1945 to the left-wing Professor, Laski, "A period of silence from you would be welcome." Nothing would darken the economic future of the country more effectively than politics of the pendulum.

The cement industry is passing through a difficult period. Despite its growth in terms of production capacities, its financial health has been gravely impaired. Some companies are already in the intensive care unit, others are *en route.*

In the years prior to 1982, total control on the price and distribution of cement was the great begetter of corruption and black money. The present policy of partial control — when there is a glut of cement — represents only the triumph of obstinacy over experience.

(December 21, 1988)

*T*his month Europe celebrated the centennial of the birth of Jean Monnet, who as a private citizen did far more to ensure the formation of the European Economic Community than men in high public office. (Incidentally, when the First World War was raging, Sri Aurobindo spelt out the imperative need for a union of the States of Europe and, therefore, the inevitability of it. In 1916, Sri Aurobindo spoke of "The United States of Europe". In 1946 when Winston Churchill used that phrase, he was applauded on the assumption that it had never been used before.)

*I*t would be most appropriate if the centenary of Jean Monnet could see the strengthening of a similar organization in our part of the world — the South Asian Association for Regional Co-operation (SAARC). At present SAARC may be truthfully described as a pregnancy rather than a birth. Bangladesh, Bhutan, India, the Maldives, Nepal, Pakistan and Sri Lanka must come together and work in a spirit of friendly co-operation with the conviction that they have to share a common future. The economies of all the seven countries would then benefit greatly. (For instance, the potential market in Pakistan, Sri Lanka, Bangladesh and Nepal for surplus Indian cement is two million tonnes per annum). Enormous resources which are wasted by India and Pakistan annually on defence and armaments could be diverted to economic and social uplift of our peoples. It would really transform the entire future of more than one-fifth of the human race who inhabit these countries. It would result in the technological and industrial rebirth of the whole region. The foundation of our regional prosperity would be the binding tie of cohesive sentiment.

The democratic elections in Pakistan this month offer a golden opportunity which should not be missed. India — by far the strongest nation in the group — can afford to be not only fair but generous and magnanimous. We should stretch our hand of friendship and goodwill to the new Pakistan government. Goodwill is communicable and friendship is infectious.

If active co-operation between India and Pakistan seems a hopeless dream today, let us go back in history and see how often the dream of one generation has become the accepted common-place of the next. If Japan and the USA can live together in amity after the holocaust of the Second World War, if France and Germany can regard themselves as each other's most valued trading partner after more than a century of bitterness and belligerence, if the Soviet Union and China can forget their differences of decades — it should be much easier for the SAARC countries to become firm allies. Sri Aurobindo who had predicted the formation of the United States of Europe when the idea seemed to be wholly chimerical, expressed his firm conviction on August 15, 1947 that India and Pakistan (which included Bangladesh) were bound to come together in some sort of confederation, if not a federation.

With the elections soon or late next year, economic wisdom will probably be asked to take a back seat. The claptrap of socialism is likely to be heard more frequently in the months to come. Our politicians, who were never renowned for the acute sensitivity of their economic antennae, revel in the eighth deadly sin — ideology. Myth matters more than reality in electoral politics.

When will the nation wake up to the fact that the administration of direct and indirect tax laws is today in a more chaotic state than ever before in this century? The painful truth is that in the vast arsenal of Indian bureaucracy, justice and fairness are negotiable commodities. A sense of justice and fairness is not inherent in the Indian psyche, — witness the institutions of *sati* and untouchability, and the squalor in which millions exist in stinkingly rich cities.

The evil is compounded by the fact that we lack the requisite political culture — the set of institutions, attitudes and habits needed to make democracy work efficiently. The one-man-one-vote rite flourishes, but government flounders.

Sandwiched between rising costs of inputs and declining prices of products, the cement industry is going through a difficult phase.

As the installed capacity of the cement industry has doubled since 1982, there is today an excess of two million tonnes of supply over effective demand. In spite of this surplus which will stay with us for a while, the government continues the four-decade old strangulating control over the industry, in the mitigated form of levy cement. It cannot be too often repeated that the citizen has to continue subsidizing the purchases of cement by the government at a price below the cost of production. The last remnant of the controls of a bygone era — the pork barrels for political patronage and corruption — must now be ended. With the glut of cement as a universally admitted fact, the industry should at least now be allowed to breathe freely in the free market.

The Jute Packaging Materials (Compulsory Use in Packing Commodities) Act, 1987, is typical of the aberrations to which a government is prone when it puts politics in front of economics. The Act compels the industry to pack 65 per cent of its cement production in jute bags if the plants are located beyond 1200 kms from Calcutta, and 70 per cent if the plants are within 1200 kms of Calcutta.

New technology swamps the world, but time is made to stand still in India. Consumers in all continents now get cement packed in high density polyethylene (HDPE) bags which are far superior. Cement being a fine powdery material and the texture of jute bags being porous, the seepage in transit and on multiple handling can be as high as five per cent when the product in jute bags reaches the consumer. The estimated loss on account of jute packaging would be to the tune of one and a half million tonnes out of a targeted production of 43.5 million tonnes for 1988-89. The jute packaging order is a disgrace to any progressive country. It is neither reasonable nor in the interests of the general public.

(September 28, 1989)

I have to begin on a sad note. Sumant Moolgaokar is no more. He was one of the main builders of your Company, and served the cement industry with rare distinction for 58 years. The fall-out from his dedicated labours was "innovative quantum jumps in India's technological progression", as one of your Directors put it. We shall endeavour to ensure that your Company will always maintain the high standards that Sumant established. To improve upon them is beyond hope.

After four decades of strangulating controls, total decontrol has been the most propitious development this year for the cement industry. I heartily welcome the long-delayed decision on decontrol for this vital industry which can now organize itself to achieve higher standards in the free market.

We should have no difficulty in adopting remedial measures which are so obvious that they almost cry aloud for adoption:

First, the imperative for the cement industry is to scout for new markets in semi-urban and rural areas where the demand for cement has remained largely untapped. Cement should be placed outside the purview of the Essential Commodities Act which makes it obligatory for dealers to go through the arduous process of obtaining licences at considerable cost in time and money. Unless cement selling is delicensed, penetration into the rural markets is bound to remain dishearteningly difficult.

Secondly, active measures need to be taken to promote the use of cement for housing. It is a sad commentary on our plans and public policies that, on the one hand, we have a glut of cement and consequent sickness in the industry, while on the other hand we view with equanimity the homelessness of tens of millions of our people as a regular feature of the bleak national landscape. Recently, the Chairman of the National Housing Bank put the existing housing shortage at 29 million units, and estimated that an additional 36 million housing units will be required to be constructed by the year 2000. In other words, 65 million housing units will have to be constructed over the next twelve years if the shortage is to be met in full.

Thirdly, the Central and State governments should implement a priority programme of constructing concrete roads and using cement for the lining of canals for irrigation purposes. International financial agencies have shown an active interest in plans for concreting our roads. While the initial cost of concrete roads may be a little higher, (a) the savings in maintenance cost and the longer life of the roads, and (b) the savings in operation costs of plying the ever-increasing number of vehicles, would far outweigh the extra initial outlay. While we mentally accept that roads are the road to national growth, we are content to have the most woefully inadequate system of roads of any comparable country in the world. Only about 1.3 per cent of our surfaced road length is laid out in cement concrete, while—as the Planning Commission's Report recently pointed out—almost one-third of the length of our national highways has only a single-lane road pavement.

I have no doubt that the depression in the cement industry will not last long. The governments will be obliged by compelling circumstances to adopt the three remedial measures. The foresight of those who, like your Company, are expanding their capacity, will be fully justified by events.

In the competitive situation today, we are fully geared to stay ahead of the others. In production, our accent is on quality; in distribution, on availability of the product at a fair price.

We strive to live up to the motto — "It is good to be big; it is better to be good; it is best to be both." We shall maintain our premier position in the field; and the good quality of our product is witnessed by the better price it commands in the free market.

(September 13, 1990)

*O*n the moral plane, India—which has the potential to be the Light of Asia—has become a black hole. Our country is dangerously drifting towards the position of a state without a nation. Not content with risking the loss of national identity by sustained bouts of religious fundamentalism and linguistic and regional fanaticism, we are now whipping up a frenzied confrontation between the urban and rural sectors, and between the backward and "forward" classes. The Circle of Divisiveness is complete. We can do no more to ensure the fulfilment of Miss Jean Dixon's clairvoyant prediction of India's disintegration before the end of the century.

Ages ago India evolved the transcendent concept of *buddhi*. Today no country can claim to have less of it than the originator of the concept.

The stock exchange has gone through the roof. Now is the chance of getting money without earning it! Never mind that more than 90 per cent of all activity on the stock exchange is purely speculative. Anyway, no one reads Lord Keynes who warned: "Speculators may do no harm as bubbles on a steady stream of enterprise. But the position is serious when enterprise becomes the bubble on a whirlpool of speculation. When the capital development of a country becomes a by-product of the activities of a casino, the job is likely to be ill done."

Last year I had pleaded that cement should be placed outside the purview of the Essential Commodities Act which makes it obligatory for dealers to go through the arduous process of obtaining licences at considerable cost in time and money. The good news today is that at long last the government has delicensed the sale of cement.

The laying of concrete roads in Bombay has been a sensible step. Marine Drive, constructed decades ago (incidentally with ACC cement), has cost the Bombay municipality less to maintain than any other artery of the city and is the least pock-marked with potholes.

This year falls the bicentenary of Adam Smith who preached the profound truth that the market would, literally, deliver the goods and should, by and large, be left alone. There is only one cure for the evils which newly acquired freedom produces; and that is continued freedom.

(September 18, 1991)

*I*n the Soviet Union, communism lived for 74 years. When the end neared, it died within three days of the administration of artificial respiration. Thanks to the Second Russian Revolution, we now have a larger percentage of free people on the earth than ever before in world history.

The kaleidoscopic changes in the USSR have three lessons which, I hope, will be written as with a sunbeam on Indian consciousness.

First, the thirst for freedom can never be quenched in the human breast. But the one-man one-vote rite is not enough to make a democracy meaningful. It is the aristocracy of calibre which must take to public life, however distasteful it may be, because "the success of democracy depends upon an informed citizenry, not on the participation of every inmate in the asylum".

Secondly, *laissez faire* capitalism and arthritic communism have both been tried and have failed. In the USSR, as in India, Taiwanese/Singaporean liberalism remains to be tried.

Thirdly, national integration lives in the hearts of men. When (a) States are treated as vassals of the Union; (b) ninety-three per cent of organized industries are controlled by the Centre while the Constitution enacts that "Industries" shall be a State subject; (c) governors function as servile stooges of the Union, barring exceptions like Mr. C. Subramanian; (d) Chief Ministers of States (ruled by the same party as at the Centre) are chosen at Delhi; (e) State Assemblies are dissolved and President's rule is imposed shamelessly to serve party ends — the Constitution is put 41 light years behind us, and it is a sure prescription for national disintegration.

Other countries have graduated to the higher stage where the government actively pursues a fruitful, nutritive policy to promote technological development and industrial growth. India is still at the lower stage where the best we can hope for is that the strangulating controls and restrictions would be removed. Dr. Manmohan Singh is a man of vision and courage, combined with unusual competence and an extraordinary capacity for hard work. With him as the Finance Minister, there is every likelihood of the promise of liberalism being translated into action, despite the inevitable bureaucratic resistance. We should bid goodbye to the nanny state, without casting a longing, lingering look behind. Then there would be a distinct possibility of India—the tiger—emerging from its self-made cage.

*I*n addition to several pollution control measures, your Company has taken other positive measures, including afforestation programmes and landscaping, to enrich and beautify the environment. At the Gagal plant and the Jamul mines every single employee from the General Manager down to the *mazdoor* has a tree after his name with the responsibility of caring for it.

What a splendid transformation would be achieved if each citizen exercised his right to a clean and green environment: EACH ONE — PLANT ONE.

(August 26, 1992)

*T*he explanation for our endless predicament is to be found in the basic fact that we are born of risen apes, not of fallen angels. Our conflicts and crimes, our missiles and murders, should cause no surprise when we remember our predatory animal origin.

Though all of us belong to the same species of creation — *Homo sapiens* — we are at different stages of evolution. Some are closer to the brute from whom our species is believed to have evolved, and some to the supramental beings who will emerge after aeons of existence. The miracle of man is not how far he has sunk, but how magnificently he has risen. We are known among the stars by the *Mahabharata*, not by our riots and massacres.

If the capacity of India to march forward on the economic front is to be speedily translated into reality, it can only be by following the present government's policy of liberalization. The motive of some of our leaders in the past forty years in adopting socialism might have been honest. "A lively sense of wrongs crying for redress", is how the socialist intellectual, G.D.H. Cole, defined the will to socialism. But it has been found that, like prohibition, socialism is a good idea which does not work in practice. "We are all socialists now", said a British Prime Minister almost a century ago. It would be true to say the exact opposite today: we are all anti-socialism now.

The Eighth Five-Year Plan (1992-97) identifies six areas of strength in the Indian economy, and cement is one of them.

But, deplorably, the concreting of roads has no priority. After four decades of independence, as many as 98 per cent of our national highways are non-motorable by world standards. Although they constitute only 1.5 per cent of our total road length, they carry 35 per cent of the road traffic.

Recent cuts in governmental expenditure on a whole range of development programmes will mean a significant reduction in demand, since the government — with 40 per cent offtake — is the biggest single consumer of cement.

The Eighth Plan lays great emphasis on export of cement, in view of the fact that our neighbouring countries are net importers of this commodity. The Plan projects cement exports to increase from one million tonnes in 1991-92 to 5 million tonnes in 1996-97.

The true index to a company's greatness is not only its turnover, not only its quantum of profits, but its human resources. Under the high-powered stewardship of Dr. S. Ganguly and his colleagues — backed by a loyal and dedicated workforce — your Company has proved itself an expert in the management of change. Its success will be judged not merely by the market value of its shares, but by the pride of place your Company occupies in the hearts and minds of the people it seeks to serve.

In the final analysis, I believe we shall be measured by an even more stringent yardstick: how effectively did your Company play its role in helping India achieve the transition from a developing to a developed nation.

(September 22, 1993)

Globalization, democratization, and liberalization will be counted as the three great powerhouses of change in our times. In the words of Chris Patten, the Governor of Hong Kong, "On every continent, in nearly every land, hope is turning on the lights."

Never before in world history have the economies of different countries attempted to come together to commence the concept of the global village. The twilight of communism has compelled even a diehard like Castro to concede that democratic reforms would eventually have to come to Cuba. Three-fourths of the 47 countries south of the Sahara are in various stages of a democratic surge. Liberalization is to the nineties what socialism was to the forties. Socialism is as outdated as the dinosaur. We now have insignificant ideologies; and our commanding heights have been reduced to molehills.

Without whole-hearted public support for Dr. Manmohan Singh's liberalization policies, we shall only bear out the recent comment of *The Economist* (July 31, 1993) that India is "Asia's big laggard". Such unthinking demonstrations as were staged against the New Economic Policy on August 19 and 20, merely give point to Dr. Einstein's observation that to many people the Creator gave brains by mistake — the spinal cord would have been amply sufficient!

Unfortunately, while the world is celebrating the 2500th anniversary of the birth of democracy, the grim crisis facing the free world is the lacklustre leadership. Politicians have been reduced to mere mortals. When did so many heads of state have so little public backing and evoke so little public respect? The free world has lost confidence in its politicians. We do not believe in them any more.

Winston Churchill referred to the times of Lord Rosebery as "an age of great men and small events". We are living in an age of small men and great events. Talking about the G-7 Summit, a shrewd political analyst observed, "What we have in Tokyo is a meeting of the world's strongest countries but the world's weakest leaders."

India partakes of this world trend. Mistrust of government as an institution broods over the nation. Very few people are aware that for months our Union Cabinet has functioned without a Commerce Minister, or a Defence Minister, or a Law Minister, or a Foreign Minister in normal health. Leaders are not missed when there is no leadership worth the name.

7

Taxation

Paucity of Foreign Investment in India
The Law Permits What Honour Forbids

*T*he general public are not aware that the greatest single factor responsible for the paucity of foreign investments in India is the insensate instability of our laws, specially tax laws, and the total absence of honour and good faith on the part of the government.

The number of non-resident Indians (NRIs) residing abroad would be close today to 15 million. Their accumulated wealth, at a conservative estimate, would be not less than 100 billion in US dollars, the equivalent of Rs. 312,000 crore.

A week after the Budget for 1993-94 was introduced in Parliament, I visited Muscat and Dubai to speak on the Budget and to persuade NRIs to invest in India. I pointed out the benefits of further liberalization and the new tax concessions which afford attractive incentives to invest in new enterprises. The general impression I gathered was that NRIs are not only willing but eager to help India. Their strong emotional attachment to their mother-land is beyond question. They find the policy of liberalization sufficiently attractive and the tax reliefs in this year's Budget sufficiently generous.

But the most perturbing part of their reaction was their mistrust of the government, born of their bitter experience of the maddening changes in Indian laws and their painful consciousness that the law permits what honour forbids. They bluntly ask—can we trust the Government of India? If they start an undertaking on the strength of the tax holidays proposed in this year's Budget, can they be sure

(The Times of India, April 9, 1993)

that the basis on which they decide to embark on the venture will continue to be the law of India at the time when production commences three years later? The majority of chartered accountants practising in the Arab countries are NRIs themselves and they have full knowledge of what has been happening in the recent past.

Prior to the Finance Act, 1986, the then existing Section 32A(8) of the Income-tax Act provided that the Central Government might notify the discontinuance of investment allowance in respect of any ship or aircraft acquired or any machinery or plant installed after a specified date "not being earlier than three years from the date of such notification". The Finance Act, 1986, shamelessly discontinued investment allowance without the three years' notice which was mandatory under the law, by the simple expedient of omitting the statutory words which required three years' notice. The force of high-handedness could go no further. Indians have no option but to submit to such strident injustice. But NRIs and other foreigners who can venture in any part of the world are understandably averse to investing in a country where a sense of honour has become totally anachronistic.

In a profound sense, the issue of abolition of investment allowance without the statutory notice involved the honour of the Government and of Parliament. The tax evader breaks the law. The Government which abolishes investment allowance without three years' notice equally breaks the law. Does it make a difference that the Government has the power to pass an amendment which is the fig leaf to cover the flagrant breach of faith? Is there much to choose between a tax-evading citizen and a promise-evading Government?

Incidentally, in the last twenty-five years, brazen breaches of promise have been perpetrated by governments and public authorities all over India. State Electricity Boards promise exemption from electricity duty for a specified period to attract industries to backward areas even as municipalities promise exemption from octroi to entice new industrial undertakings to their region, and then go back on their written assurance. Our standards of public behaviour have become so degraded and depraved that such tactics are openly adopted without the slightest fear of public outrage.

The belief that the government will act on principles of honour and good faith is an invaluable but fragile national asset. The greatest mistake men in power make is to destroy that asset at their arrogant whim and fancy. The fiscal system must have not merely legality but also legitimacy. It is denuded of all legitimacy when there are breaches of faith on the part of the government in its dealings with taxpayers.

A similar breach of faith was involved in the abolition of reliefs by the Finance Act, 1990 which dealt with certain provisions of the Income-tax Act. It abolished, without notice, reliefs under Section 33A (development allowance for tea bushes planted in new fields); Section 80HH (establishment of new industrial undertakings or hotels in, or shifting of existing units from cities to, backward areas); and Section 80HHA (establishment of small-scale industrial undertakings in rural areas). Those sections had been in operation for a long time—ranging from 13 to 25 years. The Government refused to consider the palpable injustice entailed as regards schemes which had been in the process of implementation and which had been undertaken by trusting taxpayers on the basis of existing law.

Not surprisingly, the total NRI direct investment during the period 1975 to 1992 has amounted to a meagre Rs. 582 crore (or 188 million dollars at the current rate of Rs. 31 per dollar). This was only ten per cent of the total foreign investment in India during those years. In the case of other foreigners who have no ties with India, the erosion of international confidence, resulting from the mindless instability of our governmental policy, acts as an even greater deterrent to investment in India. In the year 1992, approvals for direct foreign investment in India amounted to only 1.25 billion dollars, as against ten billion dollars in China, six billion dollars in Mexico, three billion dollars in Malaysia, and 1.8 billion dollars even in small Thailand.

*T*he question may be asked—how can any finance minister ensure that such breaches of faith are not committed by his successors? In Mauritius they amended the Constitution and provided that changes in certain policies could not be made without a special majority needed to amend the Constitution. India need not go to that length. There is a simple expedient to deal with the situation. The Government should declare its economic and fiscal policy for the remaining term of its office. It should apologize for the breaches of faith committed in the past and publicly avow that its policy hereafter would be to ensure that those who act on the faith of the existing law would be protected. Such a solemn assurance would give rise to the doctrine of "promissory estoppel" which, in jurisprudence, means that the Government is estopped from going back on its promises. The equity of promissory estoppel can be enforced in the High Courts and in the Supreme Court by any aggrieved citizen or foreigner.

This is the only way of attracting large foreign investment. Otherwise, in the prevailing atmosphere of fully justified mistrust of the Government, which NRI or other foreigner will invest on the basis of the proposed amendment of Section 10A of the Income-tax Act which promises a tax holiday to a new industrial undertaking for production of hardware or software in technology parks, or of Section 80-IA which promises a tax holiday to any industry started in the sixteen specified areas and to any undertaking which generates or produces electricity in any part of the country?

Let us never forget that large countries and small minds go ill together, and that absence of a sense of honour can never be compensated by politicians however able or by bureaucrats however astute. We should be stung by shame in committing a breach of faith by changing our laws to the detriment of those who act on the basis of our existing enactments.

Octroi — The Levy that has Every Vice

*O*ctroi was introduced more than 2,000 years ago in the days of the Roman empire when the world was far less civilized and the value put on time was infinitely lower than it is today. This led Sir Charles Trevelyan to remark that octroi represents "the remains of a barbarous system of universal taxation".

The world has changed beyond recognition and two whole generations have flourished and perished since the Indian Taxation Inquiry Committee declared in 1925, "No country can be progressive that relies to any extent upon octroi which has nearly every vice." Sixty-two years later, nine of our States are witness to the fact that the levy, like a famous monarch, has taken an unconscionable time a-dying.

Octroi has the signal distinction of having four "qualifications" which no other levy possesses. It is the only tax which has been unanimously and unequivocally condemned by high-powered bodies specifically appointed to consider the desirability of its continuance. It is the only tax which has generated an epidemic of political schizophrenia. It is the only tax which has institutionalized corruption on so vast a scale that a strong lobby has grown up against its abolition. It is the only impost which taxes the people to a tolerable extent in terms of money and to an intolerable extent in terms of time and energy.

First, the universal disapproval. After 1925, no less than two dozen other commissions and committees have expressed their view that the collection of octroi is working dead against the national interest.

The Motor Vehicles Taxation Enquiry Committee (1950) noted the highly deleterious effects of octroi on trade and commerce and remarked, "Evidence before the present Committee indicated that in some areas the ill-effects on trade of local octroi, terminal tolls and similar taxes on goods in transit are today perhaps even greater than they were when the 1924-25 Committee commented so adversely on this form of taxation."

The Road Transport Reorganization Committee (1959), under the Chairmanship of Mr. M. R. Masani, commented that the system of octroi duties was a "national waste" and strongly recommended its immediate abolition.

The Committee on Transport Policy and Co-ordination (1966), appointed by the Planning Commission and presided over by Mr. Tarlok Singh, a Member of the Planning Commission, observed, "There has been general agreement on the vexatious and inhibitory nature of octroi duties and the abuses to which they are prone . . . . From the point of view of intra-state movement, the first recommendation we would reiterate concerns the need to do away with octroi duties."

The Rural-Urban Relationship Committee (1966) said, "Octroi constitutes a major hindrance to the free flow of traffic and trade and hence it retards the growth of commerce and industrial activities. It is in the national interest that octroi and terminal taxes should go."

The Committee on Road Transport Taxation Enquiry (1967), under the Chairmanship of Mr. Keskar, expressed its strong belief that octroi is an impost "of the greatest hindrance in the way of commercial and economic development of the country. Advanced countries realized it long ago and abolished octroi." The Committee condemned the "canker of octroi" which had spread through the body politic of local administration and called it "a grave danger to the civic life of the community".

The Bhoothalingam Committee (1969) appointed by the Karnataka Government was clearly in favour of abolishing octroi.

The Estimates Committee (1975) of the Lok Sabha renewed the plea for the abolition of octroi and stated, "One of the main obstacles in the way of quick and rapid movement of road transport in the country is the multiplicity of checkposts and payment of octroi duties at these checkposts."

The Jha Committee on Indirect Taxation (1978) reported strongly against octroi and thought it should be ended.

The National Transport Policy Committee (1980), under the Chairmanship of Mr. Pande, opined, "There are no two opinions that octroi is harmful, obnoxious and inhibits efficiency of road transport and that the socio-economic cost of octroi is much more than the revenue yielded by it."

Secondly, the political schizophrenia. Men in power time and again talk of the urgent need to abolish octroi and express their firm conviction that octroi should no longer be allowed to hinder trade and commerce inter-state or intra-state; and then have a spell of convenient amnesia which makes them forget to act upon their own pronouncements.

Abolition of octroi was in the election manifesto of the Janata Party in 1977 and was also in that of the Congress Party in 1980. But our political leaders are so lacking in courage and intellectual integrity that they know what is right but will still do what is wrong. It is a case of paralysis of political will — the incapacity of the party in power to relate action to words.

The Committee of Ministers on Augmentation of Financial Resources of Urban Local Bodies (1965) pleaded for the abolition of octroi. In their words, the impost "constitutes a restriction on through trade. The national economy should be safeguarded as an entity by facilitating the smooth flow of trade and commerce among states and also among different parts of the same state and preventing the raising of bottlenecks through local government regulations."

In February 1970, Mr. Raghuramaiah, the then Minister for Parliamentary Affairs and Transport, while inaugurating the Eighth Meeting of the Transport Development Council emphasized the necessity of abolishing octroi. The Meeting "reiterated the necessity of abolishing octroi and its replacement by other duties".

The Committee of Five Chief Ministers in 1976 re-endorsed the suggestion for discontinuing octroi.

Likewise, the Conference of Chief Ministers and State Ministers in charge of sales tax in New Delhi in September 1980, took a decision in principle to abolish octroi. Addressing that Conference, Mrs. Indira Gandhi called octroi a regressive and retrogressive levy.

At the All India Businessmen's Convention held in New Delhi in January 1984, Mr. Rajiv Gandhi, the then General Secretary of the Congress Party, welcomed the promise of Congress (I) Chief Ministers in the states to abolish octroi. Later, as the Prime Minister, Mr. Rajiv Gandhi expressed in April 1986 strong views in favour of scrapping the levy and directed the states to take prompt action in the matter.

O, the years we waste, and the tears we waste! We have got used to a comfortable time-lag of years and years intervening between the consciousness that a certain thing is required to be done and a serious attempt to do it.

In Maharashtra itself, three years after the condemnation by the Keskar Committee, a study group headed by Mr. S.K. Wankhede, after labouring for about seven years, recommended in 1970 the immediate abolition of octroi. In January 1974 the State Cabinet (in which Mr. S.B. Chavan then held, inter alia, the portfolio of State Transport) promised in principle that octroi would be abolished. After Mr. S. B. Chavan became the Chief Minister, he promised that octroi would be abolished in the state not later than May 31, 1988.

Thirdly, the canker of corruption. This point needs elaboration only to those who are either unforgivably ignorant or inexplicably determined to see no evil.

The Keskar Committee (1967) referred to above, conducted detailed investigations of which the result was summed up by the Committee in the following words: "Side by side with detentions, a general practice has developed to give some sort of gratification to the peon or clerk-in-charge of the post, without paying which the vehicle is not allowed to cross the barrier."

Likewise the Estimates Committee of the Lok Sabha (1975), which has been mentioned earlier, came to the conclusion that the present system of octroi "tends to generate nepotism and corruption and also results in a large scale leakage of this revenue."

One historical fact would suffice. In early 1970s there was a strike by the employees of the Municipal Corporation of Greater Bombay. To break the strike, the Corporation had the octroi checkposts manned by temporary recruits, while the regulars were away. The Corporation had the startling experience that during the period the *nakas* or checkposts were controlled by the raw recruits innocent of the usual practice, the collection of octroi duties increased fourfold!

Finally, the cost of the levy in terms of the time and energy of the nation. Delays at *nakas* or checkposts have been found to range from 30 per cent to 73 per cent of the effective travelling time of commercial vehicles. The 4,000 checkposts where octroi is collected in different states result in 15 per cent of fuel consumption being wasted.

A study of the transport industry by the National Council for Applied Economic Research in 1979 pointed out that these checkposts virtually involve the carrying capacity of 80,000 trucks being rendered idle. The waste of fuel itself entails an annual loss of hundreds of crores of rupees in foreign exchange. According to the Save Energy Committee, headed by Mr. K. C. Pant, the annual wastage of fuel on account of detained vehicles may be put at Rs. 1,000 crore at today's prices.

Reliable statistics show that for every rupee of net revenue derived from octroi, the net burden on the nation is Rs. 6.27

Several committees have satisfactorily reported on the possibility of imposing other levies in lieu of octroi. Various States which have scrapped octroi have suffered nothing, since they have adopted alternative measures of taxation which are fair and reasonable and roughly equivalent to what used to be collected by way of octroi.

Entry tax is one such measure. It is payable on goods which cross the State borders. Other alternatives are surcharge on sales tax, increase in property taxes, extra stamp duty/registration fees on urban immovable properties, entertainment tax to be passed on to local bodies, etc. The Kasbekar Committee, appointed by the Maharashtra Government, should be able to go into this subject in detail and suggest ways and means of making up the loss of revenue consequent upon the abolition of octroi.

But one must guard against the tendency of avaricious State governments to adopt such alternative sources of revenue and then appropriate the proceeds of such imposts for themselves. Twice in the past, the industrialists and traders of Maharashtra went out of their way to suggest some alternative measures of revenue *in substitution* of octroi. However, to their dismay, the State government accepted the alternatives, pocketed the proceeds of such new sources, and *continued the octroi!*

Octroi is covered by Entry 52 in the State List in the Seventh Schedule to the Constitution — "Taxes on the entry of goods into a local area for consumption, use or sale therein." To insulate the State governments from undue political pressures, the best solution would be to amend the Constitution and provide that after a specified date no taxes shall be imposed on the entry of goods into any locality even if the goods are intended for consumption, use or sale therein.

In a country where time is of no consequence and the word *kal* is used in the national language to denote both yesterday and tomorrow, such a constitutional amendment is the only safeguard against the perpetuation or revival of fiscal policies for which the nation has paid so heavily for so many years.

In the affairs of nations, as in the affairs of men, there is a providential margin of error; you may take wrong turns at the crossroads, misuse time, take gold for dross and dross for gold, and yet somehow stumble along to your destination. But the margin and period of permissible error need to be carefully watched. You overstep them at your peril.

Tax Avoidance is Legal

*A*mong the propositions sanctified by the case-law of a century are the following. The citizen has the legal right so to dispose of his capital and income as to attract upon himself the least amount of tax. Avoidance of tax is not tax evasion and it carries no ignominy with it; for it is sound law, and certainly not bad morality, for anybody to so arrange his affairs as to reduce the brunt of taxation to a minimum.

The subject cannot be taxed by ignoring the legal position and regarding "the substance of the transaction". The supposed doctrine that in revenue cases "the substance of the matter" may be looked at as distinguished from the form or the strict legal position, has been given its quietus by the House of Lords, by the Privy Council and by our Supreme Court in a catena of decisions.

The principles set out above represent the correct state of the law, today as always in the past. However, in *McDowell v CTO* (154 ITR 148), the Supreme Court took the view that the legal position in cases of tax avoidance should be taken as altered in the light of three judgments of the House of Lords — *Ramsay* v *IR* (54 TC 101); *IR* v *Burmah Oil* (54 TC 200); and *Furniss* v *Dawson* (55 TC 324).

In McDowell's case the Supreme Court had to decide a simple question under the Andhra Pradesh sales tax law — the uncomplicated issue being whether excise duty voluntarily paid directly to the state by the buyer should be charged to sales tax.

(The Times of India, June 29, 1990)

The manufacturer contended that sales tax was payable only on the contractual sale price which did not include excise: the law permitted the buyer to pay excise directly and did not include excise so paid in the artificial definition of "sale price". The court had merely to decide whether the manufacturer could legitimately reduce the sales-tax liability in this manner.

This article is not concerned with the correctness or otherwise of the Supreme Court's decision on the question arising under the sales tax law. But it is of great public importance to consider the validity of the ruling of the Supreme Court blurring the distinction between tax avoidance which is legitimate and tax evasion which is not. It is submitted that the court's pronouncement obliterating such distinction is patently incorrect and proceeds on a total misreading of the three decisions of the House of Lords.

First, the three decisions of the House of Lords were rendered in the context of facts which were entirely dissimilar to the facts before the Supreme Court. Those decisions do mark a significant change in judicial approach — but only in cases where "the safe channel of acceptable tax avoidance shelves into the dangerous shallows of unacceptable tax evasion". The House of Lords was dealing with sham cases of "readymade schemes" (usually purchased off the shelf) which involved a series of inter-connected transactions which were "self-cancelling", i.e., the taxable gains were artificially neutralized by a pre-arranged loss, the loss being "the mirror image of the gain". Thus the loss was not real — it was "manufactured" or "created" or "produced". Several transactions (basic to the schemes) were commercially inert, only intended to be fiscally active on the assumption that a make-believe scheme is sufficient to produce a tax effect.

Secondly, the House of Lords expressly reaffirmed the basic principle, "A subject is entitled to arrange his affairs so as to reduce his liability to tax. The fact that the motive for a transaction may be to avoid tax does not invalidate it unless a particular enactment so provides."

Thirdly, the House of Lords expressly reaffirmed the cardinal principle of *Duke of Westminster v IR* (19 TC 490, 520, 524).

"Given that a document or transaction is genuine, the court cannot go behind it to some supposed underlying substance". They only ruled against the principle being overstated or overextended.

Fourthly, both the Court of Appeal and the House of Lords have unanimously upheld in a recent case the assessee's right to form a partnership with a foreign company, expressly ruling that the fact that "the course adopted by the assessee could reasonably be described as a device to avoid tax" was irrelevant.

Fifthly, in a later judgment — *Craven* v *White* (183 ITR 216) — the House of Lords made it clear that the principles laid down in the earlier three cases did not apply to a single, genuine transaction even if the motive was tax avoidance, but were confined to only preordained or prearranged schemes involving a series of inter-connected transactions entered into for no purpose other than the mitigation of tax. In fact, in those earlier cases, the Law Lords themselves were at pains to state expressly that they were not laying down the law for a single transaction of tax avoidance.

In Britain itself, the three House of Lords cases have never been sought to be applied by the Inland Revenue to the type of facts which existed in McDowell. In India unfortunately, the misinterpretation of those cases in McDowell has been compounded by the indiscriminate and thoughtless manner in which that judgment has been sought to be applied to genuine and legitimate cases of tax avoidance.

It is reassuring that the Supreme Court itself has decided to reconsider McDowell's case and has already held in a later judgment that when the language of a deed of settlement is clear, an attempt to invoke McDowell would be futile even if the deed results in tax avoidance (*CWT* v *Arvind* 173 ITR 479, 486-7).

While McDowell's case is pending reconsideration by the Supreme Court, the High Courts have sensibly refused to apply that ruling to cases of tax planning. Is the Income-tax Department entitled to ignore a genuine partition of a Hindu undivided family where the members are honest enough to admit that the partition was motivated by a desire to reduce tax liability?

Considerations of justice, equity and the rule of law — as well as the true interests of the public exchequer — demand that the Supreme Court should categorically reaffirm the clear distinction between tax avoidance and tax evasion.

In the words of Sabyasachi Mukharji, the Chief Justice of India, "One would wish that one could get the enthusiasm of Justice Holmes that taxes are the price of civilization and one would like to pay that price to buy civilization. But the question which many ordinary taxpayers very often, in a country of shortages, with ostentatious consumption, and deprivation for the large masses, ask is, does he with taxes buy civilization or does he facilitate the waste and ostentation of the few. Unless waste and ostentation in government spending are avoided or eschewed, no amount of moral sermons would change people's attitude to tax avoidance" (*CWT* v *Arvind* 173 ITR 479, 487).

8

Annual Ritual of
Union Budgets

The Union Budget 1984-85

Aside from income-tax rates which are to be annually pre-scribed, budgets are cumulative in their effect since their legal provisions continue to be in operation indefinitely. Budgets come, heavy with suspense, in single file, but they stay with the nation except only to the extent that their provisions are superseded by a new law. The Union Budget for 1984-85 has done little to terminate, or even to mitigate, the pernicious effects of a long procession of previous budgets.

We have virtually administered euthanasia to the textile mill industry. To impose a handicap on the mills in order to encourage powerlooms and handlooms is one thing; to strangulate the mills is another. The recent prolonged strike in Bombay has deprived the textile mill industry even of the right to die with dignity.

It is amazing how many wealthy individuals have shrugged off their due share of the excise burden by being ostensibly engaged in the small-scale sector. That "small is beautiful" has passed into a byword. But we must pause to consider whether in some places small has become ugly.

The late Mr. H. V. R. Iengar publicly expressed his opinion after four decades of Government service that, generally, about 40 per cent of Government expenditure went down the drain. Mr. Leslie Chapman, a former civil servant of Britain, came to the same conclusion in his interesting book *Your Disobedient Servant*.

(Extracts from Annual Public Addresses in Bombay arranged by the Forum of Free Enterprise, and in other cities in India and abroad)

Private agencies which have a fine record of dedicated public service, like the Ramakrishna Mission and Mother Teresa's Sisters of Charity, would do a far better job of administering the anti-poverty programmes than the government departments.

The health of our economy will not improve until we inject the 'S' factor into our fiscal laws, and make them Sane, Simple and Stable.

The Union Budget 1985-86

*T*he Union Budget this year represents a silent and unheralded revolution in economic policy and fiscal thinking. The monumental task of redesigning India has begun.

The Budget is epoch-making. It is the finest among the budgets of the last three decades. It will probably provide the biggest economic story of Asia for the current year.

The years of the locusts are over. The Budget affords a refreshing contrast to the series of regressive budgets that preceded it for so many years.

There are two types of persons who frame the budget—the tinkerers and the structuralists. Most officials in the Finance Ministry have always been tinkerers. This year's Budget presents the handiwork of a structuralist who realizes that mere tinkering is useless, unless the underlying structure of the fiscal system is made sound. Our political values have got so debased that while it needs no courage to do the wrong thing, it needs a lot of courage to do the right thing. And this year's Budget is a very courageous budget.

The Budget represents a mood—the people's new mood of optimism and self-confidence.

As regards relaxation of controls, the Budget and the parallel economic policies of the new Government have taken energetic steps in the right direction.

In many parts of the world, socialism is in retreat. Western Europe's six socialist governments— Greece, Italy, Portugal,

Spain, France and Sweden— have swung noticeably to the right. It is the clash of socialist ideology with obstinate reality which has brought about the change. Jean Monnet said, "Men will only accept change in the face of necessity; and they see that necessity only when confronted by crisis."

One of the few eternal verities of economics is that growth takes place fastest under conditions of economic freedom. West Germany and East Germany, South Korea and North Korea, are classic examples of how two segments of a single people, alike in every respect, reach vastly different levels of development when one operates under conditions of freedom and the other has a state-controlled economy.

The Budget has wisely cut the corporate rate of tax. It has reduced the rates of income-tax on individuals at every slab, the maximum marginal rate being 50 per cent. It has abolished estate duty, giving a poignant significance to the line of Keats, "Now more than ever seems it rich to die". It has discontinued the compulsory deposit scheme. It has slashed the wealth-tax rates, with two per cent as the maximum marginal rate. India must never go back to the days of oppressive taxation.

The tax cuts are bound to prove economically efficient. No theory of socialism can get over the basic fact, hard as granite, that high rates of taxation inevitably result in the citizenry resorting to tax evasion.

Over the years, tax evasion has been the national sport of India. Direct taxes had reached or exceeded the point where their impact on effort and evasion far outweighed their value to the exchequer. The rich have been sheltering their wealth in the underground economy.

> "Agents of the Fisc pursue
> Absconding tax defaulters through
> The sewers of provincial towns."

This year the Government has rightly realized that when the law comes into conflict with the basic forces of human nature, the law is engaged in a losing struggle. Tax evasion is a worldwide phenomenon; no country has been able to eradicate this evil.

Predictably, the extreme leftists have voiced their protest against the reduction of tax rates. Karl Marx suggested "a heavy and progressively graduated income-tax" among the ten important measures by which the proletariat would seize power from the hated middle-class.

Dr. Gunnar Myrdal lamented that the law-abiding citizens of Sweden had been converted into tax-dodgers by excessive taxation. The same was the sad experience of the UK some years ago. In the UK 85 per cent of company accounts examined in detail in 1980 by the tax authorities showed understatement of profits. The Parliamentary Accounts Committee of the House of Commons, in its Report on Inland Revenue in 1981, referred to the disturbing growth of black money. In 1983 a working paper presented to the World Bank found, after examining the records of 20 countries, that the average unweighted annual rate of growth of gross domestic product was 7.3 per cent in the low tax group and 1.1 per cent in the high tax group.

It is interesting to note that the period of the highest Indian inflation was between 1972 and 1975 when inflation raged at a rate between 10 and 25 per cent, and that coincided with the period of the highest maximum marginal rate of income-tax, 97.75 per cent, which prevailed between 1971 and 1974. A wrong budgetary policy is followed by inflation after a time-lag of about one year or so.

In slashing taxes, India is in excellent company. In 1979, Ireland abolished wealth-tax, Germany substantially lowered it, USA cut capital gains tax, and the UK reduced its maximum rate of personal tax from 83 to 60 per cent. The maximum marginal rate matters most for incentive and hence for economic efficiency.

In 1982 Sweden brought down its maximum marginal rate of personal income-tax from 85 to 50 per cent. In 1984 the UK dropped its corporation tax from 52 to 50 per cent with further reductions in subsequent years so as to bring the main rate to 35 per cent in 1986-87; and Malaysia resorted to equally significant tax reductions.

While every Finance Minister has purported to simplify the income-tax law, it has been made more complex annually during the last 20 years. The last genuine attempt at simplification was made by Mr. T. T. Krishnamachari in 1965. This year's Budget marks a happy departure, in that it has not introduced a single complication in the ghastly mess which passes as the income-tax law of India.

"In all political regulations," said Dr. Johnson, "good cannot be complete; it can only be predominant." The Union Budget this year is an instance in point.

The Budget is intended to create the rising tide that would lift all boats, to borrow the happy phrase of President Kennedy. But it has met with criticism, some well-informed and some ill-informed. Some have criticized the Budget because they represent some special interest groups and their expectations have not been fulfilled. With special interest groups the plea always is—

"Don't tax him,
And don't tax me,
But tax that man behind that tree."

There are others who have criticized the Budget because the capacity to raise a problem for every solution is more widespread than the capacity to offer a solution for every problem. There are still others who are in the Opposition and they think that in a democracy it is the duty of the Opposition to oppose. Political parties prefer to confront each other rather than confront together the problems facing the nation.

The Union Budget 1986-87

*U*pon his elevation to the Bench an Irish judge, vowing to hold the scales of justice absolutely even, said, "I shall lean neither to partiality on the one hand nor to impartiality on the other."

I must confess to partiality in favour of the present Government. When Mrs. Indira Gandhi died, we wanted a leader, a healer, and a pilot to weather the storm. Luckily, in Mr. Rajiv Gandhi we found all the three— a leader to hold the country together and replenish its self-confidence, a healer to treat the political as well as the economic wounds which had been inflicted on the country, and a pilot (in more senses than one) guiding the country onward to its tryst with destiny. The most striking feature of his first 500 days as the Prime Minister has been the moral dimension of his liberalism.

The Finance Minister deserves public gratitude for the continuation of the lower rates of individual and corporate taxes. There is a wave, throughout the world, of low levels of taxation. Many nations have realized the wisdom of Chanakya's dictum that milk is not obtained by drying up the cow. The wisdom of introducing low rates of direct taxes in the last year's Budget is fully vindicated by the fact that the highest ever growth in direct taxes— 23 per cent—was registered in 1985-86.

Pakistan has done even better than India—its rate of corporate tax is 40 per cent, the maximum rate for individuals is 45 per cent; shareholders are not liable to any tax in respect of dividend income; and gift tax has been totally abolished. An international study conducted last year of 20 developing countries showed that the nations which levied lower rates of tax registered, without exception, a faster rate of growth than those with high taxation.

Among the countries which cut the rates of direct taxes last year or this year are — USA, West Germany, France, Norway, Sweden, Denmark, Belgium, Spain, Singapore, Thailand, Australia and New Zealand.

In his budget proposals to the Congress in May 1985, the President of the USA suggested 33 per cent corporate tax and a maximum rate of 35 per cent for individuals. Australia has cut the maximum personal tax from 60 per cent to 49 per cent. Singapore has cut the maximum personal tax and corporate tax to 33 per cent, to get out of the slough of economic stagnation. Belgium has cut the corporate rate from 57 per cent to 45 per cent.

*T*he three political tranquillizers are exactly those which characterized the Budget of 1984-85 of the previous government—the encouragement to small-scale industries, the anti-poverty programmes, and the mass loan *melas*. No right-minded person could possibly object on principle to alleviation of poverty in any form or to any encouragement extended to the small entrepreneur. But the way in which these programmes operate in practice leaves much to be desired.

In India, gestures rather than policies are practised — this is a pregnant observation by Trevor Fishlock, the eminent British journalist, who lived in India for three years. The Finance Ministry's policies and proposals reinforce his dictum. The question is—does the Budget resolve the problem of poverty or does it merely re-cycle the problem? Do we want a budget for Jobs or a budget for Doles, a budget for Self-help or a budget for State help?

We must never try to brush aside reality, however unpleasant it may be. The French National Assembly was called House without Windows, because it was totally insulated from reality.

Unfortunately myth matters more than reality in electoral politics.

There is no doubt that the economic growth of India is inextricably linked with the small-scale sector. Even in the USA, 20 million new jobs were created in the last decade in small new enterprises, whereas two million jobs were lost during the same period in the first 1,000 big corporations mentioned in *Fortune.*

But our gesture of solicitude towards the small-scale sector must not make us deliberately shut our eyes to the rampant dishonesty and tax evasion which permeate that sector.

A government survey conducted in 1973 showed that 12 per cent of the small-scale units were not traceable; while 26 per cent were permanently closed — although all of them kept on receiving critical raw materials through official agencies. In February 1975 Mr. A. P. Sharma, the then Minister of State for Industry, said in Parliament that one-third of the units in the textile small-scale sector were bogus. In March 1977 a survey conducted by the Reserve Bank showed that 34.5 per cent of the small-scale units assisted by banks represented dishonest circumvention of the law. The Fourteenth Report of the Estimates Committee of Lok Sabha (1980-81) reiterated that something must be done about the alarming rise in bogus units in the small-scale sector.

But the Budget continues the official gesture of support to the small-scale sector, including exemption from excise, without any measures to counteract the misuse of fiscal relief.

The second example of our propensity to practise "gestures" is that of the anti-poverty programmes run by the Ministry of Rural Development, including the Integrated Rural Development Programme and the National Rural Employment Programme. There can be no doubt that investment in human beings is far more important and of far greater economic value than investment in physical projects. The objection is not to the allocations but to the way in which the amounts allocated get unproductively frittered away.

The Public Accounts Committee of Parliament, in its Ninetieth Report (1981-82) has drawn attention to the fact that in implementing the National Rural Employment Programme, there were serious irregularities on the part of almost all State governments—corruption, misappropriation, false debits in the accounts, diversion of foodgrains, etc. — and it listed 36 shortcomings of the Programme in Appendix III to the Report. As the late Prof. Raj Krishna (who was a member of the Planning Commission) said, "only a small portion of the funds really trickles down to the target groups". Anti-poverty programmes have a tendency to degenerate into pro-party programmes.

The Report on Black Money by the National Institute of Public Finance and Policy which was published last year regards the anti-poverty programmes as one of the sources of black money and refers to research studies which disclose that 50 per cent to 80 per cent of anti-poverty programmes represent public money going down the drain.

*T*he third major gesture, involving a total defeat of economics at the hands of politics, is the mass loan *mela* in which branches of the nationalized banks are expected to help the poor by being compelled to grant a fixed number of applications for loans without security and later to write off the sticky loans as irrecoverable. The *mela* virtually amounts to a distribution of bank funds among persons selected according to a yardstick not defined, by a procedure not formulated, on the recommendations of politicians who are not conspicuous for their integrity. The dangers of the mass loan *mela* should be clear even to the purblind, in a country where the family comes first, the caste second, the party third, and the nation is hardly relevant at all. Inevitably, as the *mela* gathers momentum it is bound to entail a heavier tax burden on the nation.

There is a strong tendency to obliterate the distinction between the Government and the party, but we are now compounding the mischief by obliterating the distinction between public funds and bank funds. A bank is not an eleemosynary institution. It would be legitimate to employ the funds of nationalized banks for well-thought-out programmes of public benefit but not for a mass loan *mela*. The constitutional legality of the scheme is open to question; while its constitutional immorality is beyond question. It will activize evil, formalize corruption, and regularize political patronage. It is a scheme worthy of a banana republic but not of a major democracy where the rule of law, and not the rule of men, is supposed to prevail.

Banking is a profession. The banks need more autonomy and less interference from men in power. The *mela* will shake the creditworthiness of banks. Musclemen and middlemen, political opportunists and anti-social elements, will be the main beneficiaries of the *mela*. It would need a committee of archangels to conduct the *mela* in such a manner as to avoid the charge of discrimination against the supporters of Opposition parties. There are sounder and better ways of assisting the poor.

The whirligig of time brings in its revenges, and different political parties in power at different times will use the ill-conceived scheme, not for national benefit but for political mileage. Public financing of political parties can be a sensible ingredient of the democratic process, but not when it is by the backdoor. To ask whether the mass loan *mela* is good for the people is like asking whether nuclear bombs are good for your health.

The most disquieting feature of the present administration of income-tax law is the indiscriminate and barbarous manner in which raids have been conducted on taxpayers to unearth tax evasion.

In the words of Lord Denning, "No one would wish that any of those who defraud the Revenue should go free. They should be found out and brought to justice. But it is fundamental in our law that the means which are adopted to this end should be lawful means. A good end does not justify a bad means. The means must not be such as to offend against the personal freedom, the privacy and the elemental rights of property."

Raids have become such a regular, commonplace feature that they may soon lose all social stigma, and may even become a status symbol!

As I have repeatedly said, there are two defects in our national character — lack of a sense of fairness, and lack of a sense of moderation. Untouchability is the durable monument to our shameful lack of a sense of fairness, and the current raids are a distressing monument to our lack of a sense of moderation. What is disturbing is not so much the savage manner in which the raids are conducted, but the Ministry's defence of such savagery and its insistence that such raids should continue.

While it is true that no one is above the law, it is equally true that so long as our Constitution lasts, everyone is above state terrorism.

I shall not go into the question as to how far the Government's own senseless fiscal and economic policies in the past have been mainly responsible for the degradation in national character. Nor will I raise the issue — who, according to the lesson taught 2,000 years ago, has the right to cast the first stone at the businessman? The need of the hour is co-operation, and mutual respect and confidence, between the government and business, and the right response from the whole nation to the new policies so sensibly commenced last year.

In coping with evasion, there are no instant recipes. In our desire to bring about a total revolution in the mentality of the taxpayer, we must guard against the dangers of introducing the valueless values of a police state. Let us never forget that descent into a police state is deceptively easy. Excesses by the state can easily be counterproductive. They can destroy taxpayer morale which is a valuable but delicate national asset and which is a prerequisite for a tax system based on voluntary compliance.

The Union Budget 1987-88

*T*he Finance Bill, 1987, has evoked the whole gamut of public reactions — from condemnation to criticism to polite applause to standing ovation. Those who had high hopes about the budget think that they would need a magnifying glass to find traces of relief in the Finance Bill.

In order to get a proper perspective, it is necessary to cast a glance at Prime Minister Rajiv Gandhi's impact on the fiscal jurisprudence of India. In the last ten years the developed and developing countries have been going through a festival of fiscal reform, characterized mainly by the lowering of tax rates. When the history of our times comes to be written, in the chapter on fiscal legislation two events will be regarded as towering achievements — Prime Minister Rajiv Gandhi's fiscal reform in 1985 and President Reagan's in 1986. Both these leaders wrought fundamental changes. Our Prime Minister's achievement was greater — having regard to the environment in which he had to operate.

Since 1985, the seven objectives of the Prime Minister and Mr. V. P. Singh have been:

(i) reasonably low rates of taxation;

(ii) simplification and rationalization;

(iii) stability in rates and fiscal structure;

(iv) no unnecessary secrecy about budget provisions;

(v) encouraging participatory democracy by inviting suggestions from the public;

(vi) idealism involving trust in the taxpayer instead of suspicion;

(vii) educating tax gatherers in human awareness.

In the computer world, the expression "user-friendliness" means the designing of a computer with the needs and convenience of the user in mind. The objective of our present government has been to develop assessee-friendliness — i.e., tax laws should be framed with the needs and convenience of taxpayers in mind.

There are two classes of civil servants in our country. In the first class are outstanding men of vision and knowledge, who realize that a budget is not merely a measure for collecting revenue but can and should be a powerful instrument of economic growth. To call them bureaucrats would be an affront to such perceptive, thinking individuals. However, there is the other class of civil servants who are such that not to call them bureaucrats would be an affront to the English language. These bureaucrats believe that they are the "steel frame of the Indian government", as they were called in the British days, and they remain as rigid, unthinking and unbending as steel. Their participation in budget-making can seriously damage the health of the national economy.

The issue of the *Wall Street Journal* dated November 7, 1986, published an article based upon interviews with a number of such Indian bureaucrats who said that they were determined to resist our Prime Minister's new policy. This year's Finance Bill represents what may be called the Bureaucrat's Revenge. Perhaps a milder and more appropriate expression could be the "bureaucrat's uncooperative response". The bureaucrats have virtually revolted against the Prime Minister's objectives and gone their old mindless way.

The growth of India has been stunted and its public finances are in such a disquieting state, mainly because the country has been anchored far too long to the following economic illusions:

(i)   That by imposing higher rates of tax you collect more

revenue; and you can break the link between effort and reward and still get the effort.

(ii) That by state ownership and state control you can achieve economic growth with social justice. A recent issue of *The Economist* (London) rightly said that "the socialism practised in India has been a fraud". The public sector in India has 66 per cent of all fixed capital investment, but has only 27 per cent of the nation's industrial output to its credit.

(iii) That by enriching the government, you can enrich the nation. In Pakistan the government is poor while the people are rich; while in India the government is rich and the people are poor. The per capita income in Pakistan is $390 as against India's $260.

(iv) That by militant trade unionism you can raise the level of the working class and reduce or end unemployment. It was only after this illusion was exploded in Italy in 1980 that that nation has now become economically the most dynamic in Europe.

(v) That the nation can be milked to an indefinite extent; and poverty can be eliminated — faster than productivity allows — merely by making allocations for anti-poverty programmes.

Our economic problems brook no further delay. Two thousand years ago, Rabbi Hillel asked the questions — "If not us — then who? If not now — when?" We have to ask ourselves the same questions in all earnestness. The political situation in the country today is such that if we cannot achieve speedy growth under Prime Minister Rajiv Gandhi, we may find ourselves in a worse plight than merely Paradise Postponed.

The Union Budget 1988-89

*T*he 41st Budget of free India does not fulfil the great promise of the first budget of Prime Minister Rajiv Gandhi's government in 1985.

The Finance Minister has presented the country with a budget bouquet, made up of a few tiny fresh flowers at the front, and a lot of cheap greenery at the back sprayed with a soporific aroma — with some stinging nettles so well concealed that they are not easily discernible to the superficial observer.

The unbridled increase in the Government's indebtedness is truly alarming. India is already in the danger zone, if it has not yet entered the debt trap situation. As Dr. S. R. K. Rao of the Reserve Bank of India observed:

> I may define the internal debt trap as a situation when, the capacity of the market to respond to the government's borrowals being limited, the amount borrowed might be just sufficient to meet the debt servicing burden. After that threshold, the country would enter into an internal debt trap, i.e., the borrowings would not be sufficient to meet even the debt servicing charges.

Mr. A. Seshan, another officer of the Reserve Bank, comes to the conclusion that "... the annual interest payments on market borrowings will exceed the annual net market borrowings by 1992-93."

This is the greatest danger to be feared. It puts the nation at risk. The interest and repayment burdens will have to be shouldered by our children and will have to be discharged by taxation on them. For years to come, the dead hand of the excessive national debt will continue to rest heavily upon the productive energies of the country.

As a compulsive borrower, the government is mortgaging the economic future of the country. In the words of Thomas Jefferson, "If we can prevent the government from wasting the labour of the people, under the pretence of caring for them, they would be happy."

The amounts borrowed by the government under the Indira Vikas Patra Scheme, as modified by this budget, are to double at the end of five years. This means that the Indira Vikas Patras now carry compound interest at 14.8 per cent per annum. This is the highest rate of interest ever paid by the government of India. After all, the Indira Vikas Patra Scheme is, to put the truth bluntly, a scheme of bearer bonds which are mainly availed of by black marketeers and tax evaders, since the identity of the holder is not required to be disclosed. Should the government pay such an extraordinarily high rate of interest to that unworthy section of society, with every likelihood of tax being evaded on the interest?

This year's Economic Survey has strongly recommended "ruthless pruning of programmes of doubtful economic and social merit." But the government is in no mood to respect this recommendation.

In the words of Prof. K. N. Raj, a member of the late Indira Gandhi's Economic Advisory Council, "Poverty eradication schemes have become a lucrative industry giving the highest returns to those promoting them. . . Hence the enthusiasm which poverty eradication has aroused."

No fiscal locomotive can pull a deficit-heavy train. Upto 1978-79 the Indian government managed to live within its means. But since 1979-80 the nation has been living on its capital, and a deficit on revenue account has become a regular feature of the budget.

In Britain, Lord Young who is in charge of the Department of

Trade and Industry published a White Paper on January 12, 1988, in which he gave a new logo to his Department— "Department for Enterprise". His message to the business community is— "Come and see us. Find out how we can help you. Our door is open." This is the attitude of a government keen to create new productive jobs. In India if we are to have a truthful logo for our Ministries of Commerce and Industry, we would have to call them "Departments for Stifling Enterprise".

Apart from exports, another rich source of foreign exchange earnings can be tourism. India has a million tourists a year and earns annually about Rs. 1,800 crore only in foreign exchange from tourism. By contrast, Spain has 47 million tourists annually—far more than its entire population. Even Singapore has three million tourists annually, while its population is only 2.5 million. The small city of Singapore has 30,000 hotel rooms, as against 34,000 in the whole of India for tourists. Even Thailand earns annually from tourism $1,500 million, i.e., more than India's foreign exchange earnings from tourism.

The complexity of our fiscal laws — compounded by the Direct Taxes (Amendment) Act, 1987—will, if anything, be worsened by the Finance Bill. So far from putting tax consultants out of business, it will assure them continued professional prosperity.

But the complexity is a minor peccadillo compared to three indefensible provisions which cry aloud for deletion. Two of them involve breach of faith, and the third constitutes a violent assault on justice and constitutionalism. There is not a word in the budget papers to indicate to the members of Parliament and to the public that such breaches of faith are sought to be committed.

It is a sad commentary on the present low standards of public honour and public decency that investment allowance was abolished in 1986 without the three-year notice mandatory under the law which had been enacted by the same party in power. And now two more breaches of faith are sought to be committed in violation of statutory promises by the same government.

Such breaches of faith lower the credibility of the administration, and shake the trust and confidence of foreigners and non-resident Indians in the Indian government.

The budget has left untouched the incredible damage which is bound to be inflicted on the economy by the Direct Taxes (Amendment) Act, 1987. That Act proceeded on the assumption that the state has the first claim to everyone's income, and the after-tax income permitted to be retained is a gift by the state to undeserving and ungrateful citizens. That arrogant assumption is left undisturbed by the Finance Bill.

The Union Budget 1989-90

*U*nfortunately, the last Budget of this Government is purely an exercise in political symbolism. It takes the form of election rhetoric and party manoeuvre. There is no policy underlying the Budget.

In point of complexity and poor quality of administration, our direct tax laws—with the myriad rules and notifications which are beyond count or care—must surely rank as the very worst fiscal system in the Third World. If taxpayers were dogs, the officials of the finance ministry would undoubtedly be convicted under the Prevention of Cruelty to Animals Act.

*S*tability is anathema to the North Block. To preach the virtue of stability to our finance ministry is like seeking to preach the value of peaceful coexistence to Genghis Khan.

Organized industry, which contributes 80 per cent of the revenues of the central government, should be deeply perturbed by the fact that since April 1987 more maddening changes have been made or proposed in direct taxes than in the first forty years of India's independence. It is my firm conviction that if we had made no such changes after 1962 (barring removal of a few injustices), the tax collection would have been much higher, the economic growth much greater, and the lot of taxpayers much easier. Who has benefited from the chronic tinkering with the law, except lawyers and chartered accountants?

The Income-tax Act is a national disgrace. Yet more and more half-baked changes every few months are "received calmly" by our people as part of their collective *karma*. We perpetually mistake amendment for improvement and change for progress.

Our laws are changed on the assumption that there is no intelligent life outside the North Block. The arrogance of power is such that amendments are made without considering public suggestions or criticisms which are presumed to represent the ranting of vested interests.

We have now reached the danger point when the laws are made almost entirely by the bureaucracy, and Parliament has only a formal role to play in law-making. Bureaucratic legislation— masquerading as parliamentary legislation—is the barbarous off- spring of the party whip system mating with a brute majority. Let us never forget the savage laws in total denial of human rights passed by Parliament during the Emergency—laws without a parallel in the history of any democracy in this century.

The partial exemption of profits from poultry farming proposed by the budget is a striking example of our erratic laws. The Indian monsoon is far less erratic than Indian legislation. From 1965 to 1975, the profits of poultry farming enjoyed total exemption under Section 10(27) of the Income-tax Act. That Section was deleted and partial exemption was given from 1976 to 1986 under Section 80-JJ of the Act in respect of 15 per cent to 33 per cent of the profits in different years. Then the exemption was totally abolished from 1986 onwards. Now one-third of the profits are proposed to be exempted under Section 80-JJ which is to be reintroduced.

The capricious and whimsical changes in our laws are also well illustrated by the reintroduction of investment allowance. To promote industrial expansion and economic growth, development rebate was very wisely introduced in 1955 and continued till 1974 when it was irrationally abolished. Initial depreciation took its place—1974 to 1976. That was replaced by investment allowance from 1976 to 1986. In 1986 investment allowance was abolished—even without the three years' notice which was required to be given by law, a clear breach of faith which severely shook the credibility of the government. In its place investment deposit account was introduced in 1986. And now investment allowance has been reintroduced as an alternative to investment deposit account. The Prime Minister's basic idea, announced at the commencement of his regime, to put tax consultants out of business remains a distant dream.

The great French thinker Montesquieu said that often taxes are imposed due to the crankiness of men in power. Crankiness—or worse—is obviously responsible for the same instability in laws dealing with indirect taxes.

W ith the right policies, India could become a world leader in technology base. It may not be out of place to reproduce here the essence of some articles in foreign journals:

> India is a leader in off-shore software. Its productivity level is 50 per cent higher than that of UK counterparts. — *Director*, September 1988.

> India has the potential to be a world leader in software, just as Japan is a world power in manufacture of hardware. This is because India's fundamental strength is in mathematics.— *Time*, August 10,1987.

> India, with its tremendously talented business class, has the potential to be a very effective export competitor.— *Forbes*, February 1986.

> Sanskrit is best suited to the computer age, particularly in the area of Artificial Intelligence.— *AI* (Artificial Intelligence) *Magazine*, April 1985.

What a transformation would be effected if we could only

follow the policy dictated by knowledge and vision, with which the present government started!

Unfortunately, the Budget does not take a single step in the direction of the promised retreat from an overweening State. With eleven new programmes, schemes and funds envisaged in the Finance Minister's speech, the bureaucracy will be larger and more intrusive than ever before.

The Union Budget 1990-91

*P*rofessor Madhu Dandavate, the Finance Minister, belongs to a rare species in India's public life. He has a well-equipped and well-furnished mind—in contrast to the overwhelming majority of our politicians, of whom it may be said that their minds are some of the under-developed regions of the states they represent.

The budget which he has introduced in Parliament is that of an honest humanist. It is not a budget to make you deliriously happy or to drive you to the verge of suicidal despair. It may be regarded as a good budget in bad times, though it might have ranked as a bad budget in good times.

The darkest shadow brooding over the national economy is that of the national indebtedness. There has been an unbridled increase in the total liabilities of the government, which include not only what is narrowly and misleadingly called "the national debt", but also the liabilities to repay to the citizens the amounts due to them on account of provident fund, small savings, etc.

The figures are so mind-boggling that it is desirable to have comparative figures of an affluent nation, which may afford a measure of our own government's extravagance. Taking all relevant factors into account it would be fair to say that a dollar is to the United States what a rupee is to India. The debt of the United States government increases at the rate of $8,000 per second — to the American public's great dismay and concern. The indebtedness of the Indian Government increases at the rate of Rs. 11,000 per second. The inescapable conclusion is that India's public debt increases 40 per cent faster than that of the United States.

In order to arouse public sentiment against the grave financial crisis, I suggest that we have a KALIYUG CLOCK in different parts of India to indicate each day the figure of national indebtedness which is mounting at the rate of Rs. 110 crore a day. Every day in every way India goes another Rs. 110 crore into debt.

Article 292 of the Constitution enables Parliament to prescribe by law the limits within which the executive can borrow upon the security of the Consolidated Fund of India. The time has come for Parliament to prescribe such a check. The fixing of ceiling on the borrowing power of the Union government was suggested by the Chakravarty Committee appointed to review the working of the monetary system. It was also recommended by the Public Accounts Committees in their Ninth Report (1962-63), Thirty-Sixth Report (1964-65), Fifty-Second Report (1965-66), and Sixty-Fourth Report (1968-69). The Comptroller and Auditor-General made the same recommendation in his Report published in 1988.

The people must bring strong and sustained pressure on their MPs to ensure that curbs on borrowing powers are fixed by Parliament. The good sense of the government has proved to be a non-existent substitute for legal compulsion.

The Finance Minister deserves the nation's gratitude for his public pronouncement that he would not be averse to an appropriate law being passed by Parliament under Article 292.

*I*t is not surprising that India's performance on the export front is so dismal compared to its potential. World trade is a race in which India has to run in a potato sack, while other countries compete with no such handicap. In 1950 our exports were substantially higher than those of Brazil and South Korea. Today the exports of Brazil are three times, and those of South Korea are five times larger than India's.

*T*he Finance Minister should have total public support in his endeavour to "launch a sustained and multi-pronged drive against proliferation of black money which is a social sin and an economic evil." However, what is wrong with India is the pathological obsession displayed by the law-makers who frame laws only with the tax evader in mind, regardless of the enormous inconvenience and harassment to the far larger section of honest taxpayers. It needs to be borne in mind that 96 per cent of all direct taxes collected by the Union government is on the basis of voluntary self-compliance by the taxpaying public. Only four per cent of the collection is involved in unending appeals to the tax authorities and references in the court of law.

Under-estimation of income is a worldwide phenomenon. India has a lot to learn from other countries where the laws operate fairly and reasonably on honest taxpayers and are not framed with excessive and obsessive concentration on the tax evader.

The latest investigation in the United Kingdom of corporate taxpayers showed that the income disclosed by 91 per cent of them was under-estimated. The European Economic Community estimates that at least ten per cent of the income earned in its member countries escapes tax. In Japan, an examination made by the revenue in 1988 of the accounts of 2,206 companies showed that all but one had under-estimated their income!

The phenomenon is not peculiar to free societies but is discernible even in totalitarian countries where the penalty for several economic offences is death. Last year, the communist regime in China seized the books of registered businessmen of Shanghai and found that 86 per cent of them had returned income which needed to be adjusted upwards! In the Soviet Union, the "unofficial sector" flourishes no less stridently than in India.

In these matters one must have a balanced approach and a sense of proportion. A departmental store which is wholly preoccupied with prevention of shoplifting is a sure candidate for stagnation.

The reduction of tax on the corporate sector from 50 to 40 per cent (43.2 per cent if surcharge is taken into account) is a very welcome feature. All over the world, reduction of corporate tax is now used as the instrument of economic growth. Sweden has decided to reduce it from 57 to 30 per cent, and in Japan it will now be 37.5 per cent. Singapore has reduced it (in the budget presented in March 1990) to 31 per cent. The rate of 35 per cent prevails in the UK, the Netherlands, Portugal and Spain.

A step in the right direction is the total exemption of inter-corporate dividends under Section 80M of the Income-tax Act — but subject to the condition that inter-corporate dividends would be entitled to exemption only if the company receiving the dividend declares an equal amount by way of dividend to its own shareholders. The budget should have abolished, or in any event substantially reduced, the tax on dividends which are paid out of profits on which the company has already paid tax, even where the shareholder is a non-corporate entity, e.g., an individual. Such a system prevails in a large number of countries, including the UK, France, Germany and Japan. In Pakistan, all shareholders are exempt from tax in respect of all dividend income. Public interest demands that we enlarge "the democracy of shareholders", instead of increasing the holdings of the public financial institutions in the private sector.

The abolition of investment allowance is a retrograde step. *Investment allowance is investment by the government in national growth.* Developing countries find it indispensable. Pakistan allows a deduction of 40 per cent above the cost as an investment incentive, Malaysia 60 per cent, while in South Korea the incentive is as high as 100 per cent.

In 1950 India had an average income higher than that of Thailand or South Korea. Today, Thais have an average income of $ 900 a year, and South Koreans $ 2,370. Indians languish on $ 290. Our bureaucratic over-planning has entrenched poverty.

As of December 31, 1987, the Reserve Bank of India identified 2,06,098 units — large, medium, and small-scale — as sick. Since such sick units are increasing at the rate of 188 every working day, there must be at least three lakh sick units today, and 93 per cent of them are terminally ill.

The number of persons seeking employment through the 840 Employment Exchanges is rising at an alarming rate. It exceeded 30 million at the end of 1988; while the actual strength of the army of the unemployed must be double that figure

The aggregate number of persons in the organized sector is 26 million. Here the organized sector mèans (a) the private sector employing more than 25 persons, and also (b) the public sector, i.e., the Union and State governments, municipalities, local authorities and public sector corporations. Thus, for every one person employed in the organized sector, there are two who are jobless!

Futurologists all over the world are predicting that the countries of Asia will be the economic power-houses of the future. There is a scramble to board the Orient Express to the twenty-first century which is less than 3,600 days away. But there is not an uncontrollable rush to enter India.

The total foreign investment of Rs. 3,000 crore in India over the last forty years is less than the annual investment made in China or Australia in recent years. This year's budget will not dispel our socialist stagnation.

In several parts of Africa when the rains do not come, the tribal chief conducts a ritual dance watched by the anxious members of the tribe. The dance does not bring rains, but it consoles and satisfies the people who feel that their chief is doing something to alleviate their misery. Our feverish changes in the law are intended to serve the same purpose as the tribal chief's rain dance.

At a recent meeting of the World Economic Forum at Davos, Prime Minister Lee Kuan Yew of Singapore said to a leading Indian businessman: "The Indian economy is like a sleeping giant which, if awakened, could by itself transform the face of the global economy. India has the potential to form an independent economic

block on her own, without too much dependence on anybody else."
But in keeping with our forty-year hallowed tradition, the budget
this year will not be so rude as to disturb the slumber of the
sleeping giant.

The Union Budget 1992-93

*T*his year's budget is not a budget for the greedy, paid for by the needy. The budget provisions properly so called (as distinct from the proposed amendments to the direct tax laws) are well-conceived, and deserve the support of the well-informed irrespective of party affiliations.

Liberalization is the key to the budget. It is a watershed budget which marks the beginning of a new chapter in India's economic history. It was our ideological socialism which had been responsible for India remaining the twentieth poorest nation on earth. Our gross domestic product is smaller than that of Greater Los Angeles (population 14 million). This year's historic budget for the first time reflects the consciousness of our government that fast economic growth would be impossible with outdated socialism.

Dr. Manmohan Singh has rightly emphasized that unless certain values are adhered to by the nation, it cannot come out of the recession. The Finance Minister has no Midas touch; he has no snake oil which can be used as having a magical healing power in matters economic.

The proposed integration of India into the global economy has not come a day too soon. The emerging world economy has erased national boundaries. Capital and companies no longer stop at the border. If India is to grow and prosper, it has no alternative but to be integrated into the world economy.

Reduction of taxes is one of the avowed aims of the budget. In a global economy, cutting taxes has become a matter of national interest: high tax countries inevitably lose out. The days when the Government could adopt any tax policy, as if the nation existed within a vacuum, are over.

If India is to have a stable and healthy balance of payments, it can only be through increased exports. Even Holland, one of the tiny countries of the world with a population of 15 million, has six times the exports of India!

*T*he least justified criticism of the budget is that it has been framed under the dictates of the World Bank and the International Monetary Fund. The censure is levelled by those whose critical perception does not exceed forty watts. They should credit India with enough intelligence to make the right decision for itself after forty years of mistaken policy. Some of the ablest men in the two international institutions are Indians: to say that the Indian Government cannot think for itself is gratuitous self-condemnation.

In any event we must judge the policy underlying the budget on its merits, and it is wholly irrelevant to be concerned about who suggested the path of wisdom. One of the great failings of democracy is the mistaken belief that it is the duty of the Opposition to oppose.

Secondly, the fear has been expressed in some quarters that India will be swamped by multinationals. The truth is that India runs no risk whatever of being dominated by foreign corporations. We must get rid of the illusion that we are still fighting the East India Company.

Thirdly, the view has been expressed that the Budget has not done enough to check inflation or to counter recession. To control inflation is possible, but to eliminate it is beyond hope at this juncture. The last time we had "negative inflation" (to use bad English) was when Mr. Morarji Desai was the Prime Minister (1977-79). The spirit of the nation — the spirit of national dedication and confidence which then emerged after the tyranny of the Emergency — had as much to do with the fall in prices as any budget.

Inflation is a worldwide phenomenon. A dollar today is worth only 13 cents in 1945 money; a pound is worth six pence. Even the Deutschemark is only one-third of its value in 1948 when it replaced the worthless Reichsmark.

Again, the world economy is going through a period of recession. The current economic depression in the United States is billed as "the mother of all recessions" — the longest since 1945. General Motors, the giant among corporations, incurred a loss of $ 4.5 billion in 1991 — unparalleled in the Company's 84-year history. The critics claim that in Britain the recession is deeper than in any other country. About 20,000 companies went into liquidation in 1991, which works out to one in every 50 British companies.

*T*here are several points on which the budget deserves to be commended.

(1) It is the first budget which aims at breaking the shackles of the bureaucratic command system.

(2) It reflects consciousness of the risk to the nation of an unbridled increase in the total liabilities of the government. We are stealing from the future. No less than Rs. 32,000 crore will be spent next year merely on servicing the loans. That would constitute almost one-fourth — 23 per cent to be precise — of the total governmental expenditure: more than what will be spent on Plan or Defence.

(3) It has restored the balance of payments to a less critical level than before. We have a reserve of $ 4.4 billion. The risk of defaulting or having to ask for rescheduling of debts no longer looms over the horizon.

(4) Partial convertibility of the rupee is a sensible step. That this step is in the national interest is proved by the example of

Pakistan.

(5) The confidence of foreign investors has been restored. The scramble by non-resident Indians to withdraw their deposits from banks has ceased.

(6) The abolition of the office of the Controller of Capital Issues is an essential step in the process of liberalization.

(7) The decision to abolish deduction of tax from interest on term deposits with banks is in the public interest. When Bonn introduced ten per cent withholding tax from interest on bank deposits, there was a flight of capital. Deposits worth DM 100 million vanished from West German banks and re-appeared next door in tiny Luxembourg. The law was promptly scrapped.

(8) Permitting the import of gold is a prudent decision.

(9) The reduction of the statutory liquidity ratio from 38.5 per cent to 30 per cent would release larger bank funds for loans to business and reduce the heavy bank interest rate by one percentage point.

(10) The lowering of the vertiginous customs tariffs to a less unreasonable level is welcome. It is the inevitable step which has to be taken if India is to be integrated into the global economy.

(11) The lowering of the maximum marginal rate of income-tax on individuals would, in the long run, have no detrimental effect on Government revenues, because it would result in better compliance. Professor Lawrence Lindsey of the Harvard University has given cogent evidence to prove that income-tax revenues are most buoyant when the maximum rate is 40 per cent. This phenomenon, called "the Lindsey effect", has been accepted in the United States where the maximum rate is 33 per cent and in Britain where it is 40 per cent. The reduction of the maximum marginal rate on non-corporate assessees to 44.8 per cent (including surcharge) will bring India closer to the fast developing countries which have slashed their rates.

The Union Budget 1993-94

*O*n the whole, it is a creative and nutritive budget. Dr. Manmohan Singh is not a politician but a technocrat. He has introduced a Budget which a mere politician would have thought possible only through witchcraft or fraud, to use the words of *The Economist.*

The goals of the budget are unexceptionable. Agriculture and agro-processing industries are sought to be promoted. Another avowed objective is to promote exports.

The third objective is to curb inflation and to reduce deficit financing. Inflation which was 17 per cent in August 1991 has already been reduced to 7 per cent. Fiscal deficit, which had risen to 8.4 per cent of the gross domestic product, is now only about 5 per cent. The unborn generations are a group wholly unrepresented in Parliament, and to protect their vital interests it is essential that we bear the burden of our own debts. In the words of Thomas Jefferson, one of the outstanding Presidents of the USA, "The question whether one generation has the right to bind another by the deficit it imposes is a question of such consequence as to place it among the fundamental principles of government. We should consider ourselves unauthorized to saddle posterity with our debts, and morally bound to pay them ourselves."

The fourth goal is to increase expenditure on development —health, education, and family planning. It is development which determines the quality of life. The riots and disturbances which recently took place at Ayodhya, Bombay and Surat were the handiwork of hoodlums who made Hitler look like a juvenile delinquent. A long-term plan of value-based education alone can prevent the recurrence of such disasters. It is for the first time that an Indian budget has emphasized the need for education.

Revival of the economy is another important goal. Even the countries whose currency was weaker than India's for decades have marched ahead. Today 52 Mauritian rupees and 79 Pakistani rupees equal 100 Indian rupees.

The sixth and last goal of tax reform, remains a distant dream so far as direct taxation is concerned. It is only in the field of indirect taxes that positive measures have been taken.

*T*he Budget is in conformity with recent trends the world over. Fashions in ideas change, as do fashions in clothes. India is much less quick to follow new fashions in ideas than in dress.

It has been observed that nationalization was the fashion in the 1940s, as was privatization in the 1980s. Luckily, education has become all the rage in the 1990s. World opinion is veering round to the view that education is the universal panacea of the day. Dr. Warren Bennis, the guru of business management, said that what is needed for our competitive advantage, long-range growth and full deployment of our people are three things: education, education, and education.

Liberalization and lower taxes are again in vogue. John Smith, the new leader of the Labour Party in Britain, said last month that if his party were elected there would be no nationalization, no high taxes and no enhancement of union power. He called it "economic madness" to raise taxes and added that such an increase would be a "massive betrayal". Less than a week before our budget was introduced in Parliament, Singapore reduced corporate tax from 30 to 27 per cent, and the rate of top personal tax from 33 to 30 per cent.

*T*he shortcomings of the Budget are as obvious as its plus points.

The failure to increase the threshold for personal taxation cannot be justified on any ground. The minimum income liable to personal tax remains unchanged at Rs. 28,000.

The minimum taxable limit was fixed in 1981 at Rs. 15,000 which is equivalent to Rs. 45,000 today. In 1985 it was raised to Rs. 18,000 which is equivalent to Rs. 37,000 today. In 1990 it was raised to Rs. 22,000 and in 1992 to Rs. 28,000 — both those limits would be equivalent to Rs. 31,000 today. In order to take care of the unfolding future and to eliminate the necessity of annual revision, the limit should be raised to at least Rs. 45,000. In Pakistan the threshold is Rs. 40,000 (equivalent to Indian Rs. 50,400) and the tax at that level is only 10 per cent.

No attempt whatever has been made to achieve stability or simplicity in our tax laws. I should like to repeat the suggestion I had made earlier that there should be a separate Minister for Stability and Simplicity whose only duty would be to ensure that these two great virtues of any good government are preserved and promoted. He should be accountable only to the Prime Minister and his word should prevail.

The surcharge of 12 per cent on the income-tax payable by individuals, and of 15 per cent in the case of companies, should have been abolished, as had been promised last year.

*T*o sum up, the Budget is a harbinger of good times to come. It will not take India to heaven but it will check India's precipitate slide to hell.

9

The Age-old Curse of Casteism
The Paramount Constitutional Issue

Mandal Report — Five Fatal Flaws
Unity and Security of the State at Stake

*P*erhaps there is no other country which has such a genius for creating torture and tribulations for itself as modern India — the inheritor of the age-old practice of self-flagellation.

Physicists describe the relationship of oxygen to fire as "necessary but not sufficient". Casteism and its prophet Mandal, are necessary *and* sufficient to ignite an unprecedented national conflagration. His Report will create two nations neatly balanced numerically — and never the twain shall meet.

The avowed decision of the Indian government to implement "without any dilution" the Mandal Report (which had been wisely kept in cold storage for more than a decade), is a Himalayan blunder. Since people are convinced that the government listens only to the language of violent agitation, there has been an explosion of violent mass revolt in several states. It will gather momentum in the days to come, with unforeseen consequences for the integrity and unity of India.

*T*he Mandal Report suffers from five fatal flaws:
(a) It contemplates rich and rigid reservations for employment under the State in its infinite variety, and in business undertakings and educational institutions, where merit would be unable to find a berth. The sub-standard has to replace the

(The Indian Express, August 28, 1990)

standard, and the reins of power are to pass from meritocracy to mediocrity.

(b)   It enjoins reservations based exclusively on caste, as if a poor Brahmin or a rich Dalit is a contradiction in terms. It firmly ignores the stark reality that there are no backward castes but only backward individuals. Economic backwardness or the opposite is treated as wholly irrelevant.

(c)   Not only employment but even promotions are to be reserved for the privileged (euphemistically called 'backward') castes. That would be disastrous enough for the civil administration, but far worse for the military. Our armed forces are the pride of the nation — the only institution which we have not devalued and degraded. What kind of an army, navy and air force shall we have, when field marshals and generals, air marshals and admirals, have secured their promotions on caste considerations? This raises the most momentous of all issues — the security of the State.

(d)   The only known solvent of casteism is change in the national consciousness: harmony among, and social intermingling of, the anachronistic castes. Petrified and ossified for centuries, casteism should be put on the scrap-heap of Indian history. Instead, the Mandal Report emphatically ensures a fresh lease of life to the canker of casteism for a long, indefinite future.

(e)   The progress of India has been from casteism to egalitarianism. It has been from feudalism to freedom; and equality is the very heart of a free republic. There never was, and never will be, a free democracy without equality of all citizens. The foundation of a true republic, the source of its inspiration, the criterion for its citizenship, the hope for its welfare, all lie in the incandescent ideal of equality. (It is the exact opposite of what prevails in totalitarian states where you enjoy privileges as card-holding members of the ruling party.) The bedrock of the Mandal Report is discrimination in reverse; it is discrimination against merit and calibre.

The challenge to land reforms legislation could be staved off by inserting an item in the Ninth Schedule to the Constitution which insulates the law from judicial invalidation on the ground that it violates the fundamental rights. But implementation of the Mandal Report would go against the basic structure of the Constitution. Therefore, any constitutional amendment to avoid judicial scrutiny would itself be unconstitutional and void. Our thoughtless action — to achieve the thoughtful object of doing justice to the "backward" castes — can be allowed to prevail only by scrapping the noble Constitution and promulgating a backward Constitution for a backward nation.

Supreme Court's Judgment in the Mandal Case

Future historians of the Indian republic will regard 1992 as one of the saddest years in the history of our jurisprudence. This is the year in which the Supreme Court, by a majority, continued, virtually in perpetuity, the scourge of casteism.

Over the last thousand years, the greatest curse which had afflicted the Indian nation had been the curse of casteism, as Justice Kuldip Singh has pointed out in his minority judgment. Historians are agreed that the reason why foreign invaders — the Afghans, the Turks, the Moghuls — succeeded in subjugating this country was because casteism divided Indian society and assigned military duties to one caste only.

Dr. B. R. Ambedkar was luckily the Chairman of the Drafting Committee of free India's republican Constitution. He ensured that caste would be anathema to our noble Constitution and strove single-mindedly to bring about the social integration of India.

In Dr. Ambedkar's own words, "Fraternity means a sense of common brotherhood of all Indians — of Indians being one people .... Castes are anti-national: in the first place they bring about separation in social life. They are anti-national also because they generate jealousy and antipathy between caste and caste. But we must overcome all these difficulties if we wish to become a nation in reality. For fraternity can be a fact only when there is a nation. Without fraternity, equality and liberty will be no deeper than coats of paint."

(The Hindustan Times, November 30, 1992)

After celebrating the centenary of Dr. Ambedkar's birth only last year, we have now impaired and desecrated his greatest monument — the Constitution of India.

The majority judgments of the Supreme Court held that reservations in government service on the basis of caste are permissible under Article 16(4) of the Constitution, in spite of the fact that discrimination against any citizen on the ground of caste in respect of any employment or office under the State is prohibited under Article 16(2).

The minority judgments of Justices Thommen, Kuldip Singh and R. M. Sahai state the correct law. They rule that casteism can never be the basis of reservations for employment under the Government.

It is submitted that the majority judgments in the Mandal case are patently erroneous, and need to be overruled in the public interest and in the long-term interests of the backward castes themselves.

The basic structure of the Constitution envisages a cohesive, unified, casteless society. By breathing new life into casteism the judgment fractures the nation and disregards the basic structure of the Constitution. The decision would revitalize casteism, cleave the nation into two — forward and backward — and open up new vistas for internecine conflicts and fissiparous forces, and make backwardness a vested interest. It will undo whatever has been achieved since independence towards creating a unified, integrated nation.

The majority judgments will revive casteism which the Constitution emphatically intended to end; and the pre-independence tragedy would be re-enacted with the roles reversed — the erstwhile underprivileged would now become the privileged. (The desperate tale of the forward caste woman in Kerala who, merely with a view to gaining admission for her son in a medical college, deposed before a magistrate in the presence of her husband that the son was her illegitimate offspring by a harijan, does not seem to have attracted the attention of our unawakened people.) Caste will be given precedence over merit and calibre. Article 16(4) has been virtually rewritten by substituting "caste" for "class". The majority judgments which upheld reservations on the basis of caste, prescribe the following qualifications and conditions without which the reservations cannot be allowed to continue. The judgments enjoin that (a) the "creamy layer" of backward classes should be excluded, because otherwise they would lap up all the benefits of reservations meant for that class; (b) within four months the Government of India should "specify the basis of exclusion — whether on the basis of income, extent of holding or otherwise — of the creamy layer"; (c) the inclusion or exclusion of a caste or a section of a caste would have to be periodically reviewed to take care of changing circumstances; (d) permanent commissions should be appointed within four months by the central government and by the state governments to decide regularly the cases which would arise involving questions whether a particular caste or a section of a caste was rightly included or excluded; and all further proceedings in such matters can be taken only in the Supreme Court; (e) it is advisable to have armed forces, and some higher civilian posts to be selected by the government, outside the purview of caste reservations.

The crucial point is that under the majority judgments of the Supreme Court it is the members belonging to certain castes only, who are eligible to be considered for reservations. When you have removed the creamy layer, what you are left with are still the members of certain castes only. The sections of society which fall outside those designated castes do not qualify for reservations, however socially and educationally backward they may be.

It is undisputed that 45 years of independence have changed the social, educational, and economic landscape beyond recognition. There are crores of backward individuals in forward castes and crores of forward individuals in backward castes. By making caste the essential condition, the majority judgments have (a) included for reservation all members of backward castes who do not belong to the creamy layer, and (b) excluded all members of forward castes, however backward and deserving. Such a classification patently discriminates against those who do not belong to those castes which are listed as backward.

A backward class may be given the benefit of Article 15(4) or Article 16(4), but the class must consist of a homogeneous group— the element of homogeneity should be the backwardness characterizing the class. In other words, the link or the thread holding the class together should be the backwardness of the members. Such a link or thread can never be supplied by caste. Excluding the creamy layer of the caste would not get rid of the vice that the only link or thread binding the benefited class together is caste. In other words, a classification may be justified on the ground that it is a backward "class", but never on the ground that it is a backward "caste" or "a section of a backward caste". This principle was precisely enunciated by the Constitution Bench in *Triloki Nath* [(1969) 1 SCR 103], *Pradip Tandon* [(1975) 2 SCR 761], *Jayashree* [(1977) 1 SCR 194], *Akhil Bhartiya Soshit* [(1981) 2 SCR 185]. These judgments were cited before the Supreme Court and are referred to in the majority judgments without disapproval, but they are inexplicably overlooked.

The majority judgments did not pause to consider the reasons why for all the past decades the Union Government had not made reservations on caste basis in areas of employment, admissions and promotions. The practice of mentioning the caste in service records was discontinued by the Government of India by 1951. The last census records to proceed on caste basis are those of 1931 which, though hopelessly obsolete, were relied upon by the Mandal Commission because they were the latest census records to proceed on the caste basis.

Kaka Kalelkar's own letter forwarding his Report (1955) to the President said, "I am definitely against reservations in government services for any community, for the simple reason that the services are not meant for the servants but they are meant for the service of society as a whole." Kalelkar's Report, which was not accepted by the then government, had listed 2,399 castes as backward. Dealing with this list the Union Government said, "If the entire community, barring a few exceptions, has thus to be regarded as backward, the really needy would be swamped by the multitude

and hardly receive any special attention or adequate assistance."
This objection would apply *a fortiori* to the Mandal Report which
lists (not exhaustively) 3,743 backward castes. Like the expanding
universe the list of backward castes is ever expanding. Many more
are already waiting in the wings to receive attention.

The last word on the subject may be left with Pandit Jawaharlal
Nehru who, in his letter to the Chief Ministers sent on June 27,
1961 said, "I dislike any kind of reservation, more particularly in
service. I react strongly against anything which leads to
inefficiency and second-rate standards . . . . The only real way to
help a backward group is to give opportunities for a good
education . . . But if we go in for reservations on communal and
caste basis, we swamp the bright and able people and remain
second-rate or third-rate . . . . It has amazed me to learn that even
promotions are based sometimes on communal or caste considerations. This way lies not only folly, but disaster. Let us help the
backward groups by all means, but never at the cost of efficiency."

Reading Article 16(4) and Article 335 together, it is evident
that when efficiency of administration cannot be sacrificed even
in favour of the scheduled castes and the scheduled tribes, much
less can it be sacrificed to favour less weak sections, viz., the other
backward classes. The majority judgments accept this proposition.
How will the Government ensure the fulfilment of the condition
of "efficiency of administration" or lay down satisfactory criteria
to exclude the creamy layer of backward castes in a country where
less than one per cent of the population are income-tax payers?

Public opinion needs to be mobilized to make the Government
realize what an imponderable responsibility lies on its shoulders.
No doubt it is bound by the law as laid down by the majority
judgments of the Supreme Court. But it is not bound to continue
the policy of reservations. The qualifications and conditions
indicated by the majority judgments of the Supreme Court are such
that they would necessarily entail unforgivable squandering of the
nation's resources, time and energy. The Cabinet would be well
advised, and undoubtedly entitled, to say that it is not in the
national interest to continue the system of caste quotas on the

fulfilment of conditions and qualifications which would involve such colossal waste.

The choice before the government is clear. It can opt for populism, carry on with the policy of reservations and, acting upon what the majority judgments have enjoined, convert this poor country into a paradise for lawyers. Or, it can give up the thoughtless policy of caste reservations.

Mr. V. P. Singh said that after the Supreme Court judgment in the Mandal case he could die in peace. But unfortunately his policy has ensured that the nation will not live in peace. The poisonous weed of castéism has been replanted "where it will trouble us a thousand years, each age will have to reconsider it".

10

Other Constitutional Issues

Election of the President of India
The Five Cardinal Rules

*I*n the words of Woodrow Wilson, the President is the representative of no constituency but of the whole people. The President of India, unlike that of the USA, has no executive power; but he represents "the majesty of the people incarnate". His office symbolizes the unity and integrity of the State. He is above the chances and changes of party politics; and his election is, therefore, of special importance in a country like India with deep political cleavages and numerous political parties. The present President witnessed two elections and three governments in a brief span of less than eighteen months between December 1989 and June 1991.

Constitutional morality dictates that merit should be the sole criterion for the election of the Head of State. But the motivations and machinations in New Delhi (the customary burial place of constitutional morality) suggest that merit has been subordinated by some groups to caste or creed.

Ours is a noble Constitution, worked in an ignoble spirit. It is inherent in the very process of democracy that men of high character and exceptional calibre do not get nominated or chosen. It is not the fault of the Constitution but flows from the innate limitations of adult franchise. One wonders what would be the chances of Ashoka or Akbar being chosen as President if they were to stand for election in India today. Commenting on American polity, Lord Bryce remarked that the one disturbing, but unavoidable, feature of democracy is that it puts mediocrity in power. The election of Abraham Lincoln was an exception that proved the rule. Will Durant observed that we forgot to make ourselves intelligent when we made ourselves free. The most under-developed territory in every continent on earth is situated between human ears.

*I*f the President has to be chosen by the democratic process, it is difficult to conceive of a more satisfactory method than that embodied in our fundamental law. There are five cardinal rules laid down in our Constitution to regulate the election of the President.

First, the voting at the election is by secret ballot. Since the Head of State is expected to be above party politics, every vote for or against him is expected to be a conscience vote. This is meant to avoid trivialization of the election process by plain parochialism of party politics.

Secondly, the election of the President is indirect. As Pandit Nehru and others pointed out in the Constituent Assembly, indirect (and less expensive) election of the President is unquestionably preferable in a country like India which does not have a presidential form of government. Direct election of the President on adult franchise basis has been wisely eschewed. Nothing would be gained by having the President elected by "the mass man" — the malleable class of people, unthinking and easily exploited. The electoral college consists of (a) the elected members of both houses of Parliament, and (b) the elected members of the legislative assemblies of the states. The reason why the members of state assemblies have been included in the electoral college is clearly to prevent the President being elected merely by the vote of the party which happens to be in power at the Centre.

Article 62 of the Constitution provides that an election to fill a vacancy caused by the expiration of the term of office of President shall be completed before the expiration of the term. In view of this mandatory time-limit, the election of the President would have to be completed even though there may be some vacancies in Parliament or in some of the state assemblies; or even if the assembly of any of the states may have been dissolved and there may be no assembly in existence in that state. The presidential election cannot be postponed beyond the time-limit which is mandatory. (The term of office of President Venkataraman expires on July 24, 1992.) Only those persons can vote who possess, at the date of election, the qualification of being elected members of either house of Parliament or of a state legislative assembly.

Thirdly, there has to be uniformity among the states inter se, as far as practicable. This is achieved by ensuring that the rule of one voter, one vote, does not apply. Every elected member of the legislative assembly of a state has as many votes as there are multiples of one thousand in the quotient obtained by dividing the population of the state by the total number of elected members of the assembly. Uniformity in the scale of representation is brought about by the members of the legislative assemblies of thickly populated states having a larger number of votes than the members of the assemblies of less populous states.

This is called "weightage" which is determined by the population of each state. Needless to add, in a democracy such weightage on the ground of population is possible, but there can be no weightage on the ground of wisdom, knowledge or insight. Human ingenuity has not discovered, and never will, how to get over the perennial injustice of "the lives of wise men at the mercy of fools". The foolish, the feckless, and the fatuous among the MPs and MLAs have the same voice in the election of the President as the most well-informed.

The *fourth* rule is that there should be parity between the states taken together and the Union. This is achieved by the provision that the elected members of the two houses of Parliament would have the same number of votes as the aggregate of the votes of the elected representatives of the state assemblies taken together.

Fifthly, the election of the President has to be held "in accordance with the system of proportional representation by means of the single transferable vote". The object of this rule is to afford the minorities a better voice in the selection of the Head of State. As Dr. Ambedkar explained —

> ... Obviously no member of the House would like the President to be elected by a bare majority or by a system of election in which the minorities had no part to play. That being so, the election of the President by a bare majority has to be eliminated and we have to provide a system whereby the minorities will have some voice in the election of the President. The only method, therefore, that remained was to have a system of election in which the minorities will have some hand and some play and that is undoubtedly the system of proportional representation."

This method is known as "the alternative vote" in a single-member constituency. At the time when the votes are cast, every member of the electoral college has to indicate which candidate he votes for in the order of preference. If a candidate gets an absolute majority of the votes cast, he would be deemed to have been elected and it would be unnecessary to have a recount. But if no candidate has secured an absolute majority of the votes cast, the subsequent preferences would have to be taken into account. This is the effect of the Presidential and Vice-Presidential Election Rules, 1952.

Development Boards —
A Dangerous Remedy

*I*t would be wise to recall the wit's saying that most politicians live in a thought-free zone. The truth of this dictum has been seldom more strikingly illustrated than by the unanimous resolutions passed by the Maharashtra Legislative Assembly and Council on July 26, 1984 requesting the President to issue an order for the establishment of separate development boards for Vidarbha, Marathwada and the rest of Maharashtra. This is symptomatic of our times when Maharashtrian politics has moved out of reality and into the world of words.

There can be no doubt as regards the necessity of ensuring that regions like Vidarbha and Marathwada are brought up to the level of development reached by some other parts of Maharashtra. The only question is of the procedure by which such an eminently desirable result can be achieved. Developmental backlog can and should be removd by efficacious, democratic means. The Constitution can be smoothly worked only by men of goodwill, with a sense of justice and fairness. But the establishment of development boards, as envisaged by Article 371, would be a disastrous substitute for such goodwill and sense of justice and fairness.

Article 371 provides that notwithstanding anything in the Constitution, the President may by order provide for any special responsibility of the Governor for (a) the establishment of separate development boards for Vidarbha, Marathwada, and the rest of Maharashtra or, as the case may be, Saurashtra, Kutch and the rest

(The Times of India, August 8, 1990)

of Gujarat; (b) the equitable allocation of funds for developmental expenditure over the said areas, subject to the requirements of the state as a whole; and (c) an equitable arrangement providing adequate facilities for technical education and vocational training, and adequate opportunities for employment in services under the control of the state government, in respect of all the said areas, subject to the requirements of the state as a whole.

There is no article in the Constitution more vague and unsatisfactory than Article 371. It is fraught with such formidable ambiguities that though it has been in existence so long, it has never been brought into operation. The only time it was invoked was in February 1977 when the President promulgated an Order which envisaged the setting up of a development board for Kutch; but the Order was not acted upon and was withdrawn twelve months later.

The demand for development boards is good rhetorical adrenalin, but their establishment would create more problems than it would resolve. It would aggravate political acrimony, and entail years of protracted litigation to decide several fundamental questions including the following:

(1)   Are the provisions of Article 371 intended to supersede the normal process of free democracy, as in the case of President's rule under Article 356 upon failure of constitutional machinery in a state?

(2)   In respect of matters covered by Article 371, can the governor exercise the executive and legislative powers which, but for the President's order under that Article, would fall squarely within the competence of the council of ministers and the state legislature?

(3)   Can development boards be invested with any administrative or executive powers or are they merely to make recommendations and submit reports?

(4)   Is the normal machinery for disbursing or dealing with state

finances overridden by functions assigned to the Governor and the development boards under Article 371?

(5) If an allocation of funds for developmental expenditure over a region is approved by the Governor, can it be debated, examined, altered or voted upon by the legislature, or does it become a sum "charged on the Consolidated Fund of the State"?

While there is ample room for doubt and debate, the just and reasonable construction would seem to be the following.

Article 371, which deals with two of the most important states of India, must be interpreted in harmony with the rest of the Constitution. It must be read not *in vacuo* but in the context of the other provisions of the Constitution which embody the basic scheme of governance of each state by the duly elected representatives of the people. Since the President's order under Article 371 may provide for nomination and not election of the members of the development boards, it is clear that while the reports and recommendations of the development boards should be given great weight, the development boards cannot be assigned the executive functions of ministers or the legislative functions of the state assembly. The matters enumerated in Article 371 are the special responsibility of the Governor and not of the development boards.

The words "special responsibility of the Governor" merely indicate that the Governor should exercise his functions in his discretion and is not bound to follow, and may in a fit case override, the advice of the Council of Ministers. But the fact that the Governor has "special responsibility" in certain matters does not mean that he has to make the regular decisions in those matters. Upon the President's order being made under Article 371, the Governor has only to *ensure* that appropriate development boards are established, and to *ensure* that equitable allocation of funds is made for developmental expenditure, and equitable arrangement is made for education and employment opportunities, bearing in mind "the requirements of the state as a whole". There is a sharp, though subtle, distinction between the special responsibility to ensure that an equitable allocation is made and the power or duty to make the actual allocation.

Article 371 cannot be read as if it provided for the Governor's rule, analogous to the President's rule under Article 356. It is significant to note that a Proclamation of President's rule under Article 356 is hedged in by various safeguards and has to enure normally for a period of only six months: whereas under Article 371 there are no safeguards whatever and the establishment of the development boards can be for an indefinite period.

*T*here are cogent reasons to support the view that it is advisable *not* to constitute separate development boards but to evolve some other machinery by which the problem of regional imbalances can be resolved.

First, politicians, by and large, have an insatiable appetite for the loaves and fishes of ministerial office. Once the development boards are constituted, the demand for disintegrating the Maharashtra state and constituting Vidarbha and Marathwada as separate states will increase, and not diminish. The development boards, with their vision necessarily confined to the region they represent, will make demands which are disproportionately large and not "subject to the requirements of the state as a whole" as enjoined by Article 371; and the non-fulfilment of the demands will only intensify the agitation for separate states.

What matters most is consciousness — the consciousness among Maharashtrians that they are one people, linguistically knit, who must live together in one state and work out a common destiny by the democratic process. Development boards will impair, not heighten, this consciousness.

Secondly, it would be difficult to resist similar demands by other regions of Maharashtra, which will ask for separate development boards. There is already a unanimous resolution of the

Maharashtra legislature passed in March 1989, requesting the government of India to amend Article 371(2) with a view to establishing a separate development board for the Konkan.

Thirdly, the establishment of development boards in Maharashtra is also bound to give rise to demands in other states for at least development boards in regions which have been clamouring to be recognized as separate states, e.g., Jharkhand in Bihar and Telangana in Andhra Pradesh.

Fourthly, it will result in constitutional and political conflict between the Governor and development boards on the one hand, and the Council of Ministers and the state legislature on the other.

Fifthly, it will drag the Governor into the political arena and considerably vitiate the normal functioning of the democratic apparatus.

*I*f action is hastily taken under Article 371 on a certain legal basis and that legal basis is ultimately held by the Supreme Court to be erroneous, it would obviously create enormous political problems, — and Heaven knows we have enough already!

In the circumstances, it is desirable, if not imperative, that the President should be advised to make a reference to the Supreme Court under Article 143 of the Constitution so that the Government and the public have clear guidance on the baffling questions which arise under Article 371. An authoritative pronouncement on the legal implications of Article 371 may induce second thoughts in the minds of the ill-informed who are today agitating for invoking that Article. In any event, if action is taken thereafter under that Article in the light of the legal position elucidated by the Supreme Court, it would then be beyond the pale of controversy.

Misconceptions about Legislative Privilege

A Commission, headed by Mr. Justice B. Lentin, one of the finest Judges of the Bombay High Court, was appointed in 1986 to inquire into deaths of patients in the J.J. Hospital due to alleged reaction of substandard drugs. The inquiry lasted for more than a year.

On June 30, 1987 while the Commission was still recording evidence, the Health Minister, Bhai Sawant, stated on the floor of the Maharashtra Legislative Assembly that Opposition members, including one Ram Kapse, were misleading the Lentin Commission by supplying false information. Immediately, Mr. Justice Lentin issued the following statement:

> While I do not have the slightest intention or desire, by way of criticism or otherwise, of impinging on the privileges of the Hon'ble Members of the Assembly or on their right to make statements or take part in discussions on the floor of the Assembly, it would not be out of place in this particular instance for me to make an observation for the record of the Commission. That I hereby do.
>
> I do not know any of these Hon'ble Members, and without meaning to be derogatory, I heard the name of Mr. Ram Kapse for the first time yesterday from these newspaper reports. Both learned Counsel appointed by

the Commission namely, Mr. N. A. Shah and Mr. J. P.
Devadhar, have requested me to say the same on their
behalf.

This Commission has kept itself above politics. No
member of any party, ruling or opposition, has supplied
information to this Commission; nor has the Commission received such information.

On July 5, 1987, a notice of breach of privilege was given,
against Mr. Justice Lentin and the two advocates assisting the
Commission, by Mr. Keshavrao Dhondge, a member of the
Legislative Assembly, alleging that the judge and the advocates
had committed a breach of the state legislature's privilege by
making observations on the proceedings of the House, particularly
since they had been depending on newspaper reports of the
proceedings instead of waiting for a version certified by the
Speaker.

On April 7, 1988, Mr. Dhondge, who had moved the motion
for contempt said, according to a newspaper report, that Justice
Lentin was "perverted, cranky and horribly unethical". For good
measure, he added that Justice Lentin was "a criminal judge".
Presumably, by calling him a criminal judge Mr. Dhondge did not
intend to say that he was a Judge trying criminal cases.

Mr. Dhondge further added, according to the newspaper report,
that "Lentin had no business to poke his nose in the business of
the Legislative Assembly. The time has come for us to stress the
sovereignty of this House. We must drag the Judge before the
privileges committee."

The law on the subject has been clearly enunciated by a Full
Bench of the Supreme Court in the Special Reference No.1 of
1964, reported in AIR 1965 SC 745.

Article 194(3) of the Constitution provides in effect that the
powers and privileges of a state legislature shall, till they are

defined by law, be those of the House of Commons in Britain at the commencement of our Constitution.

It is significant to note that in the last 300 years no judge has ever been asked to answer a charge for contempt by the House of Commons in England, although British judges have heard and disposed of quite a few petitions by citizens who were committed for contempt by the Commons. By 1950 when our Constitution commenced, the House of Commons was not armed to the teeth with privileges, but it was a House which had grown in dignity and mellowness and had allowed several ancient privileges to fade away as a result of desuetude.

In the aforesaid case, the Supreme Court laid down three basic propositions:

(1) When a privilege is claimed by the legislature, it is not enough to show that it was claimed by the House of Commons at some time centuries ago, but it is further necessary to show that the privilege was recognized by the English courts as existing in 1950.

(2) If a notice or warrant is issued by the legislature for frivolous or extravagant reasons, it would be open to the Court to examine the validity of the warrant or the notice.

(3) The Court has jurisdiction to deal with the petition of a citizen committed for contempt by a legislature, and to quash the committal where the legislature has exceeded its privilege, even if the warrant is unspeaking or general. An unspeaking warrant cannot silence the Constitution.

*I*t is to the great credit of the Bar that they reacted promptly and courageously to the aspersions cast on Mr. Justice Lentin and the two members of the Bar.

Last week, the Bar Association of Maharashtra and Goa, and the Western India Advocates Association passed appropriate resolutions. The justification for the resolutions may be summarized as follows.

First, the Bar expressed its total support to and solidarity with Mr. Justice Lentin and the two advocates. The note which formed part of the Record of the Commission had been couched in totally dignified language and contained a statement of facts which was necessary to preserve the credibility of the Commission. It was essential that the public should not get the untrue impression that the Commission's working was vitiated by wrong information supplied out of political motives. A certified copy of the proceedings of the House would not have been available for months and it was absurd to suggest that the Judge and the advocates should have allowed the public to lose faith in the Commission, by waiting till a certified copy of the proceedings of the House was made available. It was not only the right but the duty of the judge and of the advocates to refute without delay the allegations which would have shaken public confidence in the Commission.

Secondly, any attempt by the legislature to take action against such a judge would be grossly detrimental to the public interest and would deter high-minded judges from consenting to head a commission hereafter.

Thirdly, the Bar had to refute the theory that each House of the state legislature is "sovereign". The correct position in law is that only the people are sovereign and only the Constitution is supreme. All other institutions are merely the instruments or agencies to fulfil the great purposes of the Constitution. Our Constitution envisages not only a democracy of men but a democracy of institutions. The attributes of sovereign authority or unlimited power do not attach to any office or any institution. To claim sovereignty for the state legislature was directly contrary to the law laid down by the Supreme Court in the aforesaid decision.

Fourthly, the Bar emphasized that democracy can survive only if basic norms of public decency are maintained both within and outside the legislature. Unfortunately, no citizen can take legal action in respect of what happens within the legislature. But citizens are certainly entitled to criticize or condemn what is said within the House if it is untrue or misleading or constitutes a gratuitous slur on the Bar or the Bench.

Fifthly, the purpose of the Bar's resolutions was to draw the attention of the Speaker to the grave consequences if the privilege motion were to be unwisely adopted by the House.

*I*t is interesting to note that no legislature of a mature democracy today claims to exercise the type of "privileges" which Indian legislatures are so ready to exercise. The plea that larger powers are necessary to preserve the dignity and respect of the legislature, is totally unsound.

Under the American Constitution the Congress has even fewer privileges and smaller powers than those which are available to Parliament and the state legislatures under our Constitution as interpreted by the Supreme Court, and yet the Congress functions efficiently without any loss of dignity or respect from the public.

Even in England, from where we have borrowed the doctrine of parliamentary privilege, the tendency during the last several decades is to narrow and not to widen the interpretation of privilege. In fact, the Committee of Privileges appointed by the House of Commons, which submitted its Report in June 1964 emphasized that it would be in the interest neither of the House nor of the public to widen the interpretation of privilege and that privilege should not, "except in the clearest case", be invoked so as to inhibit or discourage the formation and free expression of opinion outside the House.

The Times (of London) in its issue of June 25, 1964, commenting editorially on that Report of the Committee of Privileges, pointed out that one of the paradoxes of the relation between privilege and freedom of speech has always been that unless the rights of Parliament are exercised with great discretion, the risk is run of securing the reputation of Parliament only at the expense of some part of the citizen's liberty which it is Parliament's duty to defend; and *The Times* further observed, "The frequent invocation of privilege is more likely to harm, than elevate, the reputation of Parliament." In fact, the House of Commons had wisely rejected an opportunity to extend its privileges in 1958.

One would have thought that forty years of freedom is a sufficiently long period to clear the anachronistic misconceptions about legislative privilege in India. A change of attitude on the part of our politicians on this subject is vital to the very survival of our democracy.

(I was also charged with breach of privilege for having the impertinence to publish the above article in which I tried to. set out the correct constitutional position.)

Crisis of Public Faith in the Judiciary
Time for National Introspection

World history moves in cycles. High ethical times are succeeded by low, decadent decades. Today we are at the nadir of moral values. The size of the crime wave and armed violence, which is so huge as to baffle criminologists, is symptomatic of our ethical degradation.

A commercial recession can be quickly transformed into a buoyant economy; but a moral recession cannot be shaken off for years. The rot in public life began after the death of Lal Bahadur Shastri and has been increasing at a galloping rate. It has spread so far as to contaminate the higher judiciary which is the soul of any democracy. Judges are the indispensable servants of society: without them, its most fundamental equilibrium cannot be maintained.

The poisoning of the well-spring of justice began in 1973 when the three seniormost judges of the Supreme Court, who were independent enough to decide against the executive in *Kesavananda*'s case, were superseded upon the Chief Justice's office falling vacant.

The government expressly proclaimed that it wanted "committed" Judges — committed to the ideology of the ruling party. That began an era of a judiciary made to measure. The Government looked out for pliant Judges.

Evil is more infectious than AIDS and, if unchecked, progresses with an inevitable momentum of its own. It is but one step from

(The Times of India, July 9, 1990)

forsaking intellectual integrity to forsaking financial integrity. A Judge who decides wrongly out of motives of self-promotion is no less corrupt than a Judge who decides wrongly out of motives of financial gain.

The slide on the inclined plane has been rapid and unmistakable. In the first two decades of our republic it was the compulsion of veracity, not the fear of the law relating to contempt of court, which was responsible for the fact that no charges of corruption were levelled against the judiciary. Now the compulsion of veracity dictates such charges, in defiance of the Contempt of Courts Act. The lawyers' associations of Bombay passed resolutions last month virtually charging some judges of the High Court with corruption — a move unprecedented in the history of any modern democracy.

There is undoubtedly room for debate on the issue whether the course of action adopted by the lawyers' associations was fair or desirable and whether it was right to condemn the judges without hearing them. But even those who do not approve of the *action* must approve of the *objective*. For the lawyers, it was a cry of despair. Collectively they could do with practical impunity what, if done individually, would have amounted to criminal contempt of court.

The issue affects not merely lawyers and litigants but the entire nation. All citizens are vitally interested in an unpolluted stream of justice.

It is pre-eminently a time for deep, national introspection. We must be self-critical enough to meet the truth face to face. The Bar is more commercialized than ever before. Today the law is looked upon, not as a *learned* profession but as a *lucrative* one. The due process of law has become less "due" than tortuous and unending.

Public disenchantment with judicial administration has been vastly aggravated by the recent developments in the Bombay High Court. If you lose faith in politicians, you can change them. If you lose faith in judges, you still have to live with them. The ineluctable fact is that the conduct of some judicial officers in different courts has been far from exemplary in terms of ethics.

Corruption in the upper reaches of the judiciary is illustrative of the incredible debasement of our national character. There is general public acceptance of venality everywhere as a venial idiosyncrasy. We are merely amused by the fact that the contrast between the moral tone of ancient India and that of modern India is sufficient to disprove the theory of evolution upwards!

The question is — which is the best way of dealing with a corrupt Judge in the higher courts without creating a crisis of public faith in the judiciary as is done by a Bar association's resolution publicly condemning the Judge.

The greatest illusion of our people is their infantile belief in the legal solubility of all problems. In the wise words of Lord Hailsham, the former Lord Chancellor of the UK, "We might do well to remember that in the whole realm of human relations there is no field more vulnerable to corruption, dishonesty, chicanery, and sheer quackery and charlatanism than contested litigation, criminal and civil, commercial, matrimonial, testamentary, or resulting from personal injury, real, imagined, or invented. We might also do well to consider that few of the safeguards we have achieved against these evils have been achieved by Government interference or by parliamentary legislation. They have been brought about by the steady application of self-regulatory procedures and disciplines . . . ."

Impeachment proceedings in Parliament — the only constitutional way of removing a judge of a High Court or the Supreme Court from his office — is a procedure not to be resorted to lightly. It is enormously cumbersome and is likely to bring political passions into play. A striking example of the malfunctioning of our democracy is afforded by the fact that the only impeachment proceeding* ever sought to be started in our Parliament was that against one of our finest judges, J. C. Shah, a judge of impeccable

---

* In 1993 a motion to impeach Justice V. Ramaswamy of the Supreme Court was defeated in Parliament because the Congress party issued a whip that Congress members should abstain from voting, ignoring the correct legal position that Parliament had to exercise a quasi-judicial function on an impeachment motion.

integrity. It was a move commenced by a disgruntled, dishonest civil servant against whom Justice Shah had given a judgment in the Supreme Court, and who cunningly managed to secure as many as 199 signatures of members of Parliament for an appeal to the Speaker of the Lok Sabha to start impeachment proceedings against the judge.

It would be foolish as well as dangerous to relax the rigour of the Contempt of Courts Act, 1971 and permit truth to be pleaded as a defence when an allegation of corruption is made against a judge. Character assassination is the national sport of India, and some dissatisfied litigants and lawyers will have no hesitation in making allegations which would scandalize the court and then inviting the judge to face a public inquiry.

Mr. Dinesh Goswami, the Law Minister, was right in publicly stating that the executive would keep aloof from the controversy in the Bombay High Court. In the past there have been sufficient instances of the executive interfering in matters pertaining to the judiciary for ulterior, ill-founded reasons, to dissuade an honest law minister from establishing another precedent of inter-meddling even for well-founded reasons.

Perhaps the best way of dealing with the problem is to have a law regarding the procedure to be followed when there are allegations of the type the lawyers' associations have made. The matter should be placed confidentially before the Chief Justice of the High Court for inquiring into the case. If his view is that there is no substance in the allegations, the matter should be regarded as closed. If he thinks otherwise, the case should be referred to the Chief Justice of India and the two Supreme Court judges who would be members of the National Judicial Commission proposed to be constituted by the Constitution (Sixty-seventh Amendment) Bill, 1990 which was introduced in the Lok Sabha in the last session. If the decision of the National Judicial Commission (which would be final) is also adverse, the errant judge should be compelled to regard discretion as the better part of valour and decide not to continue on the bench. This would be a dignified and quietly effective way of dealing with men unworthy of holding high judicial office.

Meanwhile, the resolutions by the lawyers' associations would have done a distinct public disservice, instead of a public service, if they have created an impression in the public mind that our higher judiciary is not worthy of public confidence and respect. Luckily, the overwhelming majority of our judges in the eighteen High Courts and the Supreme Court are men of integrity, while some of them combine character with outstanding calibre.

12

Culture and Education

Adi Sankaracharya
Builder of the Empire of the Spirit

*M*ost historians are agreed that if a count were taken of the twelve greatest men who ever lived in any country in any age, Adi Sankaracharya would be one of them. I would call him the Universal Man. He deserves to be called the Universal Man in more senses than one.

He was a poet of the first order and also a philosopher par excellence. He was a savant and a saint, a mystic and a religious reformer. He was a *karma yogi, bhakti yogi* and *jnana yogi,* and was in the forefront of each category.

As a man of action he achieved as much as persons who have attained world renown only as "doers". He did not propound a religion but propounded *the* religion which underlies all religions. He was a man of infinite faith and infinite compassion. Nothing human was alien to his nature. His knowledge was truly profound. He went to the heart of the *Upanishads,* the *Vedas*, and the *Bhagavad Gita* and could expound these scriptures in a manner which has been rarely equalled.

What was his aim in having *mutts* in different corners of India? One of his main ideas was that this is one single country. We may have different faiths, different sects, different creeds. Different communities may flourish here, and they have flourished through the centuries, but we are all members of one single family. And his objective in going round the country was to ensure that the

(Public lecture under the auspices of the Bharatiya Vidya Bhavan, Bombay, April 7, 1989)

message that we have a common and indivisible destiny and a unified culture got across this great nation.

Adi Sankara was universal in his outlook. Swami Vivekananda and Sri Aurobindo must have been thinking of him when both of them said that the destiny of India is to be the spiritual leader and moral teacher of the world.

Adi Sankaracharya did all his phenomenal work in the short span of thirty-two years; bearing out, as Bacon said, that a man may be young in years but old in hours if he has lost no time; and Sankaracharya never lost any time.

Every moment of his life was filled with thought and action. And the great *mutts* which he founded 1,200 years ago, are still continuing, still imparting the type of guidance which this country so badly needs today.

It is amazing how close Sankaracharya's teachings are to the latest conclusions reached by scientists. The human spirit can, merely by means of meditation and introspection, come to the right conclusion about the ultimate reality, which hundreds of years of scientific research might finally lead to. The main message of modern scientists like Sir James Jeans, Sir Arthur Eddington, Albert Einstein, and Max Planck (one of the authors of the *Atom and Atomic Research*) is that although the universe exists, the appearance is different from the reality. The reality, the only reality, is the spirit, the infinite spirit. Dr. C. P. Ramaswamy Aiyar believed that the essence of the theory of relativity propounded in the twentieth century was known to ancient India 3,000 years ago.

In any of our great scientists' meetings today or in meetings held twenty years ago when some of the most eminent scientists who are now dead were alive, Adi Sankaracharya would have found himself quite at home. He would have discussed, on a level of equality, the ultimate theories of science which he intuitively knew to be right.

His main contribution, summed up by the different people who have written on him, is his synthesis of all religions. It must be remembered that in his time there were already quite a few different sects, sub-sects and castes and creeds. There was the question of

Buddhism as against old Hinduism and the question arose to what extent you could reconcile the different philosophies and beliefs.

Adi Sankaracharya not only synthesized the different philosophies and ideals, but he purified them. As any creed or religion or language goes down the centuries, it gathers a crust of useless, immaterial accretions, and those trappings are mistaken for the essence of religion. He broke that crust and went to the essence of all those religions and showed how they all could be synthesized, how they could all be made to fall into one pattern. That gives his philosophy a certain completeness, a certain wholeness. You don't need to supplement Sankaracharya. As for his hymns, they are amazingly beautiful. He composed them in Sanskrit, one of the greatest languages that the human mind has ever evolved. They embody his profound vision.

It has been said in the *Bhagavad Gita* by the Lord, "When things get very bad, I reappear to re-establish *dharma*." It seems that we have sunk to such a depth now that that day is at hand.

To Sankaracharya, philosophy was not an intellectual exercise — it was the fruit of the dedication of a life. Sankaracharya looked upon every human life as the embodiment of the Ultimate Reality. And he said that human life which is vouchsafed to us is available for transmuting ourselves into an instrument of the Divine Will.

The four essences of his philosophy, as summarized by both Eastern and Western thinkers, are the following:

First, he says that you must discriminate between what is eternal and what is ephemeral. The One remains, the many change and pass; so do not get attached to what changes and passes, but get attached to the eternal, because that alone is the Ultimate Reality.

He was not against family life. He was sensible enough to realize that if there was no family life, the human race would come to an end. But his message was, "Realize that everything around you, including your wealth and your family, are all ephemeral things." Too much attachment would result in diverting your mind from what is timeless to what is evanescent.

His second message was that each one of us has to learn to

renounce the thought of reward for what we are doing. Your attitude must be that you are not interested in the reward for what you are doing. I doubt whether Sankaracharya in his own lifetime got full recognition for what he did. But he knew that ages and ages hence, people would realize the importance of his message.

Men do not recompense their greatest benefactors. Christ was crucified by the majority vote of the people around him. Socrates was put to death by his own fellowmen. That again was by a majority vote. So much for democracy. Never mistake the majority vote for a vote in favour of reason or for a vote in favour of what is right. What is right is often quite different from what the majority believes in.

The third message of Sankaracharya was moral preparation. He believed that each life has to be so lived that you are prepared to meet the Maker at the time of "crossing the bar", and to present a clean record, when the final call comes, of what you have accomplished with whatever you have been endowed with. So, you hold your talent, as much as your wealth, in trust for your fellowmen. He believed that universal compassion and universal love are essential ingredients of the moral preparation.

I would like to quote a few words which are from one of his hymns. "In you and in me and everywhere else, there is but one Vishnu." See yourself in all things, give up the false sense of difference from other human beings everywhere. This is his message of universality; the brotherhood of the entire human race.

And his last message was the longing for liberation, what St. Luke in his Epistle calls the "longing for the Eternal Life". Adi Sankaracharya said that this world is just a preparatory ground, a school where we are trying to prepare ourselves, educate ourselves, for the life everlasting.

About his year of birth and death, there is no certainty. Max Mueller believed that he was born in 788 and so we celebrated the 1,200th anniversary last year. We are also not sure in which year he died, though the general consensus is that he was perhaps thirty-two years old when he passed away. But whatever might have been the exact year of his birth or death, it is his message which counts, more than his own personal life.

He established what I would call the Empire of the Spirit. Whole generations have come and gone, empires have flourished and vanished, but Sankaracharya's Empire of the Spirit survives. And so long as his great Spirit abides with our people, there is hope for the future greatness of our country.

Ancient Insights and Modern Man

*T*he values which have been taught in India over the last 5,000 years have great relevance to the times we live in. And yet so few Indians are aware of our priceless heritage.

It has been my long-standing conviction that India is like a donkey carrying a sack of gold — the donkey does not know what it is carrying but is content to go along with the load on its back. The load of gold is the fantastic treasure — in arts, literature, culture, and some sciences like Ayurvedic medicine — which we have inherited from the days of the splendour that was India. Adi Sankaracharya called it "the accumulated treasure of spiritual truths discovered by the *rishis*." Rabindranath Tagore said, "India is destined to be the teacher of all lands."

The golden voices of ancient India have come to us down the ages in unbroken continuity through countless *rishis* and saints — some of them world famous and some of them nameless. Our culture which is primarily concerned with spiritual development is of special significance in our age which is marked by the obsolescence of the materialistic civilization. Sri Aurobindo said, "India of the ages is not dead, nor has she spoken her last creative word; she lives and has still something to do for herself and the human race."

India is eternal, everlasting. Though the beginnings of her numerous civilizations go so far back in time that they are lost in

(All India Radio, Jaipur, February 16, 1985. Based on "India's Priceless Heritage")

the twilight of history, she has the gift of perpetual youth. Her culture is ageless and is as relevant to our twentieth century as it was twenty centuries before Christ. Dr. Arnold Toynbee, after surveying the story of the entire human race observed:

> It is already becoming clear that a chapter which had a Western beginning will have to have an Indian ending if it is not to end in the self-destruction of the human race.... At this supremely dangerous moment in human history, the only way of salvation for mankind is the Indian way — Emperor Ashoka's and Mahatma Gandhi's principle of non-violence and Sri Ramakrishna's testimony to the harmony of religions. Here we have an attitude and spirit that can make it possible for the human race to grow together into a single family — and, in the Atomic Age, this is the only alternative to destroying ourselves.

Toynbee echoes the ideal placed before mankind by India's ancient *rishis* — *Vasudhaiva Kutumbakam* — "The World is One Family".

The most fundamental of all fundamental principles is that a Spirit, supreme and unchanging, pervades the entire universe and the material world is merely a manifestation of that Spirit. Thousands of years ago, India perceived this principle even more clearly, and understood its implications even more deeply, than the most highly civilized nations do today. It is precisely because the Spirit alone is the everlasting reality that the infinite mystery of the material world can never be explained merely in material terms. The vastest knowledge of today cannot transcend the *buddhi* of the *rishis*; and science, in its most advanced stage, is closer to *Vedanta* than ever before.

It would be hard to improve upon the sense of values which made ancient India so great. Our old sages judged the greatness of a State not by the extent of its empire or by the size of its wealth, but by the degree of righteousness and justice which marked the public administration and the private lives of the citizens. Their timeless teaching was that man's true progress is to be judged by moral and spiritual standards, and not by material or physical standards. Sacrifice was far more important than success; and renunciation was regarded as the crowning achievement. The citizen ranked in society, not according to wealth or power, but according to the standard of learning, virtue and character which he had attained. The finest example of that is the well-known story of Emperor Ashoka, a true follower of Buddha, making it an invariable practice to bow in reverence before Buddhist monks. His minister Yasha thought that it was wrong and improper for a great Emperor to bow before monks. Ashoka's answer was:

> After all, I am doing obeisance to them as a mark of my deep respect for their learning, wisdom and sacrifice. What matters in life, Yasha, is not a person's status or position, but his virtues and wisdom. The finest minds and hearts may be hidden in ugly mortal frames. Only when you have raised yourself up from ignorance can you recognize the greatness of a few in a sea of humanity, just as a good jeweller alone can spot a gem among worthless pebbles.

The Sanskrit word *dharma* cannot be easily translated into English. It has within it elements from the different concepts of law, righteousness, duty, and basic morality.

India has had an unrivalled tradition of religious freedom and tolerance. That tradition was born of the consciousness that truth can never be the monopoly of any one sect or creed. The words of the *Rig Veda* are world famous:

"Let noble thoughts come to us from every side."

The *rishis* realized that each man has to work out his own salvation and that everyone's own spiritual experience is vital to the attainment of the ultimate state of the soul's evolution. A blind obedience to authority is the surest prescription for spiritual paralysis. Mere acquiescence, even in the dictates of the *sruti*, is not enough. There is nothing like salvation on the cheap. There is no spiritual enrichment which money can buy. There are no fixed

11

The Law, Judges and Lawyers

International Arbitration
v
Litigation in Law Courts

*I*nternational arbitration dates back to the civil wars between the ancient Greek city states. Its modern development begins with the Jay Treaty of 1794 between Great Britain and the United States of America to settle claims stemming from the American Revolution. Commercial arbitration began in Mediaeval Europe as a means of settling disputes between individual merchants.

More than sixty years ago when the International Chamber of Commerce at Paris started offering the services of its Court of Arbitration, businessmen in different countries found it convenient to avail themselves of that facility. In course of time that *convenience* became a *preference,* and the preference has now ripened into a *necessity.* As one who has had some experience of the working of courts of law in India and abroad, and also of international commercial arbitration, let me bear testimony to the incalculable advantages of international commercial arbitration as compared to litigation in ordinary courts of law.

The 1980s has been the decade of privatization. Even socialist governments across the world are handing over to private enterprise some of their herd of white elephants which used to command the respect of socialists as State-owned enterprises. International commercial arbitration is nothing but a species of privatization. It delegates to a private agency the task of adjudicating upon disputes, specially when the courts of law are unable to perform

---

(International Chamber of Commerce, New Delhi, February 9, 1987)

that function as speedily, cheaply and efficiently as the business world is entitled to expect.

In order to appreciate the great benefits of international commercial arbitration, let us cast a glance at the prevailing state of affairs in the courts of some significant countries.

In the English-speaking world, there never was a time when such gloomy forebodings were expressed about the present and the future of the system of administration of justice: there never was a time when the legal profession was so commercialized and the courts of law so clogged.

In Britain, the office of Lord Hailsham, the Lord Chancellor, is trying desperately, and trying almost in vain, to refurbish the legal system so as to avoid the long delay before a case reaches hearing, to shorten the hearing itself and to avoid excessive costs. In March 1985, Michael Joseph, a qualified solicitor, published a book under the embarrassing but appropriate title, *Lawyers Can Seriously Damage Your Health*. There can be no doubt that litigation in ordinary courts of law can seriously damage the health of international commerce.

Coming to the United States, Warren Burger, the former Chief Justice of the Supreme Court, has been no less explicit in his criticism. In that country there has been an explosion of *lawyer-stimulated* litigation — more than 25 million new lawsuits are filed in America every year, taking the Federal, State, and local courts together.

The question which many thinking Americans are asking themselves is this: have they reduced the inalienable rights of man to life, liberty and the pursuit of litigation? The burgeoning costs and demoralizing delays of litigation in courts of law are so devastating that litigants have no hope of coming out of the intensive care unit. Unavoidably under the present system, litigation in civil courts continues to be lawyer-dominated.

May I turn to the situation in India? Former Chief Justices of India have been repeatedly warning that the Indian judicial system is on the verge of collapse. The present Chief Justice, Justice Pathak, himself said last January at a function in Allahabad that the Indian courts "now carry a burden almost beyond their apparent capacity". In India, cases drag on; they continue to drag their dreary length before the court in a manner strikingly reminiscent of *Jarndyce* v *Jarndyce* in Charles Dickens' *Bleak House*. In our eighteen High Courts we have more than 500,000 cases that have been in litigation between ten and thirty years. *The Economist* (of London) noted a case in the Karnataka High Court which had been dragging on for 38 years. The litigant was a bachelor when it began; today he is an old man with ten grandchildren, some of whom might well have to carry on the legal battle after he is dead.

International commercial arbitration has four factors to commend it — speed, finality, cheapness and justice. Let me say a word about each.

Speed — Courts of law are flooded with work, because cases are today brought to court for every conceivable relief. Four centuries ago, Gresham, the economist of Queen Elizabeth, propounded the famous maxim which is known as Gresham's Law — "Bad coins drive good ones out of circulation." Gresham's Law of Litigation is equally sound — "Bad cases drive out good ones and prevent their being heard in time." In our High Courts, for the hearing of a commercial suit (however good your case) the waiting period is seldom less than a decade.

International arbitrators know the value of time and the cost of delay. They know how to fill the unforgiving minute with sixty seconds' worth of distance run. No civil court can equal them in the promptness with which a case is slated for hearing. Once a case begins, it is brought to a speedy conclusion, without permitting dilatory tactics which are often adopted in a court of law to protract the hearing. This is possible because the arbitration proceeds without the full array of time-consuming formalities, procedural and substantive, which characterize normal litigation in courts of law.

Finality — In most arbitrations, the parties have no right of appeal to a higher forum, unlike the right of appeal or appeals which is available against the trial court's judgment. I have no doubt that finality of the award is a distinct advantage.

Let us not forget that the final guarantee of a correct decision is not the number of appeals available to a litigant, but the calibre and intellectual integrity of the man entrusted with the decision. I must say, frankly and truthfully, that I have found the calibre-cum-intellectual integrity of the arbitrators appointed by ICC, Paris, to be at least equal, if not superior, to that of the commercial judges of the highest courts of law.

Cheapness — Cheapness is a relative term. Sir A. P. Herbert said, "Justice must be cheap, but judges must be expensive." International commercial arbitration offers you moderately expensive judges but the total procedure is cheap — compared to what you spend in courts of law where judges are cheap and justice is expensive. Litigation has almost become a luxury. In two places — hospitals and law courts — there is now a haemorrhage of costs.

If justice is a commodity, you will find that in the market run by ICC, Paris (elegantly called the Court of Arbitration) you can get the best quality product at a lower cost than in courts of law. Costs are saved because you have brevity in place of length, precision instead of prolixity. The arbitrator is not in the popularity contest: he does not need to cultivate the goodwill of the Bar as an exceptionally patient judge tries to.

The American advocate, Frank Hogan, gave the following definition of the ideal client of a lawyer — "A very rich man, thoroughly scared". You don't need to be very rich, nor thoroughly scared, to seek justice before an arbitrator.

Justice — In the heated atmosphere of a court of law, the cold truth is sometimes obscured. The Court of Arbitration may be described as the place where the law approximates closest to justice. My invariable experience has been that parties with justice on their side are keen to go on with international arbitration, while parties whose case is marked, shall I say, by an "economy of merit" are reluctant to embark on arbitration and would prefer the interminable delays arising in courts of law. In other words, eagerness to have international arbitration is directly proportional to the strength of your case. I know of no greater tribute which can be paid to international arbitration.

Explaining the respective functions of the British system which comprises the High Court, the Court of Appeal and the House of Lords, Lord Asquith once said to a group of American lawyers, "It is the duty of the trial court to be slow, courteous and wrong. This is, however, not to say that it is the duty of the Court of Appeal to be quick, rude and right, for that would be to usurp the function of the House of Lords." The Court of Arbitration manages to combine the quickness and correctness of a House of Lords verdict with the courtesy of the trial judge.

To sum up, a court of law is a Rolls Royce of 1907 vintage, stately and solemn, while an international commercial arbitration is a 1987 Honda car which will take you to the same destination with far greater speed, higher efficiency and dramatically less fuel consumption.

If I were appointed the dictator of a country, in the short period between my appointment and my assassination I would definitely impose a law making international arbitration compulsory in all international commercial contracts. Arbitration would help to transform character — toward less confrontation and more consensus, less litigiousness and more understanding. Moreover, international arbitration would avoid the bias which some countries have against the multinationals of another country. When a corporation of my country goes abroad, it is animated by a high spirit of adventure and enterprise. When a corporation of another nation comes to my country, it is motivated by greed and exploitation! It reminds you of Bernard Shaw's remark, "When a man wants to murder a tiger he calls it sport: when the tiger wants to murder him he calls it ferocity."

If the law is not to be a system of tyrannical rigidity, but instead to be the efficient and useful servant of a changing society, it must from time to time be adapted and parts of it replaced. A court of law is like an ancient castle, constantly under repair. There comes a time when it no longer pays to patch it up, and it is better to resort to a new compact house built on modern lines.

The Judiciary and the Legal Profession Yesterday, Today and Tomorrow

*J*ustice and the rule of law are perhaps two of the noblest concepts evolved by the wit of man. To the Romans, Justice was a goddess whose symbols were a throne that tempests could not shake, a pulse that passion could not stir, eyes that were blind to any feeling of favour or ill-will, and the sword that fell on all offenders with equal certainty and with impartial strength. Ancient Indian culture pays a similar tribute to dispensers of justice. But in our own times there has been a precipitate diminution of admiration and a sharp erosion of the values which ought to actuate the administration of justice.

Doubtless, the law is imperfect, and it would be imperfect even if it were made by a committee of archangels. This is understandable. But according to an eminent writer, the court is no longer looked upon as a cathedral but as a casino: if you are dissatisfied with the trial court's judgment, you double the stakes and go to the Division Bench; if you are dissatisfied with the Division Bench judgment, you treble the stakes and go to the Supreme Court.

A number of observations have been made down the centuries about the legal profession, and few of them have been complimentary. G. K. Chesterton, talking of lawyers, said:

> "They fight by shuffling papers,
>   They have dark, dead alien eyes;
> And they look at our love and our laughter
>   As a tired man looks at flies."

(125th Anniversary Celebrations of the Bombay High Court, Nagpur, September 28, 1987)

I asked Sir Noshirwan Engineer, the Advocate General of India in 1947, how he viewed, in the light of his decades of experience, the legal system of administration of justice. His answer was, "I am inclined to the view that it is better to have *Kazi* justice, where one wise man decides what he thinks is right and that is the end of it."

The reasons for these somewhat disparaging remarks are not far to seek. If some people in our country believe that the difficulties we face in our administration of justice are due to British influence, I would emphatically dissent from such a view. I do not think the British should be blamed for the ailments afflicting our legal system today.

It has become the fashion to talk of Oxbridge (Oxford and Cambridge) as if they were responsible for undesirable influences. Let us not forget that some of the eminent judges of the Nagpur and Bombay High Courts, including Justice M.C. Chagla and Justice Hidayatullah to whom well-deserved tributes have been paid, were the products of Oxford or Cambridge. If we did not have the rules of British jurisprudence, it would be impossible to administer justice in this country. Our history goes back 5,000 years. More than a dozen civilizations waxed and waned in different parts of India over these fifty centuries. Which system could we have possibly adopted as the national system? We fight over everything. We fight on the issue whether towns on the boundary of one state should not belong to another state. What would become of the system of administering justice if we left it to be dealt with by historical antecedents without the influence of any foreign system of administering the law? Further, the rule of law, human rights, equality of all citizens, are not traditionally Indian concepts. If untouchability still continues in practice in our country, if *sati* continues to occur, and thousands flock to the spot where *sati* has been performed, we do have something to learn from other parts of the world.

I would like to give an example of Nigeria to illustrate what happens when the Western concept of the rule of law does not prevail. An Air-India plane was recently detained by the Nigerian forces. Air-India went to the High Court of Nigeria and asked for the release of the plane. The High Court decided that the aircraft should be released forthwith. But defying the court's order the Government of Nigeria would not release the plane, even after that Government's appeal to the higher court was dismissed. Some days later, the Nigerian Government issued an ordinance under which jurisdiction in the case was transferred to the Military Court which refused to release the plane. This is what happens when the rule of law does not prevail; and let us not pretend that the rule of law is a concept which can be regarded as a part of the Indian psyche.

Please recall the events during the Emergency. Our fundamental right to life and liberty under Article 21 of the Constitution was suspended. Our High Courts, let it be said to their great credit, ordered certain detenus to be set free — those who had been arrested under a mistake of identity, or as a result of private vendetta, or at the whim and fancy of the executive, or without being heard at all. Our Parliament, to supersede the judicial decisions, passed an extraordinary law to the effect that "no citizen shall be entitled to liberty on the ground of natural law, common law or rules of natural justice." This is typical of what can happen in India when the Western concept of common law, natural law and rules of natural justice is treated as a pernicious outside influence! Another law passed by Parliament was to the effect that "no police officer shall be *permitted* (as distinct from *compelled*) to disclose to a court of law the grounds on which an individual is detained", and that if a man was released by a court because the detention was held to be unsustainable, he could be re-arrested on the same grounds after he left the courtroom. Such are the laws passed by the Indian Parliament when it is unrestrained by the Western concepts embodied in our Constitution.

*I*t is interesting to read what has been said about the present position of the judiciary and the legal profession in Britain and the United States of America. If there is anything critical to be said, it is better to say it in respect of other countries, rather than our own. The reason is that we Indians do not mind other countries being censured, but we do strongly object to ourselves being criticized.

In Britain, Lord Benson, Chairman of the Royal Commission on Legal Services, told the International Commission of Jurists that the public was showing unwillingness to accept high costs, inefficiency, prolixity, incompetence and delay in the legal system; and that the traditional attitude of the legal profession is that "all change is bad, specially change for the better."

Lord Devlin, one of the most famous of living British judges, has pointed to the obsolescence of the British system of meting out justice, mainly on two counts - the adversary system which wastes time and effort, and the system of taking oral evidence.

Lord Gifford, QC, said last year that British judges were ignorant and biased, the bias being the product of their education and social position. In his book, *Where's the Justice?*, Lord Gifford observes that a male-dominated judiciary is unable to understand the problems of women. Personally, I think the remark was justified in view of some of the amazingly lenient sentences handed down in England in cases of rape where the rapist was let off lightly on the ground that his career would otherwise be ruined, while the judge thought nothing of the girl's career being ruined as a result of the cruel and wicked crime.

Lord Hailsham, the former Lord Chancellor, has expressed himself strongly about the heavy load of work. He even suggested that judges might have to undergo training and part-time job experience, as is necessary in the case of physicians, surgeons and engineers.

Let me come to the United States. In that country the legal profession is perhaps more commercialized than in any other country of the world, though India comes a close second. In America you can work on a contingency fee basis — i.e., a fee depending upon the monetary redress awarded by the court to your client. You will recall how US lawyers rushed to Bhopal to make money out of the miseries of the poor victims of the Union Carbide tragedy. Ambulance-chasing and acting as scavengers is thought to be perfectly in order. Small wonder that citizens of the States of Massachusetts and Pennsylvania demanded in the eighteenth century that the legal profession be abolished.

Judge Learned Hand said, "As a litigant, I should dread a lawsuit beyond almost anything else, short of sickness and death."

Justice Douglas said that 40 per cent of American lawyers were incompetent. Justice Warren Burger, the former Chief Justice of the US Supreme Court, said that 50 per cent of American lawyers were incompetent (disagreeing with Justice Douglas' estimate of 40 per cent). He believed that America was approaching a disaster area, not just a problem. He further stressed that the American judicial system "may literally break down before the end of this century." He told the American Bar Association:

> "The harsh truth is that we may be on our way to a society overrun by hordes of lawyers, hungry as locusts, and brigades of judges in numbers never before contemplated. The notion — that ordinary people want black-robed judges, well-dressed lawyers and fine-panelled courtrooms as the setting to resolve their disputes , is not correct. People with legal problems, like people with pain, want relief and they want it as quickly and inexpensively as possible.

A former Deputy Attorney-General of the United States has warned that the "legal process, because of its unbridled growth, has become a cancer which threatens the vitality of our forms of capitalism and democracy." In the United States, $30 billion is spent annually on lawyers, which comes to about 1.5 per cent of its Gross National Product. In India, thanks to our complicated laws, the percentage spent on lawyers may also well be 1.5 per cent of our Gross National Product.

*T*here are three grave shortcomings of the present system of administering justice.

First, the commercialization of the legal profession. I do not think the legal profession was ever so commercialized as it is today. When I started my practice in 1946 on the Original Side of the Bombay High Court, if a counsel made a factual statement to the judge, it was implicitly believed to be true. You seldom heard of an affidavit, filed on behalf of the Government or any public authority, which did not contain the whole truth. But now all that has totally changed. Counsel often make statements at the Bar which are factually incorrect, and affidavits are often filed, even on behalf of public authorities, which do not state the truth. Look at what was going on before the Lentin Commission, and how witness after witness perjured himself. Yet there was no surge of public disgust and outrage. Unfortunately, we accept perjury as a fact of Indian life. The worst danger is not that even persons in high public office perjure themselves. The worst danger lies in public acceptance of such degradation of national character. As a man who loves India not wisely but too well, I ask the question — Why can we not have standards as high as those of mature democracies in the world? After all, our ancient culture is the noblest ever known.

Secondly, administration of justice suffers from the intractable complexity of modern society. Life has become far more complex, and corruption and all-round lowering of standards are far more pronounced, than ever before.

Thirdly, while all the time we emphasize our rights, we do not lay a corresponding stress on our responsibilities. Part IVA of the Constitution, which deals with "Fundamental Duties", has been a dead letter from the moment it was enacted by the Constitution (Forty-second Amendment) Act, 1976.

If I were asked to mention the greatest drawback of the administration of justice in India today, I would say that it is *delay.* There are inordinate delays in the disposal of cases. We, as a nation, have some fine qualities, but a sense of the value of time is not one of them. Perhaps there are historical reasons for our relaxed attitude to time. Ancient India had evolved the concepts of eternity and infinity. So what do thirty years, wasted in a litigation, matter against the backdrop of eternity? Further, we believe in reincarnation. What does it matter if you waste this life? You will have many more lives in which to make good.

I am not aware of any country in the world where litigation goes on for as long a period as in India. Our cases drag over a length of time which makes eternity intelligible. The law may or may not be an ass, but in India it is certainly a snail and our cases proceed at a pace which would be regarded as unduly slow in a community of snails. Justice has to be blind but I see no reason why it should also be lame: here it just hobbles along, barely able to walk.

A charitable trust, with which I am connected, filed a suit to recover possession of its building. It took thirty years to get the final decision of the Supreme Court. Even after that, the trust has been unable to recover full possession, because there are obstructionists' notices in the Small Causes Court (in respect of some floors) which would take another decade to dispose of. If litigation were to be included in the next Olympics, India would be certain of winning at least one gold medal!

The fault is mainly of the legal profession. We ask for adjournments on the most flimsy grounds. If the judge does not readily grant adjournments, he becomes highly unpopular. I think it is the duty of the legal profession to make sure that it co-operates with the judiciary in ensuring that justice is administered speedily and expeditiously. It is the one duty of which we are totally oblivious.

Sometimes judges are asked to intervene on humanitarian grounds, e.g., in the case of encroachments on public property. Courts of law are there to enforce the law. But in matters relating to encroachments and similar cases the courts are expected to *prevent* enforcement of the law. Lawyers who would not allow homeless persons to stay with them in their own houses or build a hutment next to the wall of their own building, act as great champions of the downtrodden in such disputes. Double standards have become shamelessly common in the legal profession.

We take cases in mind-boggling numbers to the court of law. Small wonder that we have colossal arrears in courts. Do we not have to blame ourselves as members of the legal profession for this state of affairs? Lawyers are entitled to earn their living, but not at such an unbearable cost to society.

What are the ways in which the problem can be even partially tackled?

First, we must educate our lawyers better. We produce ethical illiterates in our law colleges, who have no notion of what public good is. In India the number of advocates today is about three lakhs. We have the second highest number of lawyers in the world, the first being the United States which has seven lakh legal practitioners. These large numbers result in a lot of lawyer-stimulated litigation in the two countries. By contrast, the number of practising lawyers in Japan is less than 14,000. About 30,000 students appear for law examinations in Japan and only about 475 succeed, i.e., less than two per cent. So stiff is the examination they have to go through! No wonder that in Japan very few cases are filed and disputes are mostly settled out of court.

Secondly, we must improve the quality of public administration which is today at an all-time low. In the last forty-five years India was perhaps never governed so badly as it is governed today. It has been said that in the state of Bihar nothing moves except the river Ganges!

In the UK there are 29 million taxpayers, while the number of tax references to the High Court there is only around thirty annually. In India there are 5 million taxpayers, while the number of references made to our High Courts annually is over 6,000, plus more than 1,000 writ petitions. The exceptionally large number of tax cases is not because the Indian people are more litigious than the British, but principally because the quality of tax administration is so poor. Nothing happens to the officer who makes an assessment which no reasonable man would ever dream of making.

Few persons know about the administrative scheme announced during the tenure of Mr. V. P. Singh as the Finance Minister. Under the administrative incentive scheme, if a show cause notice is issued by an officer asking the citizen why a certain amount should not be collected from him in addition to the amount of tax admitted to be due, the officer and his colleagues are entitled to a reward which may go up to 5 per cent of the amount specified in the show cause notice, irrespective of the final result of the case. To illustrate: a show cause notice was served on ITC alleging that a sum of Rs. 806 crore was due from that company by way of excise during a period of five years in which the company's total profit was Rs. 70 crore. On the alleged excise dues of Rs. 806 crore, the officers' reward could go up to Rs. 40 crore. This matter is still pending in the Calcutta High Court.

Thirdly, the citizenry must be better educated to evolve a higher standard of public character. Ancient Indian culture must be taught in schools and colleges. The synergic effect of the different cultures, the amalgam of which is called Indian culture, is bound to prove of great ethical value. Will Durant said that just as continuity of memory is necessary for the sanity of an individual, continuity of the nation's traditions and culture is necessary for the sanity of the nation.

formulae, no rules of thumb, no prescriptions as in a pharmacopoeia. The path of the Spirit is narrow and there are yawning abysses on either side.

In the words of the *Kathopanishad:*

> Sharp as a razor's edge and hard to traverse is that difficult path, so the sages say.

Realization of the Divine is possible through meditation and contemplation. The inner spirit must dwell serene on the heights of eternity. However, action can be as efficacious as contemplation. The way to salvation may be through prayer or it may be through action or through knowledge. Men like Sri Aurobindo are examples of the mysterious reconciliation of incessant work and uninterrupted rest in one and the same person. That is the ideal which the *Bhagavad Gita* sets before us: "He who sees rest in activity and activity in rest — he is wise among men, he is a *yogi* and a thorough man of action."

In his famous book, *Karma Yoga,* Swami Vivekananda describes the scope of *Vedanta* so as to include also all seekers of truth who are outside the pale of formal religion:

> Karma-yoga is a system of ethics and religion intended to attain freedom through unselfishness and by good works. The karma-yogi need not believe in any doctrine whatever. He may not believe even in God.

The doctrine of *Brahman*, the Ultimate Reality, must necessarily involve tolerance and understanding, peace and goodwill, and recognition of the immense variety of paths by which the soul can fulfil its ultimate destiny.

Ahimsa, peace and non-aggression were the hallmarks of Indian culture. In her crowded history of over five thousand years during which she had thrown up vast and puissant empires, India never practised military aggression on countries outside her borders. Thanks to our ethos, even today the Indian people patiently suffer miseries and endure injustices which would result in devastating explosions in any other country.

In these days of spiritual illiteracy and poverty of the spirit, when people find that wealth can only multiply itself and attain nothing, when people have to deceive their souls with counterfeits after having killed the poetry of life, it is necessary to remind ourselves that civilization is an act of the spirit. Material progress is not to be mistaken for inner progress. When technology outstrips moral development, the prospect is not that of a millennium but of extinction. Our ancient heritage is a potent antidote to the current tendency to standardize souls and seek salvation in herds.

Centuries have gone by but the lustre of that heritage remains undimmed. Invading forces have descended on this country but its culture has remained indestructible.

> "The East bow'd low before the blast,
> In patient, deep disdain.
> She let the legions thunder past,
> And plunged in thought again."

C. Rajagopalachari observed: "If there is any honesty in India today, any hospitality, any chastity, any philanthropy, any tenderness to the dumb creatures, any aversion to evil, any love to do good, it is due to whatever remains of the old faith and the old culture."

The old faith and the old culture referred to by Rajaji are not merely for Hindus, not merely for Indians, but for the whole world. Schelling, in his old age, thought the *Upanishads* contain the maturest wisdom of mankind. Today that wisdom is essential not only for the rebirth of the Indian nation but also for the re-education of the human race.

Female Education —
The Priority of Priorities

Barbara Wootton, one of the great champions of higher education for women, died four years ago at the age of ninety-one. She has written a fascinating autobiography entitled, *In A World I Never Made*. She observed, "The laughable idealism of one generation evolves into the accepted commonplace of the next." She lived to see the truth of her dictum proved right time and again, particularly in the field of female education.

Today, some of our most distinguished High Court judges are women like Mrs. Sujata Manohar; but no lady was appointed a judge of the High Court before the middle of this century. Till the last century it was assumed that women were unfit to get degrees. London was the first British University to overcome the prejudice against the fair sex. It threw its degrees open to women in 1878. The Bombay University conferred the Bachelor of Arts Degree (First Class) on the first woman student, Miss Cornelia Sorabji, in 1888. The first woman member to be nominated to the Bombay University Senate was in 1891. Oxford and Cambridge took a much longer time to get over their male chauvinism. These facts will give you an idea of the magnitude of Maharshi Karve's achievement, who founded this Women's University in 1916.

Education has been happily defined as the technique of transmitting civilization. It is shocking that the country with the oldest and greatest civilization should be so lackadaisical about the

(Convocation Address to S.N.D.T. Women's University, Bombay, December 19, 1992)

technique of transmitting it.

The Indian psyche remains today wholly untouched by any thought of the need for wider and more value-based education. Education has never been a high-priority item in any Indian political party's manifesto. The subject which should have galvanized the nation into action forty years ago is still kept in cold storage. Without the guidance which can be derived only from liberal education, a whole generation has grown up which is content to see crime and violence, casteism and communal frenzy, become the order of the day. More criminals have openly entered public life than ever before. No democracy can last long in such circumstances.

It is now acknowledged all over the world that value-based education is the only instrument for transmuting national talent into national progress. Amongst the important countries of the East, India is the least adequately educated. Article 45 of our Constitution enacts:

> The State shall endeavour to provide, within a period
> of ten years from the commencement of this Constitu-
> tion, for free and compulsory education for all children
> until they complete the age of fourteen years.

Elementary education is "free" in theory; but many one-room schools in rural areas are today without even a blackboard and chalk. "Compulsory" it is not, even in theory. Men in public life have always looked upon Article 45 as a pious platitude which is not calculated to give any mileage either to the politician or to his political party.

It is only through female education at all levels and the private initiative of well-educated women, that this country will ever be transformed into what our Constitution intended it to be. We have only to look around to see the difference between our apathy and the zeal and dedication of other nations in the field of nation-building.

The rate of literacy in South Korea is 98 per cent. Its economic development is the predictable result of its uncompromising emphasis on education.

When Lee Kuan Yew was recently asked on the BBC as to what he attributed the phenomenal success of Singapore, his answer was in one word — "Education". He added that no subject had a higher priority in his city-state.

President Mitterrand started his second term of office in 1988 with the promise to make education the "priority of priorities". His election manifesto proclaimed, "In future the nation's power will depend less on its financial wealth than on its grey matter." He was as good as his word. In France, after the Prime Minister ranks not the Foreign Minister, not the Finance Minister, not the Home or the Defence Minister, but the Minister for Education.

In February 1991, the British Prime Minister, Mr. John Major, in a major speech put education at the top of his personal agenda for the 1990s, and said that education is the key to a "mobile, dynamic and diverse society".

In 1983, the National Commission for Excellence in Education, appointed by the United States government, published a Report called "A Nation At Risk". The Report exhorted the government to take prompt and firm measures to raise the level of education, if the future of that country was not to be imperilled. If the United States can be called "A nation at risk", would it be any exaggeration to call India "A nation in dire peril"?

Five years ago, Professor Allan Bloom (who unfortunately died last October) published his volume *The Closing of the American Mind*. It has already sold a million copies. The sub-title of the book is "How higher education has failed democracy and impoverished the souls of today's students." The main thesis of Professor Allan Bloom is that the universities and schools are swamped with intellectual laziness bred from the doctrines propagated in the sixties that everything is related and all values are equal. Our obsession with openness and equality has produced a generation bereft of vision and ignorant of its own culture.

A survey was conducted in January 1988 by the American Council on Education. Students were asked about their objective in pursuing higher education. An overwhelming majority of the students said that their objective was to make more money in later years. The motive "To develop a meaningful philosophy of life" ranked the lowest. The same malaise affects Indian students. No wonder that ancient Indian culture is the subject least often chosen by our youth.

In April 1991, President Bush called for "a revolution in American education". He announced a plan for national achievement tests. The President said that he would like to see the creation of non-traditional schools, some of which might be operated by private organizations or businesses.

As *The Economist* pointed out last month, investing in education is to the 1990s what nationalization was to the 1940s and privatization to the 1980s — the universal panacea of the day. Right-wingers value education partly because it promises to make labour markets more efficient; left-wingers partly because it gives a respectable role for State activism. Economists on both sides of the political divide are agreed that human capital is the most precious form of capital there is. The skill and calibre of corporate manpower never appear in any balance sheet; but it is widely acknowledged throughout the world that the greatest asset of a company is trained manpower. In a book published recently by the famous economist, Julian Simon, the human resource is rightly defined in the title of the book as *The Ultimate Resource*.

Among the nations of the world, India ranks very high in innate intelligence, but abysmally low in wisdom — what the ancient *rishis* called *buddhi*. This is both the cause and the effect of our total indifference towards education. The criminalization of politics and the deplorably low moral tone of our public life are the direct consequences of the failure to impart value-based education.

Liberty without accountability is the freedom of the fool. Our concept of freedom will remain an impoverished one, until it is rounded and deepened by liberal education.

Education is the rock on which India must build her political salvation. Our country will be built not on bricks but on brains; not on cement but on enlightenment. If we cannot afford education, we cannot afford to remain a civilized society.

I hope and trust your University does not have reservations on communal or caste considerations and that, unlike some other colleges, it does not give grace marks in order to enable students to pass where the mark scored on merit is zero. "Firsts" should not be allowed to multiply; otherwise it would be like inflation — you start destroying the value of the currency.

At the last official count, the number of Indian universities was 181 — twice the number that existed twenty years ago. While the number of our universities and the number of our students proliferate, the level of edification does not keep pace. We continue to churn out ethical illiterates and moral idiots. Our education continues to be "value-agnostic" and "value-neutral". Dr. Mortimer Adler, the Chairman of the Board of Directors of the *Encyclopaedia Britannica*, said that true education can begin only after you have left school or college. All that a school or college can do is to arouse intellectual curiosity and prepare you for lifelong education later.

Education is an end in itself; and not merely a means to an end like financial well-being. There should be no profit motive in liberal education, any more than in friendship. Then alone can knowledge ripen into wisdom.

The timeless lesson of ancient Indian culture is that man is more than man, and there is more to the world than the world. Every age must take a step forward in evolution; but unfortunately India has been taking several steps backwards.

May I end with my best wishes to those who are passing out of the portals of this very fine University. They have been privileged to have been educated well, and they, in their turn, should resolve to return to the people a part of the benefits they have derived.

Science and Humanism

*C*ulture is what remains after you have forgotten all that you set out to learn. It is the residue which forms part of your personality. Naturalists say that there exist 193 species of primates, of which *Homo sapiens* is one. Man has been defined as a rational animal, but most of the time he behaves in a manner which belies the definition.

While education helps man to progress from superstition to rationality, it can never destroy our sense of the mysterious. I would like to recall here the lines of the Irish poet, A. E. (George Russell):

> I heard them in their sadness say
>> The earth rebukes the thought of God,
> We are but embers, wrapped in clay,
>> A little nobler than the sod.

> But I have touched the lips of clay,
>> Mother, thy rudest sod to me
> Is thrilled with fire of hidden day
>> And haunted by all mystery.

It is energy which takes the rocket to the moon, and it is energy which makes the plants sprout mystifyingly through the earth:

(33rd World Education Fellowship International Conference, Bombay, December 1986)

Fuelled by a million man-made wings of fire,
   The rocket tore through the sky...
And everybody cheered.
   Fuelled by only a thought from God
The seedling urged its way through the thickness of black.
   And as it pierced the heavy ceiling of the soil
And launched itself up into outer space...
   No one even clapped.

The rocket's performance is explicable; while the seedling's performance is inexplicable and miraculous. Yet the claps of the thoughtless mortal are reserved for the former.

The sense of the mysterious is the hallmark of a perfectly educated man who has learned to strike his spirit wide awake, and who not only knows science but humanism and human values.

Dr. Alexis Carrel who won the Nobel Prize in 1912, has described in his book *Man, the Unknown,* his experience at the world famous pilgrim centre of Lourdes in France where he saw miracles happen even when the patient did not have faith. Dr. Carrel frankly confessed that he could find no scientific explanation for such miracles.

A courageous medical man, Charles Robert Richet, another Nobel Prize winner (1913) while addressing a meeting of eminent medical men in Edinburgh said:

> Metaphysics is not yet officially a science, recognized as such. But it is going to be. . . . Our five senses are not our only means of knowledge, and a fragment of reality sometimes reaches the intelligence in other ways. . . . Because a fact is rare is no reason to hold that it does not exist.

Another great hallmark of a truly educated man is humility. If there is one thing on which all scientists are agreed, it is that they do not, and probably never will, understand the universe. So many basic phenomena are not only unknown but unknowable. The advance of knowledge at present may be reduced to what Einstein described as extracting one incomprehensible from another incomprehensible. Scientists are equally baffled by the fact that every mystery of the physical world points to a mystery beyond itself. Thomas Alva Edison cried in despair: "We don't know one-millionth of one per cent about anything." Sometimes we are inclined to agree with the scientist who said, "We do not run this place; it runs itself. We are a part of the running."

You are bound to be appalled when you come to examine the state of education generally.

The Carnegie Foundation for Advancement of Teaching, in a report prepared by them recently, have stated that the general level of education today is abysmally low. Most of the students seeking higher education, they pointed out, only aimed at achieving a higher standard of living, and very few were desirous of acquiring knowledge in order to attain a higher standard of life. Education today churns out amoral, unlettered ignoramuses.

A man is only half-educated if he has no sense of values. The poor level of education in ethics and values is partly responsible for the phenomenon of "educated" terrorists in so many countries of the world.

The educational institutions must be generators of excellence. They must aim at turning out integrated personalities. Today many students go in for Business Management because it is far less taxing on the intellect than science or philosophy or arts, while it promises richer financial rewards. Since I have been connected with business over the years, I can confidently tell you that it does not need much of an intellect to be a successful businessman.

One of the reasons for dilution of the quality of education is the unprecedented increase in the number of educational institutions and of students. To take the example of India, in 1950-51, there were around 230,000 educational institutions, whereas now there are 750,000. In 1950-51, 24 million students were being educated, while by 1984-85 the number had increased to 132 million. Despite this enormous proliferation, 66 per cent of the Indian people are still literally illiterate. I am not talking here of the educated illiterates of which there are plenty in every country.

We have in our midst today two distinguished lady Vice-

Chancellors — Dr. Mehru Bengalee of the Bombay University, and Mrs. Kamalini Bhansali of the SNDT University — both of whom are doing an excellent job of trying to cope with the lethargy, sloppiness and corruption which prevail in our educational system today, and are fighting hard to regain the standards of decorum and discipline, of dignity and decency, for which our universities were famous forty years ago.

13

The Great and the Eminent

Dadabhai Naoroji
The First Indian Member of the
House of Commons

We have gathered to celebrate the hundredth anniversary of one of the most important events in the history of the British Commonwealth — the election of an Indian to the House of Commons for the first time. If greatness consists of a combination of character and a massive mind and if it is to be measured by the lasting value of solid work done in the fields of thought and action, Dadabhai Naoroji was beyond question one of the most outstanding men in the history of the Commonwealth.

It was Winston Churchill who said that one mark of a great man is the power of making lasting impressions upon people he meets; and another is to have so handled matters that the course of after events is continually affected by what he did. Dadabhai Naoroji — loved and revered by millions of Indians as Dadabhai, the Grand Old Man of India — fulfilled both these exacting tests.

Dadabhai cast a spell on his contemporaries, including Mahatma Gandhi, and Gandhiji was the inspiring influence in Jawaharlal Nehru's life. Thus Nehru, after whom this Centre is named, was the intellectual grandson of Dadabhai.

The political and social history of India was decisively transformed by Dadabhai's ceaseless work over sixty years.

Dadabhai was an ardent advocate of free education and of the principle that every child should have the opportunity of receiving all the education it is capable of assimilating. He said, "I realize that I had been educated at the expense of the poor, to whom I

(Address at the Nehru Centre, London, July 7, 1992)

myself belonged.... The thought developed itself in my mind, that as my education and all the benefits arising therefrom came from the people, I must return to them the best I had in me. I must devote myself to the service of the people."

Dadabhai was a pioneer in the promotion of female education. Sir R. P. Masani, who has written the standard biography of Dadabhai which must be inevitably plundered when you are dealing with the subject, relates how Dadabhai used to tell his grandchildren some stories of his early days — how as a college student he would go from house to house with a friend, persuading parents and guardians to allow him and his friend to sit on their verandahs and to teach the three R's to their girls; how some of them took advantage of the offer; and how two or three irate fathers threatened to throw them down the steps for making such a preposterous proposal! The biographer adds that to capture a pupil was sometimes as difficult a task as to conquer a city: against them were arrayed the forces of stern orthodoxy and with it the misgivings of the ignorant regarding the consequences of such a movement on the social life of the people.

The mind and heart of Dadabhai put him in a class by himself. His teacher called him "The Promise of India", and in the course of a long and crowded life he fulfilled the promise with many "firsts" to his credit. He became the first Indian professor at a British university, the first to found several organizations for the social, intellectual and political uplift of the people of India, the first Indian member of the House of Commons, the first Indian to sit on a Royal Commission.

For decades, he worked indefatigably not as the enemy of the British but as one who held them in high esteem and regard and wanted them to show their true character in their dealings with India. The title of his book summed up his verdict on the government of the day: *Poverty and Un-British Rule in India.* He was aware of the advantages of the raj, which could not be counted in money. Some strange destiny had led to the intermingling of the fates of Britain and India.

He strove to put an end to the gross injustice on two

counts — the exclusion of Indians from the higher echelons of government, and the drain on India's slender financial resources for the benefit of the British people. He started with unswerving faith in the innate British sense of justice and fairness, and was convinced that if only the facts could be brought home to the British people, they would rectify the wrongs.

"We Indian people believe," he used to tell English audiences, "that, although John Bull is a little thick-headed, once we can penetrate through his head into his brain that a certain thing is right and proper to be done, you may be quite sure that it will be done." Whenever he spoke or wrote on the injustices done to India, he always did it with decorum and dignity, knowing full well that Englishmen will not be abused, however wrong they may be, *except by themselves*. Dadabhai said, "England will produce a statesman who will have the moral courage and firmness to face the Indian problem, and do what the world should expect from England's conscience, and from England's mission to humanity." Dadabhai's hope remained unfulfilled till Attlee as the Prime Minister gave independence to India in 1947.

Whatever credit was due to Britain, Dadabhai gave it ungrudgingly. Of all the Viceroys of India, Lord Ripon was unquestionably the most popular. He said that his ambition was to rule India not as a ruler but as a friend. Dadabhai paid him the following memorable tribute:

> Deep and unshakable as my faith is in the English character for fairness and desire to do good to India, I must confess during my humble efforts in Indian politics I was sometimes driven to despair, and to doubt my faith. But Ripon has completely restored it to its full intensity, that England's conscience is right and England will do her duty and perform her great mission in India, when she has such sons, so pure of heart and high in statesmanship.

His trust in British character was fortified by the support he received from enlightened Britishers themselves. Mountstuart

Elphinstone, a very perceptive Governor of Bombay, did a lot for the cause of public education, a cause most dear to the heart of Dadabhai. When Dadabhai started the Indian National Congress, the nationalist party, in 1885, it was a Britisher, A.O. Hume, who was one of the co-founders of that party.

Dadabhai contested election to the House of Commons as the surest way of arousing the British people to the plight of Indians. He stood for election from Holborn in 1886. He was strongly supported by a section of the British press, particularly the *Pall Mall Gazette* which reported, "If the 254 millions of Her Majesty's subjects in India are ever to be represented by one of their own people in the Imperial Parliament, it would hardly be possible to find among them all one more worthy of the position or more fitted than the Hon. Dadabhai Naoroji.... Mr. Naoroji is a Gladstonian on Irish policy. On all other matters he is a thorough Liberal. Into Parliament he is certain to go sooner or later, and it will reflect great credit upon the electors of Holborn if they place him there now . . . .".

Independent thinkers like Hodgson Pratt were equally enthusiastic in their support:

> "His speeches during the last few days have shown his
> complete knowledge of our home politics, so that you
> will have in him a true representative of Englishmen,
> of Irishmen, and of Indians."

But Dadabhai was defeated by a rival candidate of whom not a trace has remained in history. One is reminded of the defeat of Sir Isaac Newton in 1705 at the Cambridge constituency and of Lord Macaulay in 1847 at Edinburgh, by men whom history regards as nonentities.

Dadabhai was never the man to be disheartened by defeat. He was determined to try again to enter the House of Commons. The strongest support given to him was, unwittingly, by Lord Salisbury. In his notorious speech at Edinburgh on November 30, 1888 while trying to explain away the results of the election at Holborn, the Premier of Britain indulged in language reminiscent of that used by slave-owners to coloured people:

> I doubt if we have yet got to that point of view where
> a British constituency would elect a black man.

The biographer of Dadabhai records, "Those two words —
BLACK MAN — simply kicked Dadabhai into fame. The name
of the hitherto little-known Indian, difficult of articulation as it had
so far been, was within twenty-four hours on the lips of everyone
throughout the United Kingdom!"

It has been said that when Lord Salisbury made a speech, that
speech was sure to contain at least one blazing indiscretion. His
Lordship's sneer, remembered for years, aroused the British
conscience.

Dadabhai decided to stand from Central Finsbury as the Liberal
candidate. He reaffirmed his faith in the conscience of the British
people. The electors went to the polling booth on July 6, 1892 and,
despite all frantic efforts to stir up racial prejudice, recorded a
majority of three votes in Dadabhai's favour. There was a special
virtue in the narrow majority — it relieved the voters of the effort
to articulate the name Naoroji — they dubbed him "Narrow-
Majority". For months thereafter the nickname stuck to the Parsi
MP. "The cheering," a local report noted, "might have been heard
at St. Paul's on one side and Chelsea Hospital on the other."
Dadabhai's election was hailed by perceptive men in Britain like
Lord Morley. Gladstone said the next day, "Lord Salisbury one day
spoke in contempt of black men. It is a curious fact that what Lord
Salisbury called a black man has just been returned to my great
satisfaction."

The result of the election at Central Finsbury electrified India.
"The whole country was greatly moved by feelings of the deepest
gratitude to the English constituency that had returned an Indian
to the Imperial Parliament. Such a thing was possible only in a free
country like England. The electors had shown that the instincts of
political freedom and the fairness of the British public had
triumphed. They had given a concrete illustration of the elasticity
of the British Constitution and demonstrated, better than all official

declarations, the equality of British citizens, wherever born and brought up."

At a meeting held in London to celebrate the event attended by about two thousand friends and admirers of the Indian MP, including several leading Members of Parliament and foremost citizens of the city, R.K. Causton who presided, said, "The event is, indeed, unique in that it ushers in a new era in our relations with India. It shows that the claim of Englishmen that they are the pioneers of popular government throughout the world is not a myth but a reality."

In reply Dadabhai observed that new life had been infused into the people of India. He said, "We hope to enjoy the same freedom, the same strong institutions which you in this country enjoy. We claim them as our birthright as British subjects. We are either British subjects or British slaves. If we are really British subjects, you are honestly bound to give us every one of your institutions as soon as we are prepared to receive them. I have now no doubt from my long knowledge of this country that as soon as the British people begin to understand what we are prepared for, they will be ready to give it."

It was the culmination of the struggle for half a century by one of the noblest sons of India to bring home to the British people the facts of their un-British rule in India. It bears repetition that Dadabhai had an unshakable faith in the British sense of equity and fair play and he expressed that faith repeatedly and openly, testifying that love of liberty and a sense of fairness were part and parcel of the British psyche.

*U*nfortunately, the relentless statistics and remorseless logic of Dadabhai's countless speeches did not arouse the conscience of the British masses adequately. The ordinary citizens remained somnolent. Dadabhai pleaded for years that while he was not against the continuance of the British raj, he wanted due representation for Indians in the administration and a stoppage of the drain on the slender financial resources of India. When Dadabhai felt that his earnest pleadings had failed to arouse the rulers, he reluctantly veered to the point of view of the younger men in India who were demanding the end of British raj and the grant of freedom. He said, with disappointment gnawing at his heart, "The old days have passed and the Indian of today looks at the whole position in quite a different light. Now India has become restless and it is desirable that the Government should at once realize it." In his last active years he fought to achieve *swaraj* (or self-rule) for India, even as he had struggled ceaselessly in his earlier years to make his people worthy of self-rule, while the raj continued.

If the British had acted rationally at the time when Dadabhai was so passionately pleading India's cause for elementary justice, the whole history of the British Commonwealth would have been different.

The Morley-Minto Reforms constituted the first step towards giving a share to Indians in the governance of their own country. But it was a case of too little and too late. The more substantive reforms were delayed till Dadabhai was no more. He died at the age of ninety-two on June 30, 1917. Those reforms were promulgated seven weeks after he had died.

Dadabhai, the greatest Indian of his time, was a Zoroastrian by birth and by conviction, and he lived the religion of Prophet Zarathushtra — pure thoughts, pure words, pure deeds. A regenerated India, freed from the shackles of foreign rule, is the greatest monument to his memory.

The Enduring Relevance of Sardar Vallabhbhai Patel

I feel privileged and honoured to be asked to deliver the Sardar Vallabhbhai Patel Memorial Lecture this year. The series started in 1955, and eminent men have spoken in the past decades on various matters of vital importance and significance.

Looking to the state of our democracy today, I thought no topic would be of greater importance than the enduring relevance of Sardar Patel. More than ever before, we need to recall what he stood for and tirelessly strove to create. "My life is my message," said Mahatma Gandhi, and Sardar Patel could have said the same.

To question the enduring relevance of Sardar Vallabhbhai Patel to India today is like questioning the relevance of the sun to the solar system. You cannot conceive of a solar system without the sun, and you cannot conceive of modern India without Sardar Vallabhbhai Patel.

In recent world history, two events have thrown up a striking galaxy of talent. The first was when the thirteen colonies in America were fighting for their independence. From 1776 to 1783 the United States of America (as it came to be known later) produced an extraordinary cluster of outstanding men who were the founders of the great republic. In the twenty-five years between 1922 and 1947, India had a comparable galaxy of talent — no

(Patel Memorial Lecture under the auspices of All India Radio, October 30, 1992)

inferior to that which America produced — and our leaders combined talent with sterling character. Undoubtedly Sardar Patel was in the top rank.

Sardar Patel was one of the founders of our Constitution. Luckily, the Constitution was drafted by the Constituent Assembly which was *not* elected on the basis of adult franchise. First-rate minds were hand-picked from all parts of India — for their knowledge, vision and dedication.

The story of Sardar Patel's life is easily told. The traditional date of his birth is October 31, 1875. But really speaking, nobody knows the exact day on which he was born. The traditional date is what he gave for his matriculation examination and he never changed it — rather typical of the constancy which characterized his mental make-up.

Sardar Patel was born to parents who were deeply religious. It is remarkable how frequently the children of deeply religious parents fare well in life. Vallabhbhai himself became the architect of modern India, while his brother, Vithalbhai, was the first Speaker of the Central Legislature. Vallabhbhai was a very affectionate man, though there were not many occasions when he displayed his affectionate nature. He had a very fine sense of humour. Mahatma Gandhi has gone on record to say that during the sixteen months when he was in jail, he was kept in peals of laughter by Vallabhbhai who was a co-inmate.

Vallabhbhai never courted publicity. He never projected himself anywhere but quietly did his work. He was a true *karma yogi*. After he became a widower at the age of thirty-three, the only love in his life was his motherland to which he was passionately devoted.

*H*e had three great ambitions. First of all, he wanted to consolidate India. In the five thousand years of its history, India was never united: it had always been a group of different states. Vallabhbhai wanted to bring into existence a united, homogeneous

India when it became a republic in 1950.

The Times (of London) said that Vallabhbhai's achievement of the integration of the Indian States would rank with that of Bismarck and probably higher. *The Manchester Guardian* rightly said:

> Without Patel, Gandhiji's idea would have had less practical influence and Nehru's idealism less scope. Patel was not only the organiser of the fight for freedom but also the architect of the new State when the fight was over. The same man is seldom successful as rebel and statesman. Sardar Patel was the exception.

While launching the PEPSU Union at Patiala, Sardar Patel said:

> This is the first time in history, after centuries, that India can call itself an integrated whole in the real sense of the term . . . . We must work with unity. If we falter or fail, we shall consign ourselves to eternal shame and disgrace.

His second ambition was to ensure the survival of a united country through the instrument of a strong civil service. He conceived of the Indian Administrative Service (IAS) in place of the Indian Civil Service (ICS), and it was he who also conceived of the Indian Police Service (IPS). Both these services are very much extant today and have enabled India to survive as a democratic state, while the fortunes of political parties keep changing.

His third ambition was to make India economically strong, prosperous and progressive. This ambition was not fulfilled. After the death of Sardar Vallabhbhai Patel on December 15, 1950, the government consciously discarded the economic policies of the Sardar and adopted a barren form of socialism which was the bane of India till the present Government started its new policy of liberalization. This is one of the greatest tragedies of India.

*T*he nation has not realized the greatness of Vallabhbhai as it should have done. If Vallabhbhai had not lived, India would not be what it is today. He aimed at integration in two ways — not only territorial integration but the integration of the different communities by developing a sense of national identity. There were 554 Indian States which comprised two-thirds of India, while only one-third was British India. He brought all of them together, while continuing to remain on terms of mutual affection and respect with the former Rulers. When the Russian leader Khrushchev visited India in 1956, he expressed his surprise that India had managed to liquidate the Princely States without liquidating the Princes.

Sardar Patel was also the Chairman of the Minorities Sub-Committee of the Constituent Assembly. He sought to forge communal integration. He made different communities give up their claim for separate electorates. Even the spokesman of the Parsis had in mind a separate electorate. But Vallabhbhai merely smiled at the ridiculous idea and the matter was not discussed again. The Parsis were a microscopic minority, but the Muslims, the Sikhs and the Christians were in substantial numbers. Even in those days the Sikhs demanded Khalistan. Sardar Patel dealt with the problem with great understanding. He went to the heart of the Sikh hinterland. He talked to the Sikhs in Amritsar and impressed upon them how we all have to live together as brothers and sisters. The passionate plea of Sardar Patel worked. In a powerful speech he made at Patiala in October 1947 he said that we should not involve ourselves in endless disputes and that we could not afford to follow the mirage of 'stans' like Khalistan, Sikhistan or Jatistan. He pointed out that such separatism could only turn India into *Pagalistan*, a land of lunatics.

He was a true leader, in the sense that he did not flatter the people but plainly told them where they were wrong. In August 1947 he said again in ringing words how and why India could not be divided. India, he said, is one and indivisible. You cannot divide the sea or split the running waters of a river. He said this not merely to the Muslims and the Sikhs but also to the Hindus when the RSS made a strong plea that India should become a Hindu State. His words were:

> We in the Government have been dealing with the RSS movement. They want that Hindu *Rajya* or Hindu culture should be imposed by force. No Government can tolerate this.

Vallabhbhai was not against anybody except the fanatic. If you were a fanatic he was against you, whether you were a Hindu or a Muslim or a Sikh. It is wrong to portray him as being anti-Muslim. Vallabhbhai, as the Home Minister, had the courage to ban the RSS. That conclusively shows how totally secular and non-communal Sardar Patel was in his approach. He told the Hindu Mahasabha:

> If you think that you are the only custodians of Hinduism, you are mistaken. Hinduism preaches a broader outlook on life. There is much more of tolerance in Hinduism than is supposed.

In his speech in January 1948 at Calcutta, Sardar Patel warned the country that there could never be any serious talk of a Hindu State. India had elected to be a secular State. He solemnly declared:

> If the Government could not act as trustees for the entire population irrespective of caste, religion or creed, it does not deserve to continue for a single day.

In 1947 when people were jubilant that we attained *swaraj*, there were two persons who struck a note of dissent — Mahatma Gandhi and Sardar Patel. The response of Sardar Patel to independence gained in 1947 was memorable:

> What we have is not *swaraj* but only freedom from foreign rule. The people have still to win internal *swaraj*, abolish distinctions of caste or creed, banish untouchability, improve the lot of the hungry masses, and live as one joint family — in short, to create a new

way of life and bring about a change of heart and a change of outlook.

To Sardar Patel, the unity and integrity of India was of paramount importance. He shared the view of the Indian thinker who, when he was told that the British divide and rule, gave the profound response, "No, it is not the British who divide and rule. It is we who divide and they rule." That is why he was against the creation of linguistic states. In December 1949, the Working Committee of the Congress directed that a separate Andhra State should be created forthwith. In spite of this directive, Sardar Patel took no action. On the contrary, he criticized openly this directive of his own party. At a public meeting in Trivandrum in May 1950 he said:

> Some people say they want provinces on a linguistic basis like Andhra, Tamil and Kerala. What will be its effect in the north or in the west nobody cares to consider. We should cease to think in terms of different states or provinces. Instead we should think that we are Indians and should develop a sense of unity."

While the unification and integration of India was his greatest achievement, only next in importance was his creation of a strong and independent civil service. He trusted and respected the officers and gained their affection and deep regard. This put the civil servants on their honour to work for him to the limit of their capacity and never, as far as humanly possible, to let him down. H.V.R. Iengar in his *Administration in India — A Historical Review* relates one typical incident:

> On one occasion, I took a decision in his absence and reported it to him afterwards. He told me that if he had been consulted he would not have taken that decision. I was very unhappy about this, but he asked me not to worry and said that every human being makes mistakes. When the matter subsequently came before the Cabinet

he told them that the decision was his, and there the matter ended.

In Sardar Patel's words, "the most dangerous thing in a democracy is to interfere with the Services." If today the police force is wholly demoralized in most states, it is entirely due to the political interference by ministers and other politicians in the discharge by the police of their professional duties.

Sardar Patel never posed as a socialist. He had no property of his own, except his personal belongings. Once an ardent socialist approached him with an appeal to abolish inequality of wealth and cited as an instance that X was master of several millions. The Sardar let him expatiate on the distribution of surplus wealth. When he had finished, Sardar Patel coolly looked at him and said:

> I know the extent of X's wealth. If all of it were distributed equally among the people of India, your share would be about four annas and three pies. I am willing to give it to you from my own pocket if you undertake to talk no more about this.

He wanted to purge capitalism of its ugly face. But he realized that wealth has to be created first, before it can be distributed.

So long as Sardar Patel was alive, there was no nationalization. He said:

> Some people want us to nationalize all industry. How are we to run nationalized industries if we cannot run our ordinary administration? It is easy to take over any industry we want to, but we do not have the resources to run them, enough experienced men, men of expertise and integrity.

Sardar Patel started the Indian National Trade Union Congress (INTUC) because he wanted a fair deal to be given to labour. But he was not in the popularity contest and he had no patience with people who were. He was against the mindless calls for strikes made by trade union leaders. He said in Calcutta in January 1948:

> Regarding strikes, I feel that it is deplorable that they have been made so cheap. They are now props of leadership of labour and have ceased to be a legitimate means of redressing grievances of labour.... The maxim should be 'produce and then distribute equitably'. Instead they fight before even producing wealth. It is to restore sanity and a fair deal between labour and employers and to give a correct lead to labour that we set up the Indian National Trade Union Congress.

To Sardar Patel, the plighted word was sacred: he never broke his word. He had a sense of honour and good faith which successive governments so sadly lacked. He never dreamt that the promise contained in Article 291 of the Constitution to give privy purses to the Princes would be broken later. The aggregate amount of privy purses guaranteed to the Rulers of different States came to an insignificant sum of less than Rs. 5 crore. Rulers died in normal course, and the privy purse was reduced when their successors were recognized as Rulers. Yet, the then government abolished privy purses disregarding the constitutional mandate. Referring to the guarantee regarding pensions to the covenanted services, which was to be embodied in Article 314, Sardar Patel said in the Constituent Assembly on October 10, 1949:

> Have you read history? Or, is it that you do not care for recent history after you have begun to make history? If you do that, then I tell you we have a dark future. Learn to stand upon your pledged word.... Can you go behind these things? Have morals no place in the new Parliament? Is that how we are going to begin our new freedom? Do not take a *lathi* and say, `Who is to give you a guarantee? We are a Supreme Parliament. Have you supremacy for this kind of thing? To go behind

your word? If you do that, that supremacy will go down
in a few days.

Like Article 291, Article 314 was also brazenly deleted after
the Sardar's death.

In 1950, the last year of his life, Sardar Patel repeatedly
expressed his total disillusionment with the debased standards of
politicians and the malfunctioning of Indian democracy. On May
27, 1950 at Porbandar (Gandhiji's home town), in a mood of
introspection, he said:

> We have not digested Gandhiji's teachings. We are
> merely imitating. We have adult franchise but do not
> know how to use it. If we continue to indulge in
> personal jealousies and power-hunting, we shall turn
> into poison what Gandhiji had got for us.

> During the last three years we have worked in a manner
> which has brought us only shame. We have strayed
> from the right road and must get back to it and
> understand Gandhiji's teachings and apply them in life.

*T*he last Independence Day message which Sardar Patel delivered
was on August 15, 1950. His eloquent words deserve to be taught
and read in every school and college. They come from the deep
anguish in his heart, and require to be quoted in extenso:

> Certain tendencies and developments in our
> administrative and public affairs fill me with some
> disquiet and sadness of heart. The country can realize
> the feelings of one who has spent the major part of his
> public life in witnessing epics of sacrifice and selfless
> endeavour and feats of discipline and unity and who
> now finds enacted before him scenes which mock at the
> past.

Our public life seems to be degenerating into a fen of stagnant waters: our conscience is troubled with doubts and despair about the possibilities of improvement. We do not seem to be profiting either from history or experience. We appear helplessly to be watching the sickle of time taking away the rich corn, leaving behind the bare and withered stalks.

Yet the tasks that confront us are as complex and taxing as ever. They demand the best in us while we face them with indifferent resources. We seem to devote too much time to things that hardly matter and too little to those that count. We talk, while the paramount need is that of action. We are critical of other people's exertions, but lack the will to contribute our own. We are trying to overtake others by giant strides while we have hardly learnt to walk...

On this, the third milestone of our career as a free country, I hope my countrymen will forgive me if I have tried to turn the searchlight inwards. In my life, I have now reached a stage when time is of the essence. Age has not diminished the passion which I bear to see my country great and to ensure that the foundations of our freedom are well and securely laid. Bodily infirmity has not dimmed my ardour to exert my utmost for the peace, prosperity and advancement of the Motherland. But 'the bird of time has a little way to fly, and lo! it is on the wing'.

With all the sincerity and earnestness at my command and claiming the privilege of age, I, therefore, appeal to my fellow countrymen on this solemn and auspicious day to reflect on what they see in and around themselves and, with the strength and faith that comes from self-introspection, sustain the hope and confidence which an old servant of theirs still has in the future of our country.

He had the strength to speak out, bluntly and fearlessly, to his own party. At the Nasik session of the Congress on September 19, 1950, he said:

> The goal of *purna swaraj* must claim our constant attention. The question which every Congressman must ask himself, or herself, is whether we have met this claim or demand. If we are honest with ourselves and true to our conscience, I am afraid, the reply must be in the negative. The greatest danger to the Congress comes from within rather than without.

Our greatest tragedy is that the lessons taught by this outstanding Indian patriot and statesman who unquestionably ranks in the world class, are so little remembered today.

By the test of the impact which he made on his contemporaries, Sardar Patel must be regarded as one of the greatest Indians of this century.

"Jawaharlal is a thinker and Sardar is a doer," said Gandhiji at the Karachi session of the Congress in 1931. The Sardar was also a thinker but not an impractical visionary.

Lord Wavell wrote in his diary that Sardar Patel "is certainly the most impressive of the Congress leaders and has the best balance". The Sardar shared Wavell's belief that India can be governed firmly, or not at all.

President Rajendra Prasad wrote in May 1959:

> That there is today an India to think and talk about, is very largely due to Sardar Patel's statesmanship and firm administration.... Yet we are apt to ignore him.

The India of today is certainly not the India of Sardar Patel's dreams. After five and forty years of independence, the picture that emerges is that of a nation potentially great but in a state of moral decay. We suffer from an unchecked dissolution of values. We have no sense of shame or shock that we run a third-class democracy under a first-class Constitution.

What a transformation could be effected if we relearn the values which Sardar Vallabhbhai Patel stood for! The environment will change beyond recognition when we instal *dharma* on the throne again. The country is crying aloud for moral leadership, fearless and forthright, which will tell the people — as Sardar Patel did — what does not flatter them and what they do not want to hear.

Sir Asutosh Mookerjee
India's Greatest Educationist

*P*resident John F. Kennedy once gave a dinner party at the White House where he invited Nobel laureates in literature and various disciplines of science, and in the course of his address to them observed, "I think this is the most extraordinary collection of talent, of human knowledge, that has ever been gathered at the White House — with the possible exception of when Thomas Jafferson dined alone."

Sir Asutosh Mookerjee, the 125th anniversary of whose birth was celebrated in Calcutta last week, had an extraordinarily wide-ranging mind and a sweep of knowledge and intellectual pursuits which equalled Jefferson's. As Dr. R. P. Paranjpye, himself a Senior Wrangler, remarked, "If Asutosh had made up his mind to devote himself entirely to the study of mathematics, he was sure to have secured a place in the front rank of world mathematicians."

Like Jefferson, Asutosh was a devoted educationist. Jefferson left instructions that on his tombstone should be inscribed the epitaph which does not mention that he had been the President of the United States but that he was the "Founder of the University of Virginia". Asutosh shared Jefferson's passion for higher education. "Nothing," said Asutosh in a reminiscent mood in 1920, "is dearer to me than my University." The ambition of his life was to be a research professor in mathematics at the Calcutta University; but since money could not be collected to fund a chair for

(Speech at Calcutta under the auspices of the Bharatiya Vidya Bhavan, July 1989. Later, The Times of India, July 16, 1989)

him, he drifted into law.

He became a judge of the Calcutta High Court in 1904 and resigned in December 1923, officiating for a few months as the Chief Justice in 1920. (His son, Mr. Rama Prasad, in turn, became the Chief Justice of that High Court, and his grandson, Chittatosh, held the same august office until he assumed the Chief Justiceship in Bombay.)

Asutosh undoubtedly ranks as one of the greatest judges modern India has produced. In his own words, "The law is neither a trade nor a solemn jugglery but a living science in the proper sense of the word." As a judge he displayed "that highest kind of integrity — the integrity of scholarship".

But his claim to the nation's gratitude lies even more in the way he transformed Indian education beyond recognition. At the age of 25 Asutosh was nominated a Fellow of the Calcutta University and was elected to the Senate and the Syndicate. In 1906 he became the Vice-Chancellor. His tenure was marked by indomitable boldness, unflinching courage and incredible vigour. No other educationist of India has equalled his achievement in its span and its dynamism. At the commencement of his Vice-Chancellorship the Calcutta University had one professor and a few lecturers. When his last term came to an end, the University had 25 professors and about a hundred lecturers.

He had the intuitive gift of spotting men of unusual ability, and that enabled him to usher in the Golden Age of the Calcutta University. It was he who recruited Dr. C. V. Raman as Professor of Physics, and made it possible for Dr. S. Radhakrishnan to do his memorable work as Professor of Philosophy. He converted the Calcutta University from merely an examining institution into an academy for teaching and research, untrammelled by official control and interference. He believed that teaching should not merely impart predigested knowledge but actively ensure its advance by constant research.

With his forward-looking mind and far-seeing spirit he realized that the function of science is not to supply the means of making life a closed circuit of consumption and acquisition but to promote intellectual emancipation. The pursuit of science would enable the student to "know the Truth which would set him free from the bondage of superstition and the slavish regard for authority".

Asutosh was one of the great integrators of modern India. He took all India to be his province. He introduced the M.A. degree in various Indian languages and literatures and insisted that the degree in any vernacular would also require proficiency in some other modern Indian language such as Hindi, Urdu, Marathi, Gujarati, Tamil, Telugu or Oriya. Dr. Radhakrishnan who was particularly struck by the significance of this innovation said, "Genius anticipates experience" when he opened the Asutosh Institute of Languages in Calcutta in 1964.

One of the happy observations of Asutosh is that the word 'Sanskrit' though composed of only eight letters connotes, in the domain of knowledge, an empire by itself. But fully conscious as he was that Indian culture is an amalgam of various cultures, he gave the same impetus to Islamic and Buddhist studies as he gave to Vedic scholarship.

Asutosh wanted the university to be a generator of excellence, an institution for producing movers of people, mobilizers of opinion. In his own words, "The university is thus the instrument of the State for the conservation of knowledge, for the discovery of knowledge, for the application of knowledge, and above all, for the creation of knowledge-makers."

He was totally devoid of any insular or parochial approach and was ever ready to accept what is valuable in Western civilization. In his Convocation Address to the Mysore University in 1918 he said, "We cannot sit on the lovely snow-capped peaks of the Himalayas in contemplation of our glorious past. We cannot waste our precious time and strength in defence of theories and systems which, however valuable in their own days, have been swept away by the irresistible avalanche of worldwide changes. We can live neither in nor by our defeated past and if we would live in the conquering future, we must dedicate our whole strength to shape its course." But while he wanted the nation to appropriate all that is wholesome in the West, he did not want the elite of India to be mindless imitators of Western culture. To the young to whom he was always close, he said, "Disregard not all that is most sublime in Indian thought. Neglect not in the glare of Western light the priceless treasures that are your inheritance. In your just admiration of all that is best in the culture of the West, do not under any circumstances denationalize yourselves."

Asutosh believed that the benefit of liberal education should be made available to as wide a segment of society as possible and that the activities of the university should be assimilated with the life of the nation. His prophetic warning was, "If we do not thus bring ourselves into intimate touch with the progress of national life, we shall have a government of the many by the few instead of a government by all."

Two generations ahead of his times, Asutosh saw the necessity of interface and interaction between the university and industry. "Industry and education will march forward, more and more, hand in hand, for this is pre-eminently a time to awaken industry and education alike."

He shared the religion of Swami Vivekananda who at one time was his fellow-student at the Presidency College — "Glory to God in the Highest and Service to Man".

It is a measure of the sick and anaemic condition of our education today that the lives and thoughts of men like Asutosh are not prescribed studies in our schools and colleges which are content to churn out ethical blockheads.

(Sir Asutosh was born on June 29, 1864, and died on May 25, 1924)

Centenary of Dr. B.R. Ambedkar

*D*r. Bhimrao Ramji Ambedkar was born on April 14, 1891 and died on December 6, 1956. He was the main architect of consummate skill and fidelity who, between 1947 and 1950, designed the structure which "has been reared for immortality, if the work of man may justly aspire to such a title."

When Beverley Nichols visited India in 1945, he took the opportunity of meeting most of the great figures in India's public life; and he described Dr. Ambedkar as "one of the six best brains in India."

The country owes Dr. Ambedkar an immeasurable debt of gratitude which can never be repaid. He strove single-mindedly to bring about the social integration of India, just as Sardar Vallabhbhai Patel brought about its political integration.

The most impressionable years of Dr. Ambedkar's life were spent as an untouchable *Mahar* in conditions tantamount to slavery without society recognizing even its obligation to feed the slave. For the untouchables the harshness of life was so characterized by malnutrition, illiteracy, disease, squalid surroundings, high infant mortality and low life expectancy as to be beneath any reasonable definition of human decency.

Edwin Markham's poignant words about the brutalized toiler serve to sum up the condition of the Indian untouchable:

(Doordarshan, April 1991)

Bowed by the weight of centuries he leans
Upon his hoe and gazes on the ground,
The emptiness of ages in his face,
And on his back the burden of the world.
Who made him dead to rapture and despair,
A thing that grieves not and that never hopes,
Stolid and stunned, a brother to the ox?
Who loosened and let down this brutal jaw?
Whose was the hand that slanted back this brow?
Whose breath blew out the light within this brain? ......

Through this dread shape the suffering ages look;
Time's tragedy is in that aching stoop;
Through this dread shape humanity betrayed,
Plundered, profaned and disinherited,
Cries protest to the Powers that made the world,
A protest that is also prophecy.

Those were bitter memories; but Dr. Ambedkar laid them down when India had a rebirth. It was India's good fortune that Dr. Ambedkar became the Chairman of the Drafting Committee of Free India's Republican Constitution. He presided over the group — the galaxy of talent — who conceived for the new republic a fundamental law dedicated to justice and liberty; to equality of status and opportunity; and to fraternity assuring the dignity of the individual and the unity of the nation. Chief Justice Mehr Chand Mahajan (whose centenary was celebrated two years ago) rightly called it "our sublime Constitution".

Dr. Ambedkar was too big a man to harbour any thought of vengeance or vendetta, ill-will or revenge, towards those who had been exploiting casteism from time immemorial. He gave India a constitution which guarantees equality to all as its basic feature, and ensures a truly egalitarian society where no class would be unprivileged, underprivileged or privileged on grounds of religion, race, caste, sex, descent, place of birth or residence.

While Mahatma Gandhi called the untouchables *Harijans* —

children of God — Dr. Ambedkar was convinced that such soothing nomenclature meant nothing. He asked the people not to forget that "whitewashing does not save a dilapidated house. You must pull it down and build anew". He firmly believed in annihilation of the caste system, and wanted to rid our society totally of this canker. He drew a sharp distinction "between social reform in the sense of reforms of the Hindu family, and social reform in the sense of the reorganization and reconstruction of the Hindu society. The former has relation to widow remarriage, child marriage, etc., while the latter related to the abolition of caste."

Dr. Ambedkar's philosophy was that self-respect and human dignity were of paramount importance in a free republic. As he told his followers two years before his death, "Ours is a battle not for wealth or for power. It is a battle for freedom. It is a battle for the reclamation of human personality."

He had an unshakable faith in guaranteed Fundamental Rights. He said in the Constituent Assembly, "The Declaration of the Rights of Man... has become part and parcel of our mental make-up.... These principles have become the silent, immaculate premise of our outlook."

To Dr. Ambedkar the unit of society was the individual, never the caste or the village. He wholly disbelieved in the glib claptrap about the glories of the Panchayat Raj and observed: "...these village republics have been the ruination of India. What is the village but a sink of localism, a den of ignorance, narrow-mindedness and communalism. I am glad that the draft constitution has discarded the village and adopted the individual as the unit."

Dr. Ambedkar's great vision enjoined the abolition of casteism in every shape and form, since he was opposed to all divisive forces and aimed at strengthening the impulse of national integration. The ideals of fraternity and equality were the cement with which he wanted to bind together a totally cohesive nation.

The highest tribute we can pay Dr. Ambedkar on his centennial is to redouble our efforts to preserve the Constitution which endures as a lasting monument to the man who was one of the noblest sons of India.

It is not a fortuitous accident, but a coincidence of deep symbolic significance, that the Supreme Court has been called upon to decide, in the centenary year of Dr. Ambedkar's birth, the validity of the Mandal Commission's Report in the context of the sanctity of the Constitution.

Centenary of Chief Justice
Mehr Chand Mahajan

*I*n the current year falls the birth centenary of an unusually large cluster of great Indians, one of whom was Justice Mehr Chand Mahajan. His birth on December 23, 1889 was declared highly inauspicious by the astrologers, with the result that he was sent away from home and placed in a Rajput peasant's family.

Justice Mahajan touched life at many points. Among the roles that he filled with distinction were those of advocate, judge, educator, administrator, and political thinker. His tenure as the Prime Minister of Kashmir about the time of its accession to India was of critical importance to the future of our country. He could stand high above the storm and keep his head when all about him were losing theirs. He was a big man in more senses than one.

As a judge of the Federal Court and of the Supreme Court, Mahajan has an indubitable claim to the veneration of the nation. A man of sturdy independence and uncompromising intellectual integrity, he was the exact opposite of the "committed judge" whom one writer has described as the mouse that squeaks under the Home Minister's chair.

What struck you most when you appeared in the court of Mahajan was his massive intellect. He had the rare capacity to go to the jugular vein of every case. However complicated the matter, he could wade through hundreds of pages, cut through verbiage, and put his finger unerringly on the crucial issues. Few judges have equalled him in legal acumen and analytical faculty. It was his

(The Times of India, December 24, 1989)

grasp over the essentials which enabled him to write judgments which were exemplary in their conciseness and lucidity, and which blazed a new trail in different fields.

During his tenure as the Chief Justice of India he constituted a bench of the Supreme Court which sat during vacation in order to dispose of criminal cases quickly. When he retired in December 1954, he left no arrears for his successor.

Mahajan's lifework bears witness to his wholehearted devotion to the imperishable values of our Constitution and his total commitment to the inalienable human rights. In one of his early judgments he coined the memorable phrase — "our sublime Constitution".

The country owes him a deep debt of gratitude for the vision and courage with which he chalked out the lines of development of our constitutional law when it was still in its infancy.

Mahajan did not suffer fools gladly: he snappily put an end to any argument which savoured of cant or humbug. Detesting hair-splitting technicalities of the law, he enjoyed listening to a crisp, precise and logical presentation from counsel. He would cut short any long drawn out or illogical submission and gave short shrift to any repetitive advocate. I never found him interrupt a good argument or endure the prolongation of a bad one.

Like all great men, he was devoid of any feeling of self-importance. It was a pleasure to see him turn his incisive sense of humour often against himself. He was a great sport and never misunderstood a counsel's submission, however forcefully critical of judges and judgments.

His memory was truly astounding and his industry prodigious. He invariably read the voluminous record of every case before the hearing began and was able to recall the essential facts and figures with unfailing accuracy. Never once did I find his grasp weaken or his memory fail.

He was a true patriot to the core and was passionately convinced that the unity and integrity of India counted above everything else. He had the grand vision of the different states of India living together in harmony and goodwill. Nothing caused him greater anguish than the sight of Indian states quarrelling with one another like the barons in the Mediaeval Age. Exhibition of communal hatred, linguistic fanaticism, and regional parochialism was anathema to him. In his own words, "Our past history teaches and tells a sad tale of disintegration, mutual quarrels, bickerings and fights, and thus of becoming slaves. Our leaders and thinkers have to fight against history repeating itself and have to devise effective safeguards against any repetition of our past political condition."

In view of our deplorable divisiveness (the main flaw in Indian character), Mahajan strongly advocated a drastic constitutional change. He wanted to "end provincial autonomy and autonomous states and convert the Constitution of India from a federation to a unitary, democratic, parliamentary form with parliamentary supremacy and one central ministry"; and maintained that "that is the only sound safeguard against the future disruption and disintegration of the country and that it is the best way to meet the challenge of history repeating itself."

Almost all political pundits are agreed that Justice Mahajan's suggestion regarding the abolition of states cannot now be implemented in practice, since it would alter the basic structure of the Constitution and create an unmanageable national upheaval. But the very fact that so great a mind as Mahajan's was driven to make such a suggestion shows the extent to which he was disturbed by the fissiparous tendencies in our country.

Mehr Chand Mahajan died on December 12, 1967. The story of his crowded life is set out in his autobiography *Looking Back* which is a book of absorbing interest. It relates one incident which affords a typical example of the debasement and degradation of our national life. Mahajan as the Constitutional Adviser to the Bikaner State, along with the Chief Justice of that State, constituted a Tribunal which held a public inquiry into the conduct of the Home Minister in the matter of the grant of permits for export of gram and other foodstuffs out of the State. One of the witnesses was a widely respected businessman who gave evidence on oath that he had given Rs. 2 lakhs for obtaining a permit for export of gram and had made a profit of Rs. 4 lakhs in that deal. In his account books the sum of Rs. 2 lakhs paid to the Minister had been shown as an advance to his minor children. Mahajan angrily asked the witness whether giving a bribe was not reprehensible conduct on his part. The witness — unfazed and without the slightest tinge of shame or guilt — said, "We are businessmen. Had the permit not been given to us we could not have made Rs. 4 lakhs. What does it matter if we share this 4 lakh profit with the person who granted us the permit?"

I would like to recall three reminiscences of the cases I argued before Justice Mahajan.

On one occasion, Mr. Motilal Setalvad, the Attorney General, sought to argue that no limited company could claim the protection of Article 19 of the Constitution even if all its shareholders were citizens of India. His submission was that a limited company is a separate legal entity and it could not be called a citizen of India, while Article 19 applied only to citizens. Justice Mahajan, always impatient with hypertechnical arguments, turned to Mr. Setalvad and said, "Mr. Attorney, I do not think you should urge such a proposition which would work against the interests of the citizens of India. If you persist, we are quite willing to give a judgment against the Government and rule that citizens do not lose their rights under Article 19 merely because they get incorporated as a company." The Attorney General abandoned the argument.

On another occasion, we had a case before Justice Mahajan where the question was whether the State had the right to prevent a student from being educated in an English medium school. Politicians vied with one another in misconceived populism — they loved to send their own children abroad, while they pampered linguistic or regional fanaticism by insisting upon citizens being denied the right to send their children to English medium schools. The states of Maharashtra and Gujarat passed foolish laws to the effect that no child could be sent to an English medium school unless the child's mother tongue was English. The Attorney General argued on behalf of the State that the law constituted a reasonable restriction on the citizen's liberty and was in the public interest. Justice Mahajan, presiding over the Bench, turned to Mr. Setalvad and asked, "Mr. Attorney, where is your own son being educated?" At that time, Mr. Setalvad's only son — who has now attained eminence in the profession as Atul Setalvad — was being educated in England. Mr. Setalvad's response was, "My Lords, I am not presenting to you my own view in the matter. I am merely making submissions on behalf of my client — the State." Justice Mahajan rejoined, "Very well, Mr. Attorney, we now understand your position. Please proceed, and we are sure you would make the argument as brief as possible." Needless to add, the argument failed and the parent's right to educate the child through the medium of instruction chosen by the parent was upheld in a strong judgment.

I was once arguing a case before him where I submitted that the preamble to an Act could be referred to, for controlling the meaning of a section, when there was ambiguity. Justice Mahajan observed, "Counsel argue differently in different cases, as it suits them. If the preamble supports your case, you say it ought to be looked at; and if the preamble is against you, you say it has to be ignored. How can lawyers indulge in such inconsistencies?" I replied, "Why blame the lawyers, my Lord? Why not blame the judges? You have judgments supporting both viewpoints. When the judge finds that the preamble supports the decision he would like to give, he relies on it; but when he finds that the preamble is against his view, he rules that the preamble cannot control the section." Then I referred to judgments which supported reliance on the preamble, and also those which ruled that the preamble should be ignored. Justice Mahajan took the whole argument in total good humour.

*B*ehind a rough exterior, Mahajan hid a remarkably warm heart and a generous spirit. Not even his family members were aware of the number of people he helped and the young men and women who found their feet with his assistance at the commencement of their career. In this centenary year, innumerable persons will recall reminiscences of the best portion of Mahajan's life — his little, nameless, unremembered acts of kindness and of love.

Sumant Moolgaokar

As an architect of a new undertaking, Sumant Moolgaokar was in the world class of the most dynamic entrepreneurs. He combined a creative mind with a high-octane passion for perfection. To him perfection was a goal, never quite reached but always sought after. He had an eye for the scarcest resource of all — talent; and he could bring out the best in his team. No one worked *under* him: everyone worked *with* him. Emperors rule, but leaders motivate. He could motivate the workforce to the pitch where they became emotionally involved in the company they served. He could galvanize them into action and make the job exciting for each one of them. This was the secret of his spectacular success in Telco. With him as the head of the organization, every worker was made to feel that he was not merely a cog in a big machine; he was not attending to a forge or a furnace but was helping to build and advance a great industrial enterprise, to erect a national monument. It is this quality of leadership which enabled him to make a great success of ACC before he joined Telco.

With his razor-sharp mind, he always saw a decade ahead. Extravagance was wholly alien to his nature. It is difficult to imagine the office of the Chairman of a large company more spartan in its furnishing than Sumant's office in Telco.

Integrity and self-effacement came as naturally to him as deviousness and ostentation come to some others.

(Condolence Meeting, Bombay, July 10, 1989)

Sumant combined outstanding engineering talent with receptivity and unfeigned modesty. He would have periodic meetings of the executive officers in Bombay, Pune and Jamshedpur, where each one was free to express his own views. Sumant would listen with particular attention to views contrary to his own, and tried to see how far that opposite view was valid. He always bore himself at manhood's simple level.

Sumant loved nature — "the silence that is in the starry sky, the sleep that is among the lonely hills". He loved birds and trees and the wind upon the heath, and "saw the brightness of the skirts of God". He felt a mystic kinship with the animate and the inanimate world — in that sense he was in tune with the Infinite. Ecology and environment were to him paramount considerations which were non-negotiable. His was, par excellence, a life with a theme, a life dedicated to the great thinker's ideal:

> To see as far as one may;
> To feel the great forces that lie behind every detail;
> To hammer out as solid and compact a piece of work
> as one can;
> And to leave it unadvertized.

M. P. Birla

*I*ndia has lost a fine being — human and humane — in the death of Mr. M. P. Birla. He was an eminent industrialist who, in the years before his illness, had a business career distinguished by efficiency and dynamism. As a devoted soldier in India's struggle for independence, he had imbibed Mahatma Gandhi's qualities of rectitude, nobility and simplicity.

He gave of himself to a number of public causes which were doing quiet public service. Being totally devoid of ego, and instinctively averse to self-advertisement, he gave large sums to charitable causes without ever expecting or allowing his name to be associated with his generous donations.

Thousands of people make money; very few have the magnanimity and the discernment to spend it wisely. Mr. M. P. Birla was one of those select few. His contribution to the growth and expansion of the Bharatiya Vidya Bhavan was princely, particularly in the development of its UK Centre.

A perceptive devotee of India's priceless culture and religious heritage, he started (in the Bhavan) a Sarva Dharma Seva Pratishthan for repairing and renovating countless places of worship in various states. The fruits of his munificence, unannounced and unrelated to his name, may be found in different parts of India, including the birthplace of Adi Sankaracharya.

(Press Release, July 30, 1990)

Naoroji P. Godrej

*A*ugust 8th is a day of hallowed memory in the history of India.
On August 8, 1942, the Quit India resolution was adopted by
the Congress Party. The British did quit India. Then came the basic
task of building a free nation. One of those who played an
outstanding role in building a strong national economy and in
putting India on the industrial map of the world was Seth Naoroji
Pirojsha Godrej. Exactly forty-eight years after the Quit India
resolution, on August 8, 1990, Naoroji passed away.

In the entire history of India there have been few families
which, single-handed and without public participation in share
capital, have done as much as the Godrej family for the industri-
alization of the country.

Over 80,000 MBAs are churned out every year by American
and European schools — a stereotypical mass. Naoroji, unaided by
formal education at college, managed to take his enterprises right
to the top and compete successfully with large public companies
financed by lakhs of shareholders.

Naoroji, like other members of the Godrej clan, was a staunch
and perceptive nationalist. He combined great ability as an
entrepreneur with wide vision and sterling nobility of character. In
industry, he maintained the highest standards of business ethics
and public service. His philanthropy, like Jamsetji Tata's, was
constructively directed towards removal of the cause, and not the

(Condolence Meeting called by the Bombay Parsi Punchayet, September 27, 1990)

symptoms, of poverty and ignorance. Of him it could be truly said, "He had an intelligent heart and a kind brain."

He was deeply involved in the well-being of his workers and dealt with their problems with enlightened compassion. No industrial family has shown greater personal involvement in the problems of housing and education, medical care and welfare, of its employees than the House of Godrej. Mrs. Lillian Carter, the mother of President Carter, who worked for two years at Vikhroli as a volunteer in the Peace Corps, told me that what was being done for Godrej workers was comparable to the best achieved in the West. It is to the eternal disgrace of the militant section of our trade unionists that such an ideal employer should have had such a savage and dastardly attack made on him twelve years ago.

I first met Naoroji fifty-four years back. Around 1936 a friend of mine, who was employed as an engineer in the Godrej Works, took me to the factory at Lalbaug. He introduced me to Pirojsha's son, Naoroji. He told me that the young man who was not even twenty years old was already making an incredible mark at the Works. It was a sight to make surrounding workers stare — a concern trusted to a schoolboy's care!

In the ensuing decades I met Naoroji off and on in the course of my professional career. Neither he nor I was ever on the cocktail circuit, so our meetings were less frequent than I would have liked them to be.

A few years ago Naoroji met me when he was invited to join the Board of Trustees of the Bombay Parsi Punchayet. He asked me what I thought of his joining the Board. I pressed him hard to accept the invitation, because he was the man who could give a lead to the community instead of being led by the community. It would be so refreshing to have a Trustee who did not face backwards. It would be the good fortune of Parsis to have a leader who would make them realize that while the world moved on, their conventional orthodoxy was wholly obsolescent.

The last time I met Naoroji was at Godrej Baug when we talked about the construction of a new building. He had driven himself there in his small car, attired as always in simple clothes. I was proud to be in the presence of a man who had created such enormous wealth for the nation and spent so little of it on himself. The ideal of plain living and high thinking did not have a more dedicated exponent.

Naoroji had deep concern for his co-religionists. A man of his calibre and dedication could have done so much for Parsis if only they had been less hopelessly mired in crass ignorance, persistent unwisdom and thoughtless conformism.

Naoroji realized that the main problem facing the community was of housing. He, therefore, financed the construction of Godrej Baug on the Parsi Punchayet lands at Malabar Hill, and evolved the idea of taking modest donations from those who got the benefit of the apartments. Those donations were admittedly not intended for anyone's personal benefit but were earmarked to finance more housing schemes in order to provide shelter to the long waiting list of Zoroastrians. Naoroji was totally right, but he was far ahead of the community whom he sought to benefit. Unfortunately, his work as a Parsi Punchayet Trustee was not appreciated as deeply as it deserved to be. He resigned, painfully conscious that there was so little done while there was so much to do.

A thinker has observed that Christianity has been tried and has failed: the religion of Christ remains to be tried. The same can be said about every other religion — such is the universal propensity to encrust and encumber truth with dogma, religion with ritual, essence with trappings. Naoroji went straight to the truth behind the dogma, the religion behind the ritual, the essence behind the trappings. He not only believed in, but quietly practised, the true religion of Zarathushtra — the faith enjoining pure thoughts, pure words and pure deeds.

The Padma Bhushan was conferred on him, but it added nothing to his stature. All his life he had cared for honour, not honours.

Naoroji is no more but we will continue to feel his spirit as a living presence, full of light. He "banked his treasure in the hearts of his friends, and they will cherish his memory till their time is come."

Ramnath Goenka

*I*n the passing of Ramnathji, India has lost one of her most remarkable sons. He was a dedicated citizen who used his enormous powers as a newspaper proprietor for what he believed to be the good of the country. He acted on his conviction that the press should never be a poodle of the establishment but should act as the watchdog of democracy. He believed that a courageous and independent press is the noblest servant of society along with a courageous and independent judiciary.

He was dead against any form of tyranny by the State. He always adhered to the unshakable belief, which he shared with Bernard Levin, that barbed wire will rust, stone walls will crumble and the tyrant's club will shatter in his fist. During the Emergency, when most papers and journals capitulated, Ramnathji asserted his sturdy independence at colossal personal cost. In later years, when the Government — to its eternal disgrace — launched more than 200 prosecutions against Ramnathji and his companies in different courts of India, he faced the onslaught unflinchingly and with terrier-like tenacity.

Ramnath Goenka was one of the rare, select band of men of whom it can be truly said that they have the courage never to submit or yield. In his later years he was bent with age, but never with fear. To the end, he remained untamed and unbroken.

(Press Release, October 7, 1991)

14

The Press

The Fourth Estate

*M*y congratulations to your Society on its completing fifty years. Having completed half a century means that you have lived through more than one-fifth of the total life of the press in the whole world, since the press is less than 250 years old. Perhaps never in world history has a single institution acquired such fantastic power in such a short span of time. The press is one of the great powers of the twentieth century. Disraeli, foreseeing the growing importance of the press, called it the Fourth Estate.

Freedom is to the press what oxygen is to the human being; it is the essential condition of its survival. To talk of a democracy without a free press is a contradiction in terms. A free press is not an optional extra in a democracy.

I would like to recall the example of Winston Churchill during the last War (1939-45). As the Prime Minister of England he had limitless power to stifle criticism. Britain was fighting, for bare survival, the bloodiest of wars. Churchill permitted the press to criticize him and journalists like Malcolm Muggeridge were allowed to indulge in scathing disparagement of the Prime Minister. When various friends and foreign powers pleaded with Churchill to prevent ill-informed criticism, Churchill refused to stifle press freedom and pointed out that he wanted the world to know how a free nation could permit press freedom to flourish, even when the country's very existence was in peril. In the words of a great judge, "A cantankerous press, an obstinate press, a

(The Golden Jubilee Valedictory Function of The Indian Newspaper Society, Delhi, September 29, 1989)

ubiquitous press, must be suffered by those in authority in order to preserve the even greater values of freedom of expression and the right of the people to know."

There are 159 members of the United Nations, and all of them are signatories to the Universal Declaration of Human Rights, of which Article 19 guarantees the freedom of the press. But there is a surprising contrast between the theoretical acceptance of the Universal Declaration of Human Rights and the actual practice of nations. Out of the 159 signatories to the Declaration, only one-fifth allow freedom of the press in actual fact. We Indians are one of that fortunate one-fifth. In the whole of Asia total freedom of the press is unknown except in Japan, India and Israel, and now Pakistan.

Openness is a concomitant of a free society. Men in power try to control and corrupt the press because they would not like anything to be known by the public which would detract from the respect, the acclaim and the adulation to which they think they are entitled. This creates a conflict between rulers who are the keepers of secrets and the press who are the tellers of tales. Take, for example, Lee Kuan Yew who has been to Singapore what Jawaharlal Nehru has been to India. Lee Kuan Yew said in 1964 that he would like openness, and that a closed society produces closed minds. Yet, unfortunately, despite his greatness, he has become increasingly intolerant of a free press, bearing out the truth of Lord Acton's dictum that power tends to corrupt and absolute power corrupts absolutely.

This is not to say that the press is free from blemish. It is not. It errs, as all human institutions do. To make the press worthy of the absolute freedom it is entitled to enjoy, there must be self-regulation, just as the legal and accountancy professions have. There must be a body to which the press is accountable.

Journalism is not a business; it is a profession. A professional should be ready to accept standards and a sense of values.

Unfortunately, the 1980s has been a degraded decade — even professions like the legal, accountancy and medical professions, have become commercialized. The same evil has afflicted journalism. Professions have sunk to the lower level of business. We are living in times when professional or business ethics sounds like an oxymoron, a contradiction like a hot ice-cube or a tiny giant. Today the main idea of most newspapers, journals or magazines is to maximize readership, regardless of the higher values which ought to animate journalism.

Let me give you two examples of the higher standards which prevailed in the past. President Roosevelt was suffering from polio which made it impossible for him to walk without support. Newspapers were as free in those days as they are today and they could have published photographs of Roosevelt walking with the help of crutches or with human support. Yet newspapers did not publish any such photographs although Roosevelt continued to make news as one of the important world leaders year after year. The photographs which appeared in the press were those which showed Roosevelt either sitting or standing. This is self-regulation. There was no law which forbade the press to humiliate a great leader by showing him on crutches but it was a shining example of obedience to the unenforceable. Another example of what happened some years ago comes to the surface of my mind, when Mr. Harold Wilson was the Prime Minister of Britain. Mr. Brown, the Deputy Prime Minister was stepping out of the Houses of Parliament, after having had a drop too much, as was usual with him. As he came out, he stumbled and fell and had to be physically helped and put in his car. Unlike the tabloid newspapers, which loved to publish photographs which would titillate the baser instincts of the populace, *The Times* (of London) did not publish a photograph of the Deputy Prime Minister in his embarrassing predicament. But two days later *The Times* wrote a first editorial where it pointed out that it had decided, as a matter of self-regulation, not to publish such a photograph which would merely pander to the lower instincts of readers. Further, *The Times* added, "Mr. Brown drunk is any day preferable to Mr. Harold Wilson sober." This was a splendid example of self-regulation by a world famous newspaper. Most of us have personal knowledge of how some stories, emanating purely from the imagination of a "correspondent" are published as facts.

The press must make a sharp distinction between a story, the publication of which is dictated by public interest, and a story which is entirely sleazy and sensational. Where public interest is involved, it is not only the right but the duty of the press to expose the truth fully. Two books have recently been published which point out how the press failed in discharging this duty. The one published in the United States is entitled *On Bended Knee*. It shows how the press failed to expose to the public the intellectual limitations of President Ronald Reagan. The other book, published in Britain a few months ago, is called *The Twilight of Truth*. The theme of this book is that the press did not stand up against the inane policy of Austin Chamberlain which aimed at appeasing the monster Hitler and made the Second World War inevitable. I am proud as an Indian to say that there are quite a few newspapers in India which are truly the watchdogs of the republic and have no hesitation in speaking the truth, however unpalatable it may be to the powers that be.

If the Government of India allows freedom of the press, it is not a favour. Every government is *bound* under the Constitution to allow freedom of the press. Every intelligent Indian must be grateful to Providence for the fact that the Constitution of India was not drafted by men elected on the basis of adult franchise. Our Constitution, like the American Constitution, was drafted by men of profound learning, great vision, impeccable character, and absolute integrity, including intellectual integrity, who foresaw the unfolding future. A Constitution drafted by men elected on the basis of adult franchise would have been an absolute mess. We have seen how during the dark days of the Emergency (1975-77) the elected representatives of the people suffocated and choked the press without the slightest compunction — after having mortgaged their mind and their conscience to the party in power.

But freedom of the press can be indirectly stifled by certain governmental decisions which are not really conducive to a free press.

Our newspapers would have several times larger circulation but for the fact that the majority of our population is illiterate. In fact it has been estimated by the World Bank that by the beginning of the next century every second illiterate person will be an Indian. Eighty per cent of Indian women are illiterate, and if you take males and females together, the percentage of illiteracy is still as high as 65 per cent. Our politicians in power have a vested interest in illiteracy. The more illiterate the populace, the less chances of the truth becoming known to them. We became a republic at the same time as South Korea. In South Korea literacy is as high as 98 per cent, as against India's deplorable record of 35 per cent literacy. This is the one area where the Government of India has totally failed the people, despite the injunction in Article 45 of the Constitution that the State shall endeavour to provide free and compulsory education for all children until they complete the age of fourteen years.

The best way to liquidate illiteracy is to make our masses interested in acquiring *information* and, better still, *knowledge*. The illiterate man has to be motivated to realize how much his children are losing by not being literate. The innate intelligence of an Indian is as good as that of any other national in the world. What a criminal waste of human resources in a country where two-thirds of the people cannot read or write!

In order that the press may not only be free but have a wider circulation, it is imperative that there should be no customs duty on the import of newsprint or on the printing machinery which is necessary for newspapers. It is our moral duty to ensure that needless hurdles in the way of the press reaching as wide a segment of the populace as possible are removed.

The cost of a free press is an ongoing cost. It is never fully paid. So long as there are some newspapers and journals which have the courage and the independence to stand up for what is believed to be right, there is bright hope for the future of this country. I trust that under a system of well-conceived self-regulation, our vibrant press will continue to give the guidance to the country which it so badly needs. A far greater responsibility lies on the press in a country like India where the radio and television are not only State-owned but unashamedly State-controlled.

The Persistence of Unwisdom in Government and the Duty to Dissent

When the history of India comes to be written a hundred years hence, the name of Minoo Masani will continue to shine brightly as one of the finest exemplars of the true values so fundamental, and so rare, in citizens. He will be remembered for his patriotism, his indomitable courage and his passionate love of freedom, when the names of countless politicians who have held high public offices in our country are totally submerged in the waters of Lethe. I thought no subject would be more appropriate in a volume intended to commemorate Minoo Masani's 80th birthday than the one to which his long public life has been single-mindedly devoted — The Duty to Dissent.

According to Barbara Tuchman, twice winner of the Pulitzer Prize, who recently wrote *An Inquiry into the Persistence of Unwisdom in Government,* governments act unwisely because politicians cannot admit error; they lust for power; they lack self-confidence and magnanimity; they are more interested in image than in substance; they rarely get the right information, let alone know how to act on it.

Democratically elected representatives of the people can act no less foolishly, and often no less oppressively, than authoritarian states. Hence the necessity of the right "to freedom of speech and expression" guaranteed by Article 19(1)(a) of our Constitution. The right to dissent is at the heart of every democracy. This right becomes the duty of every knowledgeable and right-minded

(Festschrift on Minoo Masani's 80th Birthday, 1985)

citizen, when government acts in a manner detrimental to civil liberties or otherwise against the public interest. The *right* to dissent is conferred by the Constitution; the *duty* to dissent is dictated by the realization that in a democracy citizens have to practise obedience to the unenforceable.

Justice Frankfurter expressed the pregnant thought that in a democracy the highest office is not that of the President but that of being a citizen. "Democracy is always a beckoning goal, not a safe harbour. For freedom is an unremitting endeavour, never a final achievement."

A study of history, regardless of the period or the type of government in authority, makes one wonder why man makes a poorer show of government than of almost any other human activity. In the field of governmental activity, wisdom — which may be defined as judgment acting on experience, common sense, available knowledge, and a keen appreciation of probability — is amazingly absent. Why do men in high office so often act contrary to the way that reason points and enlightened public interest enjoins? Why does intelligent mental process seem to be so often paralyzed?

Why did successive ministries of George III — that "bundle of imbecility" as Dr. Johnson called them collectively — insist on coercing rather than conciliating the thirteen Colonies which, as a result, broke away and declared themselves as a republic, destined to be the most powerful in the world — the United States of America? Why did Napoleon invade Russia and Hitler repeat the same mistake? Why did the Kaiser's government resume unrestricted submarine warfare in 1917 despite the clear warning that this would result in the entry of the United States into the war? Why did Chiang Kai-shek refuse to heed any voice of reform or alarm until he woke up to find that his country had been irretrievably lost to him?

Wooden-headedness is a characteristic feature of governments. Wooden-headedness assesses a situation in terms of preconceived fixed notions while ignoring or rejecting any contra indications. In short, it is the obstinate refusal to learn from experience.

Summing up this basic lesson of all history, Barbara Tuchman concludes, "Philosophers of government ever since Plato have devoted their thinking to the major issues of ethics, sovereignty, the social contract, the rights of man, the corruption of power, the balance between freedom and order. Few — except Machiavelli, who was concerned with government as it is, not as it should be — bothered with mere folly, although this has been a chronic and pervasive problem. More recently, Woodrow Wilson warned, 'In public affairs, stupidity is more dangerous than knavery'. . . . Meanwhile, bureaucracy rolls on impervious to any individual or cry for change, like some vast computer that when once penetrated by error goes on pumping it out forever."

Gibbon observed that human history is "little more than a register of the crimes, follies, and misfortunes of mankind". The history of the Republic of India for several years upto 1984 was a sorry chronicle of the follies of our administration.

*N*o impartial mind studying the history of the Indian republic over the last thirty-five years would have any doubt that one of the fundamental obligations of the ideal Indian citizen has been the duty to dissent. But how many citizens had the integrity and courage to fulfil this obligation during the thirty-five years of our republic? If this duty had not been performed, regardless of personal considerations, by the few brave and perceptive citizens like Minoo Masani at crucial moments, the history of this country would have been tragically different.

15

Miscellany

Redesigning India for the Twenty-first Century

*C*ynics might rightly remind me that we should bring India into the twentieth century preferably before we redesign it for the twenty-first. Today India lives in a moral vacuum. Bold surgery is needed to treat the diseased heart of a nation which was once great.

It is a vast subject which has to be looked at politically, socially and economically. We may cast a quick glance at what may be called "The Seven Pillars of Redesigned India". They are considered below, not necessarily in the order of importance.

*T*he first and foremost of the seven pillars is a sense of national identity. We have not found it even after thirty-eight years of independence. We have millions of Bengalis, millions of Maharashtrians, millions of Northerners and Southerners — but very few Indians. Parochial loyalties and communal fanaticism are the order of the day. They are a sure prescription for national disintegration.

The greatest enemy of India today is not Pakistan or China, but Indians themselves. No enemy can possibly weaken the country so effectively as Indians can. The defences of our democracy may be impregnable from without, but they are dangerously vulnerable

(K. Santhanam Memorial Lecture, under the auspices of the Bharatiya Vidya Bhavan, August 8, 1985)

from within.

However, hope springs eternal in the human breast. The poets, the patriots, the prophets and the *rishis* — who have loved India deeply and intensely — have predicted that Indians will acquire a sense of national identity and unity in the foreseeable future. Sri Aurobindo said, "I believe firmly that a great and united future is the destiny of this nation and its peoples. The power that brought us through so much struggle and suffering to freedom, will achieve also, through whatever strife or trouble, [this] aim... as it brought us freedom, it will bring us unity. A free and united India will be there and the Mother will gather around her her sons and weld them into a single national strength in the life of a great and united people."

The second pillar is the maintenance of law and order, which is the basic duty of every government. Law and order has broken down in most parts of India. In some parts, the situation is so serious that the army is in occupation, not in charge. The statistics given to Parliament last year showed that on an average the army was called out in India once every four days to do some job or the other. If you have to call out the army so often, you are likely to put ideas into the heads of military officers, which ideas they had better be without. It is true that the government is on the horns of a dilemma as in a Greek tragedy: whichever way they decide, they would be wrong. If they do not call out the army, they would be unable to cope with disorder and bloodshed. If they do call out the army fairly frequently, the very survival of democracy would be endangered.

The essential point is that while we cannot avoid calling out the army, let us avoid the necessity of calling out the army. We could avoid the necessity, if we have an efficient and honest police force.

In order to have an honest and efficient police force, it is imperative that it should be fully insulated from political domination.

But in reality, in most States the professional autonomy of the police force has been completely destroyed by political directives, political influences and political interferences.

The only alternative is to make the police force as autonomous as the judiciary or the auditor-general. The Government cannot seek to influence, or give directives to, the High Courts or the Supreme Court, or the auditor-general, and the police are entitled to the same professional independence. Unless the politicization of the police is ended, the frequent resort to the army will be unavoidable.

A professional and honourable police force is valuable in every society, but it is invaluable in a society like ours which is marked by three characteristics — divisiveness, indiscipline and non-cooperation.

Look at our divisiveness. We must have something to divide us — religion, language, caste, or whatever. If we have nothing to divide us, we would invent something which can possibly feed our divisiveness.

Indiscipline is somehow ingrained in Indian character. We are all individuals, and not the citizens of a cohesive society. The way we behave with total carelessness about public property, the propensity to walk on the road rather than on the footpath, the motorist making the maximum noise with the horn in the silence zone — are some of the regular, maddening manifestations of our total lack of discipline. Disorderly and undisciplined conditions are fatal to development.

Non-cooperation is the other distressing feature. People love not to co-operate with the forces of law and order. When we were fighting for our freedom, non-cooperation was a valuable weapon. But the persistence of this habit after we became a republic is most reprehensible, whether it takes the form of non-payment or evasion of taxes or any other form.

*T*he third priority of a redesigned India has to be family planning.

India can never make significant progress so long as the population keeps on increasing at the present rate. Family planning is not only desirable but amounts to a moral duty both of the Government and the people.

It has been estimated that a couple at the level of subsistence must have an average of 6.3 children in order to have a reasonable chance that one son survives till the father is sixty-five years old. There is also the other unfortunate fact that in parts of India female infanticide is prevalent as a means of restricting the size of the family. There is no gainsaying the fact that the problem is fraught with enormous difficulties. However, methods — humane but firm and effective — have to be found to restrict the rise in our population.

I come to the fourth pillar — education. It is closely linked to the necessity of family planning — the lowest birth rate is in Kerala where the level of education is the highest.

Education is at the heart of the matter. Confucius wrote, "If you plan for a year, plant a seed. If for ten years, plant a tree. If for one hundred years, teach the people."

Literacy is not enough. It is good to have a population which is able to read; but infinitely better to have people able to distinguish what is worth reading. Education is a subject included in the Concurrent List; but it is vital that value-based education should become a national preoccupation. In 1983 the Commission for Excellence in Education, appointed by the US Government, warned the American people in its Report, "The Nation At Risk", "The educational foundations of our society are presently being eroded by a rising tide of mediocrity that threatens our very future as a nation and a people." Our self-complacency is too overpowering to permit us to entertain such a self-critical thought.

*C*onstitutional integrity, which must be sharply distinguished from constitutional fundamentalism, may be named as the fifth pillar. While Pakistan has gone in for religious fundamentalism, India's besetting sin is secular fundamentalism.

We interpret our Constitution as if it were an exercise in grammar. We are intelligent enough to know full well that we are abusing and mocking at the Constitution by merely construing it literally — e.g., when issuing ordinances, or when the Centre dismisses Governors or governments of states. But we are so lacking in intellectual integrity that we pretend to have complied with the Constitution.

*T*he sixth column of a redesigned India should be egalitarianism. Fecund egalitarianism is in sharp contrast to the moss-grown, outworn creed of socialism. I wish India would be the first country in the world to call itself not socialist but egalitarian. We are in desperate need of a new route-map. Today India is the poorhouse of Asia; it can, and should, become the powerhouse of the continent. When a country is bumping along the bottom, there are only two ways to make the economy buoyant — change the policy and change the policy. As I have said before, egalitarianism means the investment of human and material resources in an imaginatively planned manner which can contribute to the vitality and progress of the whole nation, keep it in the mainstream of self-generating growth and development, raise the standard of living of the masses, and enhance the quality of life. While ideological socialism is within the reach of any fifth-rate politician, the translation of egalitarianism into action demands intellect and knowledge, character and dedication, of a very high order.

The late Mr. G. D. Birla once said, "I am interested in anything that creates more wealth, more employment. I am a capitalist, but I believe in a socialism which means equal opportunity, more employment and fairer standard of living for everyone. Socialism does not mean socialising poverty but raising the quality of life for one and all."

"Socially responsible business" may be termed the seventh pillar of a redesigned India. What a transformation one could effect in this country if only business houses were socially responsible!

As Vinoba Bhave pointed out to a group of businessmen some years ago, in ancient Indian society the businessman was looked upon with respect for many centuries. He was considered to be next only to the king. The king was known as Shahenshah while the businessman was known as Shah. People confidently left their property with the businessman, when they went for a *yatra* (pilgrimage). If they died, they were confident that the businessman would make a fair distribution among the heirs. If they returned, they were equally confident that the businessman could be trusted to return safely all their properties.

Today the malpractices of many businessmen have made society hostile to the class. Let the business community try to recapture that image of honour and integrity which made the trader the repository of implicit public confidence in centuries past.

"Fragrant Memories"

*T*his is an extraordinary book about an extraordinary soul. Dilip Kumar Roy — known as 'Dadaji' to his countless followers — was a most remarkable human being who spread light and joy wherever he went. Dadaji strove to make the earth a world of harmony, beauty, and love. He was a profound seer, philosopher, thinker and poet; but all his life he remained as simple as a child — unspoilt by the veneration and reverence in which he was universally held. His magic was not far to seek — he was so human! He had a transparent sincerity and unswerving regard for Truth. I had the privilege of knowing him, and the indelible impressions of his nobility and greatness remain etched upon my memory.

Sri Aurobindo had many disciples, and Dadaji was the most outstanding of them all. Despite all his greatness and scholarship, Dadaji had unfeigned modesty and humility. His work was an offering of love to his Creator. He was a living example of the fact that the higher a man is in Grace, the lower he will be in his own esteem.

As Dadaji said, "Grace involves responsibility". And he discharged that responsibility by ceaseless work. To quote Dadaji, "Work is *sadhana*". He wrote books which ranked only next to Sri Aurobindo's in their sweep of thought, spiritual insight and beauty of expression.

In the following pages, Indira Devi — more affectionately known as 'Ma' or 'Didiji' — has recalled Fragrant Memories of

(Preface to Indira Devi's Memoirs, 1993)

happenings and Dadaji's sayings which would otherwise have been lost to posterity. Indira Devi was to Dadaji what The Mother was to Sri Aurobindo. There was between them a relationship of ineffable beauty, enriched and ennobled by their deep spiritual impulse. In Indira Devi's own words, it was a relationship not only of a guru and disciple, a father and daughter, a teacher and pupil, but the relationship between two friends, two fellow pilgrims of eternity, with one goal and one path.

Dadaji and Indira Devi were originally in Sri Aurobindo Ashram and thereafter jointly ran Hari Krishna Mandir in Poona. In this book, Indira Devi has put down her recollections as they came to her mind or welled up in her heart. This spontaneous record of reminiscences seems preferable to a pre-arranged plan involving a strict logical order or sequence. As Indira recalls the various incidents and her conversations with Dadaji over a period of thirty-one years — 1949 to 1980 — she cannot help revealing the evolution of her own character and the transformation which she went through as a result of her association with Dadaji. Indira had the responsiveness, the nobility and the courage to give up a life of great luxury and comfort, and even her deep attachment to her dear ones including her children, after she came in contact with Dadaji. It is clear that she shared Dadaji's total sincerity and constant devotion to Truth.

Indira Devi had her consciousness raised to a higher plane which was in the realm of clairvoyance. She could see events before they manifested themselves and see things at a distance which the physical eye could not reach. On a number of occasions she heard the music and songs of Mirabai which she was able to reproduce later after she came out of the trance. Sometimes the songs came to her one at a time; sometimes they came in a torrent. Undoubtedly, there are more things in heaven and earth than are dreamt of in the rationalist's philosophy.

Dadaji had a soul saturated and dripping with music, and the devotion of Indira Devi to music was no less intense. Truly, both were Music incarnate. Indira authored hundreds of songs which Dadaji set to music.

One of the passages in this book has a bearing on the need for harmony between Hindus and Muslims, and is poignantly appropriate today. Our people must be spiritually dead if they are not moved by the fact that according to Dadaji one of the best translations of the *Gita* is by Professor Dil Mohammed, the Principal of the Islamic College, Lahore. In his Preface, Professor Dil Mohammed writes in Urdu, "*Gita* is one of the greatest spiritual books in the world. It explains to us what man is, what God is, what Love is, what knowledge is, what is the right way to work."

On his last day on earth — January 6, 1980 — Dadaji was his usual cheerful self, although aware of the impending end. Dadaji said, "Wash my hands. I have to touch the Lord's feet."

These Fragrant Memories are filled with echoes of the Lord's feet.

"The Days of My Years"

*T*his is the gripping story of a man who worked his way up from scratch to vertiginous heights. A displaced person, who had lost practically everything, rose to become a first-generation entrepreneur with the second largest industrial complex to his credit.

Hari Nanda had chosen his parents wisely. His father had an irrepressible spirit of adventure and an inexhaustible fund of good humour; and the eldest child inherited these qualities in his genes. Unfortunately, the father knew as much of ill-luck as Hari was ordained to know of good fortune.

It is an absorbing saga, filled to the brim with human interest. The book is marked by candour, veracity and sincerity, and with malice to none. It should serve as a source of encouragement and inspiration to those who are at the threshold of their careers and to whom the India of tomorrow belongs.

The historical importance of this autobiography is considerable. One of the builders of a new democracy out of an old nation tells the tale in his own words. The serried, kaleidoscopic changes follow in quick succession. The inhumanity and the mindless horrors of the Partition. The refugee — his faith and courage inviolate — determined to play his part in the land which gave him refuge. The urge to become a surge. Tractorloads of destiny's favours in an unending caravan.

Over the decades, well-deserved tributes have been paid to Hari Nanda and his achievements. High honours came to him thick and

---

(Preface to Hari Nanda's Autobiography, 1992)

fast from home and abroad. The unknown refugee was rubbing shoulders on equal terms with the greats of the world.

"And one man in his time plays many parts". Hari Nanda once ventured into the mired and treacherous field of politics. He lost the election at Gurgaon/Faridabad so dismally that he had to forfeit his deposit. This tells you more about the common voter's aversion to meritocracy than about Hari's own fitness to be a lawmaker. He began to understand the psychology of the "mass man", a malleable class of people, unthinking and easily exploited. As Bryce remarked, the greatest drawback of democracy is its tendency to throw mediocrity into power.

After his defeat, Hari Nanda adopted several villages in his erstwhile constituency and upgraded their infrastructure. He gave them improved roads, sanitation, and medical care centres; he planted trees and dug tubewells. In short, after he lost he did all the things that politicians piously promise when seeking election and invariably forget after they win.

The raid on Hari Nanda's residence and offices, and the Caparo incident, provide two of the most disgraceful examples of the raw abuse of power, which must make every Indian hold down his head in shame.

The section on Caparo — THE F(R)IGHT OF HARI'S LIFE — deserves the close attention of every student of public administration and public ethics. The only way to preserve democracy, said James Reston, is to raise hell about its shortcomings. The Caparo episode is a disgusting chapter in the history of our public financial institutions. It affords a striking illustration of the depths of degradation and favouritism to which India's public life had fallen: the arrogance of power, the shameless servility of the bureaucracy, the spinelessness of the spectators (the Indian business community) who knew what was right but did what was wrong. Only the press stood up courageously for the basic norms of decency in our public life. It was one man who suffered the onslaught of the entire governmental apparatus, and still remained unbowed and unsubdued. Strength comes as naturally to the strong as weakness comes to the weak. Hari Nanda had the inner strength, the courage never to submit or yield: the tiny yet searing flame which no Niagara of oppression, no dereliction of duty by those in authority, no miscarriage of justice, could ever extinguish. In the end, it was the victory of that one man over overwhelming odds.

The most lasting and valuable contributions of Hari Nanda have been prompted by his enlightened awareness of social responsibility both to his employees and to the community at large. You give back to the people in time, energy and care a part of what you have received from them. "Escorts' bottom line is not profits," says Hari, and even the most sceptical and unsympathetic of his readers will agree. If he had done nothing but founded the Escorts Employees Ancillaries Ltd., a historic venture in industrial democracy, and the Escorts Heart Institute and Research Centre, the finest institute of its kind in India, he would have deserved the lasting gratitude of the nation.

> "No man lives life so wise
>   But unto time he throws
> Morsels to hunger for
>   At his life's close."

In the case of most hardworking men, the price of their success is neglect of their closest and dearest. The majority are insensitive to the enormity of the price. But Hari, a fine human being, is one of the few to whom this consciousness has come home in the evening of his life. His self-effacing helpmeet, Raj, passed away two years ago. As he casts a longing, lingering look behind, his wisdom aerates.

This warm-hearted man looks back on the tumultuous years gathered to the past — 75 crowded years of adventure and enterprise — and singles out friendship as his enduring treasure.

> From quiet homes and first beginning,
>   Out to the undiscovered ends,
> There's nothing worth the wear of winning,
>   But laughter and the love of friends.

So, read on....

Role of Social Service in Society

I think the word "Talk" would be preferable to "Oration". A talk can be serious, but an oration is usually solemn. I propose to be serious; but I hope I will not be solemn.

In seven years' time we shall reach not only the end of the decade, not only the end of the century, but also the end of the millennium. When centuries later the history of our times comes to be written, the twentieth century will be referred to as the Age of Compassion and Social Service. The awakening of the heart is reflected in the worldwide urge to activize character, to channelize service, and to institutionalize fellowship. Today there are more organizations dedicated to social service than ever before. In this century we have seen the birth of private global movements like the Rotary International, the Lions International, and the Giants International which strive to live up to the ideal of human unity.

Even communism and socialism, though totally misguided in their methods, had their roots in compassion for the poor and in the ideal of a just and fair society. They strove to give a fair deal to

> the ranker, the tramp of the road,
> The slave with the sack on his shoulders
> pricked on with the goad,
> The man with too weighty a burden,
> too weary a load.

(First Leela Moolgaokar Oration, Bombay, May 20, 1993)

Social service is the offspring of compassion and of love, when it is not rooted in self-advertisement.

Mother Teresa in her Acceptance Speech at Oslo in 1979, on being awarded the Nobel Peace Prize, said, "Humanitarian service brings peace to the heart." In that Address, the Mother related two stories which deserve to be etched on our memories:

The Mother gave a bowl of rice to a *Hindu* beggar woman with eight children. The beggar said she would like to excuse herself for five minutes. She went and gave a part of the rice to a *Muslim* woman whose children were also starving. Such is the harmony and goodwill among the common people of India.

The second story told by Mother Teresa is, in her own words, the following; "I shall tell you the story of a man picked up from the drain, half-eaten with worms and brought to our home. He said, 'I have lived like an animal in the street, but I shall die like an angel, loved and cared for.' It was so wonderful to see the greatness of that man who could speak like that, who could die like that, without blaming anybody, without cursing anybody, without complaining about anything — this is the greatness of our people."

More and more people are having the Vision of Voluntarism. They realize that their life belongs to the whole community, and as long as they live they should regard it as their privilege to do whatever they can for the community. Bernard Shaw expressed this sentiment in memorable words:

"This is the true joy in life, the being used for a purpose recognized by yourself as a mighty one; the being a force of nature instead of a feverish, selfish little clod of ailments and grievances complaining that the world will not devote itself to making you happy.

"I am of the opinion that my life belongs to the whole community, and as long as I live it is my privilege to do for it whatever I can.

"I want to be thoroughly used up when I die, for the harder I work the more I live. I rejoice in life for its own sake. Life is no 'brief candle' to me. It is a sort of splendid torch which I have got hold of for the moment, and I want to make it burn as brightly as possible before handing it on to future generations."

T here are two types of people in the world: those who expect the political system to produce humanity and care, and those who practise humanity and care knowing that one distant day it will produce the system. Those who rely upon the government to alleviate the miseries of the people are indulging in a pipe dream.

Again, your own life is within your control and you can put it to such useful purpose as you think fit. If you start caring, others will. Always keep before your mind's eye, Buddha's last words to his disciples — "Look not for refuge to anyone besides yourself." It is typical of the sloppy individual that he expects in his neighbour the standard of behaviour which he will not impose upon himself. The lines of the versifier who imagined the typical attitude of the self-centred man at a time of invasion, are worth recalling:

"I was playing golf the day
    The Germans landed.
All our soldiers ran away,
    All our ships were stranded;
And the sense of England's shame
    Nearly put me off my game."

Character is integrity plus altruism. Fame is a vapour; popularity an accident; riches take wings; and those who cheer you today will curse you tomorrow. Only one thing endures — character.

Business has four great advantages in the field of social service. It can give leadership, can supply organization, can marshal human resources, and provide financial support. This represents the attractive face of capitalism. The nation needs to have men in business without a mercenary outlook — those who are as keen to add to gross national happiness as to gross national product.

Professionals should cultivate their mind — without the sole motive of offering it as a commodity for sale in the marketplace. No professional is worthy of his profession if he has become only an animated cash-register.

All great thinkers have emphasized the 'S' factor — 'S' for Service — service to society. Dr. Einstein maintained that it is a higher destiny to serve than to rule. Mahatma Gandhi was never tired of emphasizing that you must not only hold your money in trust but also your talent in trust for society. Luckily, in the midst of all corruption and degradation, decadence and degeneration, India has today a vast number of men dedicated to the ideal of humanizing the human race.

Parsis in India

*H*istory affords no parallel to the role of Parsis in India. There is no record of any other community so infinitesimally small as Parsis, playing such a significant role in the life of a country so large.

A hundred years ago the fertility rate among Parsis was the highest in India. The highest figure of the Parsi population in India was 1,14,890 recorded in the Census of 1941. But over the last fifty years the number has been dwindling. Today the total number of Parsis throughout the world is estimated to be a little over 1,00,000. Of this number about 70,000 live in India, 18,000 in Iran, a little over 3,000 in Pakistan, and another 15,000 are scattered over Europe, America, Africa and the Far East.

There is no doubt that Parsis came to India as boat people, i.e., as people who crossed the seas in unsafe boats as refugees from another land. They came originally in seven ships from Iran after their country was conquered by Muslim Arabs. There is a lot of controversy as to whether the Parsi refugees first arrived in 936 A.D. or in any earlier year. Tradition has it that they initially landed at Sanjan and were given refuge by a Hindu Raja, Jadi Rana.

Till the eighteenth century, Parsis led a secluded life as a religious minority and their influence was not felt on the broad stream of India's life. About the end of the eighteenth century they began to gravitate towards the cities and today the Parsis are the

(All India Radio, August 23, 1993)

most urbanized community in India — 94 per cent of them live in cities. It is an interesting historical fact that in 1780 Bombay was inhabited by only 33,444 persons, of whom no less than 3,087 (i.e., 9.2%) were Parsis. Today out of the 70,000 Parsis in India, about 45,000 live in Bombay.

The role of the Parsis in India may be considered under four heads — education and the professions, social reforms, economic development, and politics.

The foundation of the Bombay University in 1857 opened up a new chapter in the history of Parsis. They dominated the professions and fields of higher education to an extent wholly disproportionate to their minuscule number. They played a major role in promoting the cause of education and they were pioneers in the learned professions. The first Indian Professor at the Elphinstone College in Bombay was Dadabhai Naoroji who was appointed Professor of Mathematics in 1852. In 1898, 46 out of 100 qualified Indian advocates, and 40 out of 73 Indian attorneys in Bombay were Parsis. In the same year, out of seventeen principals of secondary schools in the Bombay Province, seven were Parsis. In 1891, six out of seven Indian surgeons employed in the Bombay Province were Parsis, and of a total of 52 medical assistants (including the British) 23 were Parsis. In 1898, four out of the twelve higher non-English civil servants in the Bombay Province were Parsis.

In the field of social reforms Parsis took the initiative. In 1848 young reformers under the leadership of Dadabhai Naoroji, started the "Students Literary and Scientific Society", the principal aim of which was to raise the educational standard of the population by providing school facilities and voluntary teachers who gave their time and energy to the great social cause of disseminating literacy and knowledge. The newly founded Society considered the education of young women to be specially important. In the education of girls, Parsis proved to be decades ahead of all other Indian communities.

In the field of labour welfare, Jamsetji Tata and his enterprises introduced a number of innovations which are today given statutory expression in the Factories Act, the Employees' Provident Fund Act, the Employees' State Insurance Act, the Workmen's Compensation Act, the Payment of Bonus Act and the Payment of Gratuity Act.

Parsis played a significant role in the economic development and growth of the country, despite their numerical insignificance. They were leaders in industry, trade and banking. For the assessment year 1905-06, among assessees of Bombay with an annual income of Rs. 1 lakh or more, there were seven Hindus, six Parsis and four Muslims. In 1854, the first steam-powered cotton mill was established in Bombay by a Parsi named Daver. Parsis were not only prosperous themselves but they were the cause of prosperity in others.

The Census of Bombay of 1864 does not record one single Parsi beggar. Unfortunately, today the economic plight of the community is pathetic. It affords an object lesson in how a great community can decline when there is a failure not of resources but of the wisdom to use them, a failure of the will to utilize the material and human resources for the community's uplift.

Jamsetji Tata heralded the dawn of the Age of Technology in India. This "One-Man Planning Commission", as Pandit Jawaharlal Nehru called him, laid the foundation for India's industrial growth, not only by establishing enterprises which needed long periods of gestation and involved considerable risk but by establishing scholarships and technological institutions which would educate scientists, engineers and other technocrats for generations to come. No Indian had a greater or deeper concept of a technologically developed India than Jamsetji Tata. The Indian Institute of Science at Bangalore is one of the several great monuments to his memory. Beyond question, he was the most important pioneer entrepreneur in all of India. Jamsetji Tata, single-handed, repaid to India, many times over, the debt which the Parsis owed to this fabulous country a thousand years earlier when their forefathers were given shelter and refuge on the shores of Western India.

In politics, the role of Parsis has been truly significant. Incidentally, only three Indians were ever elected to the British

Parliament before 1980 and all three of them were Parsis — Dadabhai Naoroji, Mancherji Bhavnagari and Shapoorji Saklatvala.

This tiniest of all communities has been content to enrich India without asking for any special rights, privileges or reservations for itself.

Dadabhai Naoroji was a Colossus. For him, belonging to the Indian nation was even more important than his membership in the Parsi community. I quote his words: "Whether I am a Hindu, a Mohamedan, a Parsi, a Christian, or of any other creed, I am above all an Indian. Our country is India; our nationality is Indian."

Sir Pherozeshah Mehta gave the same expression to the total involvement of Parsis with India. In his own life he personified the identification of Parsis with the great march of events moulding the lofty destiny of this sub-continent. To quote Sir Pherozeshah Mehta's own words: "To my mind, a Parsi is a better and truer Parsi, as a Mohamedan or a Hindu is a better Mohamedan or Hindu, the more he is attached to the land which gave him birth, the more he is bound in brotherly relations and affection to all the children of the soil."

This microscopic community has produced world renowned personalities in the last hundred years — among them are Jamsetji Tata to whom I have referred earlier, Dr. Homi Bhabha, the Father of India's atomic energy programme, and Zubin Mehta, the maestro who reaches out to *Brahma* through music. The question arises — do Parsis locate their golden age in the past, or can they locate it in the future and greet the unseen with a cheer? The answer is in their own hands. It depends entirely on the present generation of Parsis whether they will prosper economically, culturally and socially, and create the conditions in which they can continue to produce great men, or whether they will become a decadent community with a glorious past, a perilous present, and a dim future.

16

Democracy or Boobocracy?

Panorama of the Lost Decades

*T*here is a strong case for recalling — periodically, soberly and sombrely — events that have been gathered to the past and have become increasingly distant, remote and forgotten. Nations which do not remember their past are condemned to repeat it.

Fernand Braudel, the French historian, said that history is like a river. On the surface it flows rapidly and disappears; but down below there is a deep stream which moves more slowly and does not change quickly but is the more important level because it drives the whole river. The crowded years of this century have been momentous. The rapid flow on the surface has been sinking daily into oblivion. But *The Times of India* also mirrored the deep stream below as it flowed silently each night. Here are gathered those reflections in the mirror which are of more than evanescent interest.

The panorama extends over eighty years. The first forty years (pre-independence) represent the period when India rightly asserted that good government is no substitute for self-government. In the last forty years, thinking India became equally conscious that self-government is no substitute for good government. "Dost thou know, my son," asked Count Oxenstierna, "with how little wisdom the world is governed?"

H. L. Mencken described American democracy as a "boobocracy" of , by and for the "vast herd of human blanks" who have neither the interest nor the capacity for intelligent self-government. This

(Introduction to 'Viewpoint', The Times of India Sesquicentennial Publication, 1992)

style of expression is both impolitic and impolite. But as you thumb through these pages and see how government after government succumbed to populism when what the country needed was leadership, you are tempted to tell yourself that even what is impolite and impolitic has to be said in a country whose national motto is "Truth Shall Prevail".

A story of deep human interest is compacted and telescoped within the covers of the book. Each piece has the special imprint of the author's style. Here are movers of people, mobilizers of opinion, dealing with events which have helped to shape history and mould the future. They write for a country which can launch a medium range ballistic missile but where forty million families do not have a steady income; a country where, in the late Dr. H. D. Sankalia's words, "the past lives with the present".

"Footfalls echo in the memory...." The evocative flavours and colours of times past, the concerns of the moment and the concerns that will not go away, are all arrayed here. The story of resilience and endurance, and of what is truly vital when life is pared down to its essence. The pattern of alternation, the ebb and flow of human history. The saga of wars — the hell where youth and laughter go. The death of Stalin — recalled without regret in these heady days of *glasnost* and *perestroika*. The brief, unhappy interlude of the Chinese war. Ephemeral political upheavals which had once loomed so large and then shrank to insignificance. The problems of going nuclear. Communal tensions leading to the partition of India and its unending backlash. Violence and fanaticism, fundamentalism and belief in the single truth. The dread night of the Emergency when freedom was measured out with coffee spoons. A nation with an imperishable heritage, but still in search of its national identity. The sleeping sickness of theological socialism afflicting a country rich by nature but poor by policy.

The pitiless lesson is, what was taught two thousand years ago, that "there is no new thing under the sun". The problems of today have been with us all through the corridors of decades. Poverty and unemployment have haunted India continuously within living memory. The cities may now be dotted with pockets of enormous affluence, but the lot of the small farmer, the rural labourer, remains unchanged:

> His speech is of mortgaged bedding,
> On his vine he borrows yet,
> At his heart is his daughter's wedding,
> In his eye foreknowledge of debt.
> He eats and hath indigestion,
> He toils and he may not stop;
> His life is a long-drawn question
> Between a crop and a crop.

This volume deserves to be commended to those who have lived through time past, and also to others who look to time future. The collage provides a veritable feast for the reader, no matter what his special interest may be. He will leave the table — enriched and fulfilled, and come back for more when the mood takes him.

INDEX